Writing Matters!

Introduction to Writing and Grammar

Lorraine Dubois McClelland & Patricia Hale Marcotte

McGraw Hill

Writing Matters!, 1st Edition

Published by McGraw-Hill/Contemporary, a business unit of The McGraw-Hill Companies,
Inc., 1221 Avenue of the Americas, New York, NY 10020. Copyright © 2003 by The
McGraw-Hill Companies, Inc. All rights reserved. No part of this publication may be
reproduced or distributed in any form or by any means, or stored in a database or retrieval
system, without the prior written consent of The McGraw-Hill Companies, Inc., including,
but not limited to, in any network or other electronic storage or transmission, or broadcast
for distance learning.

This book is printed on recycled, acid-free paper containing 10% postconsumer waste.

11 12 13 14 WDQ/WDQ 14 13 12 11 10

ISBN 978-0-07-255279-9
MHID 0-07-255279-4

Editorial director: *Tina Carver*
Developmental editor: *Jennifer Monaghan*
Cover image: © *Amy DeVooqd/Artville/Getty Images*
Interior designer: *Ellen Pettengell*
Typeface: *11/15 Meridien Roman*
Printer: *Worldcolor Dubuque*

INTERNATIONAL EDITION ISBN 0-07-121385-6
Copyright © 2003. Exclusive rights by The McGraw-Hill Companies, Inc. for manufacture
and export. This book cannot be re-exported from the country to which it is sold by
McGraw-Hill.
The International Edition is not available in North America.

To the Teacher

Writing Matters! is a high-beginning writing text for high school, community college, and adult students of English as a Second or Foreign Language. It offers an introduction to academic writing for students with relatively limited English skills as well as those students who are somewhat proficient with spoken English but need to improve their writing skills. *Writing Matters!* is unique in that it integrates in one book a structured approach to the standard three-part English paragraph and the supporting sentence skills which enable beginning students to communicate their ideas in clear, error-free English.

RATIONALE

As we worked with hundreds of students over many semesters, we became more and more conscious of the fact that our students brought a wealth of personal experiences and perceptions to the classroom yet did not have the skills to express their ideas in writing. While it was clear that our students still needed to learn basic sentence skills, grammar, and vocabulary, these alone would not enable them to communicate in writing about meaningful issues and personal experiences. Thus, it became a challenge to us not only to teach our students the basic rules of English sentence structure, grammar, and mechanics but, at the same time, to introduce them to the basic organizational skills needed to write clear, well-developed paragraphs.

ORGANIZATION

The basic objective of *Writing Matters!* is to develop both sentence skills and paragraph skills simultaneously in one textbook to enable beginning students to communicate in writing as soon as possible. Therefore, the overall organization of *Writing Matters!* is based on the approach of alternating between paragraph skills and sentence structure, first teaching grammatical points and then introducing students to the utilization of those points in the larger context of the paragraph.

In the **paragraph** chapters, students learn to develop the basic three-part English paragraph (topic sentence, body, conclusion). They study different kinds of paragraph development and learn to use reasons, examples, description, and narration to support a topic sentence. Students also learn that writing is a process and that there are specific steps they can follow to help them write a well-developed paragraph:

Step 1: Prewriting for ideas (clustering, listing, note-taking, brainstorming)

Step 2: Making an outline to plan a paragraph

Step 3: Writing the first draft

Step 4: Revising and editing

Step 5: Writing the final draft

In the earlier chapters, students are asked to write about their own experiences and opinions. We have found that when beginning students write about familiar topics, they experience the greatest success. In the later chapters, the models and writing assignments become more objective and less controlled.

In the **sentence structure** and **grammar** chapters, students concentrate on basic sentence skills, such as the accurate use of verb tenses, subject-verb agreement, and the avoidance of run-ons, comma splices, and sentence fragments. Students also learn to use a variety of sentences (simple, compound, and complex) to make their writing more interesting and effective. Grammar concepts are presented and practiced in context. Frequent reviews enable students to check their understanding of the concepts they have studied, and student paragraphs provide models for the writing assignments found at the end of each grammar chapter. The variety and flexibility of the activities allow students to work on an individual basis, in pairs and peer groups, or as an entire class.

ACKNOWLEDGEMENTS

We are very grateful to our many friends and colleagues who helped and supported us through the long process of completing *Writing Matters!* Our sincere thanks to:

Pat Moll, for her enthusiastic support, her many ideas and contributions, her flair for the written word, and her willingness to help whenever we called on her;

Rita Karlsten, Dean of English at Evergreen Valley College, for making it possible for us and several of our colleagues to classroom-test the materials, and to Renee Walsh and Jim Murray for generating stacks of beautifully copied handouts, often at the last minute;

Sylvia Rucker and Martha Blackwell, who tested the materials over several semesters and whose valuable suggestions, along with those of Michael Grove and Valerie Whiteson, contributed to the final form of the book;

The many students we have had over the years, for their enthusiasm and desire to learn and for the gift of their paragraphs to serve as models in our book;

Jennifer Monaghan, our friend and editor, and Sheryl Sever, who first brought our manuscript to McGraw-Hill/Contemporary;

Ed and Ann Bartlett, who thought that our project had outlasted our original computer and who sent us a new one to help us finish *Writing Matters!*

Thanks to you all!

Dedication

To Joe, who is surely the most patient husband of all time, and to the loving memory of the two Jims, who teased and supported us from the very first.

Contents

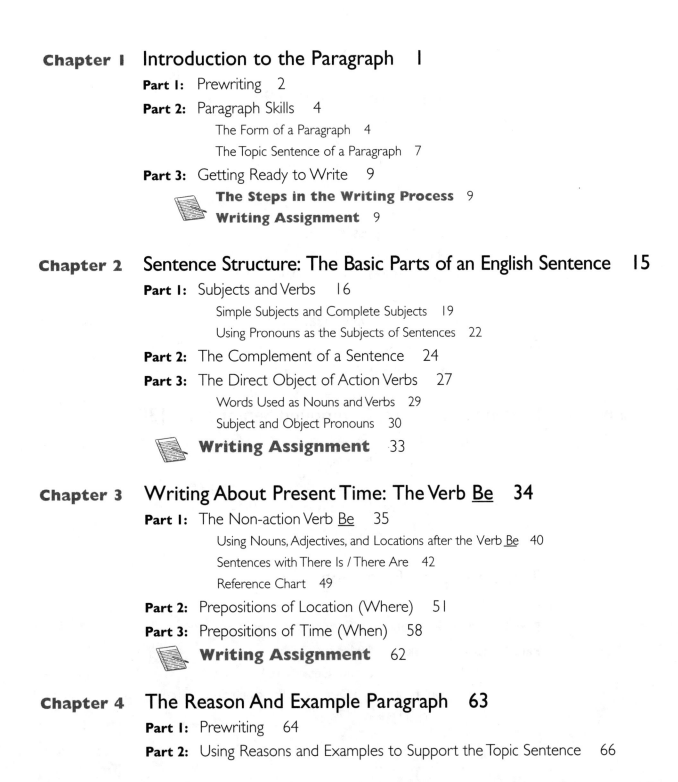

Chapter 1
Introduction
to the Paragraph

Part 1: Prewriting

Part 2: Paragraph Skills

      The Form of a Paragraph

      The Topic Sentence of a Paragraph

Part 3: Getting Ready to Write

      The Steps in the Writing Process

      Writing Assignment

To the Student:

    In all areas of life, in your personal life, at school, and in business, writing is an important form of communication. The purpose of this book is to show you how to communicate your ideas simply and clearly in paragraph form.

    This book will help you to improve your writing in several ways: you will learn how to get your ideas down on paper, how to organize your ideas, and how to express your ideas as clearly as possible.

    You will study different kinds of writing in this book and have many opportunities to practice what you are learning. Chapter 1 begins by introducing you to the form of a paragraph and to the basic steps in the writing process.

Part I
Prewriting

GETTING READY TO WRITE

➤ Before you start to write a paragraph, it is a good idea to do some kind of _prewriting_. (Prewriting means <u>before you write</u>). Prewriting is a way to help you to get ideas to write about. One good way to get ideas about a topic is to talk about the topic with your classmates. When you share your ideas and listen to the ideas of other students, it is easier to decide what to write.

➤ In this chapter, your writing assignment will be to write a paragraph about the things that you like about this school. Is it near your house? Do you have friends here? Does it offer a variety* of classes? Why do you like this school? What are your reasons? In order to get ready to write your paragraph, follow the prewriting instructions on the next page.

Vocabulary Note   *<u>variety</u>: different kinds*

PREWRITING

▶ What to do ◀

1. Form a group with three or four other students.

2. In your group, talk about the reasons that you like this school. Why is this a good school? What is special about this school?

3. Share your ideas with your classmates and listen carefully to the ideas of each person in your group.

4. On the lines below, write down a list of your ideas. Write as many ideas as you can. Do not worry about grammar or spelling. You do not need to write complete sentences. You will use these notes later to help you to write a paragraph.

NOTES

_____

_____

_____

_____

_____

_____

_____

_____

_____

_____

_____

_____

_____

Part 2
Paragraph Skills

THE FORM OF A PARAGRAPH - WHAT DOES A PARAGRAPH LOOK LIKE?

➡ Before you write your own paragraph about why you like this school, it is important for you to review the form (shape) of a paragraph. What does a paragraph look like?

1. A paragraph often has a **title** to tell the reader what the paragraph is about. In this book, each paragraph will have a title. Capitalize the important words in the title. Do not use quotation marks (" ") or put a period at the end of the title. Do <u>not</u> write the title as a complete sentence.

2. **Skip a line** (leave a space) between the title and the first line of a paragraph.

3. **Indent** the first sentence of a paragraph. Indent means to begin the first sentence to the right.

4. Leave **margins** on the left side and the right side of the paragraph. Do not write in the margins.

5. There is no rule for how long a paragraph should be. The length of the paragraph depends on what you are writing about. However, the average length of an English paragraph is about **150 - 200 words**.

6. In this class, double space your paragraph (skip a line) so that you will have room to make changes and corrections.

margin	skip a line title ───►Planning Ahead	margin
indent ►	I chose to attend adult education classes at Overfelt High School for three	
	reasons. First, I need to get my high school diploma. A high school diploma is a	
	requirement in order to get a good job. I will probably have to work for a long time,	
	and I do not want to work at low-paying jobs for the rest of my life. I am	
	currently a cook at a fast food restaurant, and it is not an easy job. Second, I	
	also need to take some computer classes. There are many good jobs in the	
	business world, but I need computer skills in order to get an interview at any of	
	the high technology companies in Silicon Valley. Finally, the tuition in the basic	
	education classes is free, and the time for the classes is convenient. There are	
	classes in the morning, afternoon, and evening. This is my first step toward a	
	better future.	

THE FORM OF A PARAGRAPH

➠ **Activity I** The form (shape) of the student paragraph below is not correct. The student did not follow the paragraph rules on page 4. Read the paragraph. Then write the paragraph correctly on the next page.

<u>the first Week of School</u>

The first few days of school are often difficult for new students for three reasons.

First of all, everything is strange and new. The school campus seems large and confusing. Students often get lost and come to class late because they cannot find their classrooms. They also have trouble locating the financial aid office, the student health center, and the bookstore.

For another thing, it is often difficult for new students to make friends. Students come from many different countries and speak many different languages such as Spanish, Japanese, Chinese, and Vietnamese. As a result, new students often feel alone and shy because it is difficult to communicate with their classmates.

Finally, when students meet a new teacher, they do not know what to expect. Is the teacher hard or easy? Is the teacher kind or impatient? Does he or she give a lot of homework?

Although teachers are usually friendly and helpful, students are always nervous the first few days of class.

THE FORM OF A PARAGRAPH

➠ **Activity 2** The form (shape) of the paragraph on page 5 is not correct. Write the paragraph correctly on the lines below. If you need help, look back at the paragraph rules on page 4.

THE TOPIC SENTENCE OF A PARAGRAPH

▶ A paragraph is a group of sentences about <u>one</u> main idea. We call the main idea sentence the **topic sentence** of the paragraph. The topic sentence tells the reader what the paragraph is about. In U.S. academic writing, the topic sentence is usually the first sentence of the paragraph. All of the other sentences in the paragraph explain, describe, and support the topic sentence.

In the student paragraph below, the topic sentence is *I like Evergreen Valley College for three reasons*. The student then gave three reasons to explain why she likes her school:

first reason:	For one thing, it has a good child-care center.
second reason:	In addition, it is easy to get to campus by bus because the bus stop is only a block away.
third reason:	Finally, the school is a friendly place.

▶ Read the model paragraph below. Then answer the questions on page 8.

MODEL PARAGRAPH

Evergreen Valley College

[1]I like Evergreen Valley College for three reasons. [2]For one thing, it has a good child-care center. [3]This is very important to me. [4]I am a young mother with a two-year-old daughter, and the child-care center gives me the freedom to take one or two classes a semester. [5]In addition, it is easy to get to campus by bus because the bus stop is only a block away. [6]My car is old, and it is not always reliable*. [7]If I have car trouble, I have another way to get to school. [8]Finally, the school is a friendly place. [9]Most students do not know each other at the beginning of a semester, but they have many opportunities to become acquainted* through school clubs, sports, and group work in class. [10]The teachers are also very friendly and usually have a good sense of humor*. [11]It means a lot to me to have such a good school in my neighborhood.

Dao Nguyen

Vocabulary Notes   *<u>**reliable**</u>: dependable   *<u>**become acquainted**</u>: get to know someone   *<u>**sense of humor**</u>: ability to laugh*

QUESTIONS ABOUT THE MODEL PARAGRAPH

▸ **Activity 3** Answer the questions below about the model paragraph on page 7, **Evergreen Valley College**.

1. What is the title of Dao's paragraph? _____

2. Did Dao write the title correctly? _____ yes _____ no

3. What is the topic sentence of Dao's paragraph? _____

_____

4. Did Dao indent the topic sentence? _____ yes _____ no

5. What are the reasons Dao gave to support her topic sentence? Write Dao's reasons on the lines below. Use complete sentences.

Reason 1: For one thing, it has a good child-care center. _____

_____

Reason 2: _____

_____

Reason 3: _____

_____

6. Are Dao's reasons clear and easy to understand? Do you know why she likes Evergreen Valley College? _____ yes _____ no

7. The last sentence of a paragraph is called the *concluding sentence*. The concluding sentence usually repeats the idea of the topic sentence in different words. Write the concluding sentence of Dao's paragraph on the lines below.

_____

_____

Part 3
Getting Ready to Write

✎ Writing Assignment

➠ In this chapter, your writing assignment will be to write a paragraph about why you like your school. To help you write your paragraph, you will study the basic steps in the writing process.

STEPS IN THE WRITING PROCESS

➠ Most good writers do not just sit down and start to write. They go through several steps before they are ready to write their final paragraph. On the next few pages, you will study four steps that most writers follow when they sit down to write.

STEP I - PREWRITING

➠ At the beginning of this chapter, you worked in a group with three or four classmates and discussed why you like this school. Go back and read the notes that you wrote on page 3.

Complete the topic sentence below. Then choose three reasons from your notes to explain why you like this school. Write your reasons on the lines below. Write complete sentences. Begin each sentence with a capital letter and end each sentence with a period.

Topic Sentence: *I like* _____ *for three reasons.*
                                          (name of your school or college)

Reason I: _____

_____

Reason 2: _____

_____

Reason 3: _____

_____

Writing Assignment

STEP 2 - WRITE A FIRST DRAFT (PRACTICE PARAGRAPH)

➡ A first draft is a <u>practice</u> paragraph. It is not your <u>final</u> paragraph. You will have to make corrections and changes on your practice paragraph before you write your final paragraph.

► What to do ◄

1. On the lines below, write a practice paragraph about why you like this school.

2. Your paragraph should be about 150 to 200 words long.

3. Double space your paragraph (skip a line) so you will have room to make changes or corrections.

Name _____

skip a line _____   title _____

I like _____ for three reasons.

Writing Assignment

FIRST DRAFT (CONTINUED)

Name _____

STEP 3 - REVISE AND EDIT YOUR PARAGRAPH

⟶ When you are finished writing your practice paragraph, the next step is to **revise** and **edit** your paragraph. Revise means to add new sentences or take out sentences. Revise also means to rewrite any sentences that are confusing or unclear. Edit means to correct any mistakes in grammar, spelling, capital letters, or periods.

▶ **What to do** ◀

1. First, read your practice paragraph to yourself.

2. Are all of your sentences clear and easy to understand? Do you want to add new sentences or take out sentences? If you want to make any changes, make them on your practice paragraph.

3. Are there any mistakes in grammar, spelling, capital letters, or periods? Did you use correct paragraph form? If you need to make any corrections, make them on your practice paragraph.

4. When you are finished revising and editing your paragraph, write your name on the Review Sheet on page 12, and give your book to a partner. Your partner will read and review your paragraph.

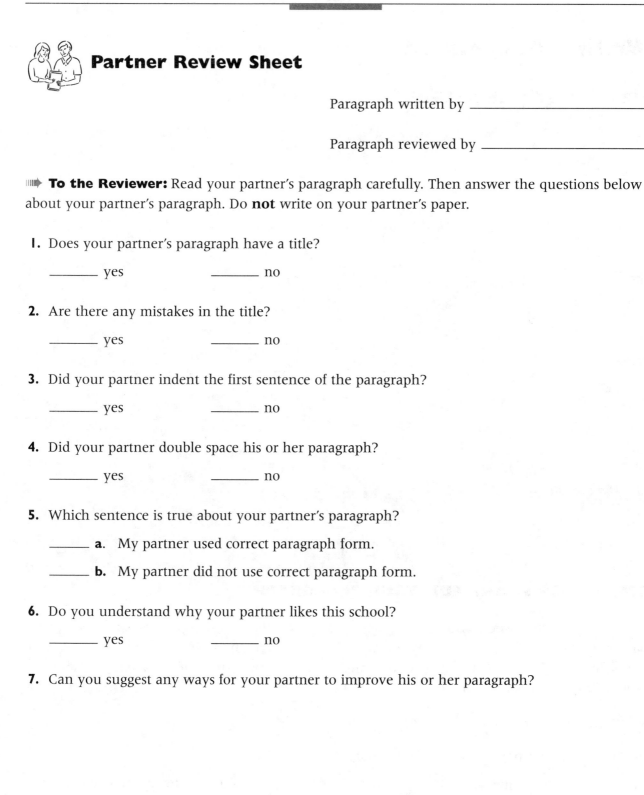

Partner Review Sheet

Paragraph written by _____

Paragraph reviewed by _____

➡ **To the Reviewer:** Read your partner's paragraph carefully. Then answer the questions below about your partner's paragraph. Do **not** write on your partner's paper.

1. Does your partner's paragraph have a title?

   _____ yes   _____ no

2. Are there any mistakes in the title?

   _____ yes   _____ no

3. Did your partner indent the first sentence of the paragraph?

   _____ yes   _____ no

4. Did your partner double space his or her paragraph?

   _____ yes   _____ no

5. Which sentence is true about your partner's paragraph?

   _____ **a.** My partner used correct paragraph form.

   _____ **b.** My partner did not use correct paragraph form.

6. Do you understand why your partner likes this school?

   _____ yes   _____ no

7. Can you suggest any ways for your partner to improve his or her paragraph?

➡ **To the Reviewer:** When you are finished reviewing your partner's paragraph, return your partner's book.

Writing Assignment

STEP 4 – WRITE YOUR FINAL DRAFT (FINAL PARAGRAPH)

⇒ When your partner returns your book, make any necessary changes or corrections on your practice paragraph. Now you are ready to write the final draft of your paragraph.

▶ **What to do** ◀

1. Write your final paragraph in ink. Write as neatly as possible, and use correct paragraph form.

2. Double space your paragraph.

3. Begin each sentence with a capital letter, and end each sentence with a period.

	Name _____
	I like _____ for three reasons.

Writing Assignment

FINAL DRAFT (CONTINUED)

Name _____

Chapter 2
Sentence Structure:
The Basic Parts
of an English Sentence

To the Student:

One of the most important ways to improve your writing is to write clear, correct, error-free sentences. If you omit words or use the wrong word order or forget to use capital letters and periods, your readers will be confused. They will not be able to understand your ideas. This chapter will help you to strengthen your basic sentence skills.

Part I
Subjects and Verbs

THE PARTS OF A SENTENCE

▥▸ A sentence is a group of words that expresses a complete thought.

Example: At a school near my house.   **(not a complete thought ⟶ not a sentence)**

I study at a school near my house. **(complete thought ⟶ a sentence)**

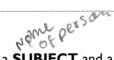

▸ **Learning Point**

A complete sentence must have two parts – a **SUBJECT** and a **VERB**.

1. **Subjects** are the <u>actors</u> in sentences. Subjects perform (do) the action. Subjects are words such as *students, teachers, Kim, Mr. Warner*.

2. **Verbs** are <u>action words</u> in sentences. Verbs tell what people do. Verbs are words such as *walk, speak, buy, help*.

▥▸ The subject usually comes before the verb in an English sentence.

1. Counselors help students with their class schedules.

      ↑   ↑
    subject   verb
    (actor) (action)

2. Students buy their textbooks at the bookstore.

     ↑   ↑
    subject   verb
    (actor) (action)

3. Teachers take attendance and answer students' questions.

     ↑   ↑   ↑
    subject   verb   **verb**
    (actor) (action)   **(action)**

4. Students and teachers eat lunch in the cafeteria.

     ↑   ↑   ↑
    subject   **subject verb**
    (actor)   **(actor) (action)**

▥▸ Sometimes the subject of a sentence is not a person.

The cafeteria sells sandwiches, salads, ice cream, cold drinks, and snacks.

     ↑   ↑
    subject   verb
    (actor) (action)

SUBJECT - VERB

▶ **Exercise 1** Write the <u>subject</u> and the <u>verb</u> on the lines after each sentence.

First find the verb (action word). Then, to find the subject, ask **who** or **what** did the action.

A Busy First Week of School

	subject(s)	verb(s)
1. Everyone works very hard during the first week of school.	*everyone*	*works*
2. Counselors meet with students and give them advice about their classes.	*counselors*	*meet, give*
3. Clerks and secretaries help students with financial aid forms.	*clerks secret.*	*help*
4. Advisers give placement tests to new students.	*Adiversers*	*test.*
5. Custodians clean the classrooms and check the heat and air conditioning.	*Custodians*	*check*
6. Colleges offer a full schedule of day and evening classes.	*Colleges*	*offer*

▶ **Exercise 2** Follow the same directions as in Exercise 1. Then study the sentences for dictation.

	subject(s)	verb(s)
1. Students greet* their friends and talk about their summer experiences.	_____	_____
2. Students compare their class schedules with their friends.	_____	_____
3. Teachers explain class requirements to their students on the first day of class.	_____	_____
4. Teachers write class assignments on the board.	_____	_____
5. Librarians take new students on tours of the library and issue* library cards.	_____	_____
6. Police sell parking permits at the Campus Police Office.	_____	_____

Vocabulary Notes   *<u>greet</u>: say hello*   *<u>issue</u>: give*

SUBJECT - VERB

➡ **Exercise 3** Circle the subjects and verbs in the paragraphs below. Then write the subjects and verbs on the lines under each paragraph.

> First find the verb. Then, to find the subject, ask **who** or **what** did the action.

Paragraph 1

¹(Students)(come) to the U. S. from all over the world. ²For example, (Ayako) and (Kenji)(come) from Japan. ³(Ayako)(studies) mathematics and computer science at San Jose State University. ⁴(Kenji) (studies) business administration and (works) part-time at IBM. ⁵(IBM)(offers) a special program to college students to (give) them experience in the workplace. ⁶(Ayako) and (Kenji)(enjoy) college life in the U. S. and (plan) to stay here for two years.

	subject(s)	verb(s)
1.	students	come
2.	Ayako kenji	Come
3.	Ayako	studies
4.	Kenji	studies works
5.	IBM	give offers
6.	Ayoko Kenji	enjoy plan

Paragraph 2

¹(Christa)(comes) from Berlin, Germany and (lives) with her sister Helga in San Jose, California. ²(Helga)(helps) Christa with her English every day. ³In addition, (Christa)(watches) American TV and (speaks) English as often as possible with Helga's American friends. ⁴(Christa)(plans) to enter college in the fall. ⁵(She)(wants) to be a doctor and intends to live permanently in the U. S.

	subject(s)	verb(s)
1.	CRistina	comes
2.	Helgas	lives
3.	CRistina	helpes
4.	CRistina	watches
5.	She	speaks
		plants, wants

Note: In Paragraph 1, *to give* in sentence 5 and *to stay* in sentence 6 are infinitives. An infinitive is **to + the simple form of a verb**. In paragraph 2, *to enter*, *to be*, and *to live* in sentences 4 and 5 are also infinitives. An infinitive is never the verb in a sentence. We will study infinitives in Chapter 14.

SIMPLE SUBJECTS AND COMPLETE SUBJECTS

> ▶ **Learning Point**
>
> **1.** Sometimes the subject of a sentence is more than one word. When the subject of a sentence is more than one word, we call the whole group of words the **complete subject**.
>
> **2.** We call the most important word in the complete subject the **simple subject**. The simple subject is always a <u>noun</u> (a person, place, or thing) or a <u>subject pronoun</u> (*I, you, he, she, it, we, you, they*). The simple subject tells *who* or *what* did the action.

⇒ Study the examples below.

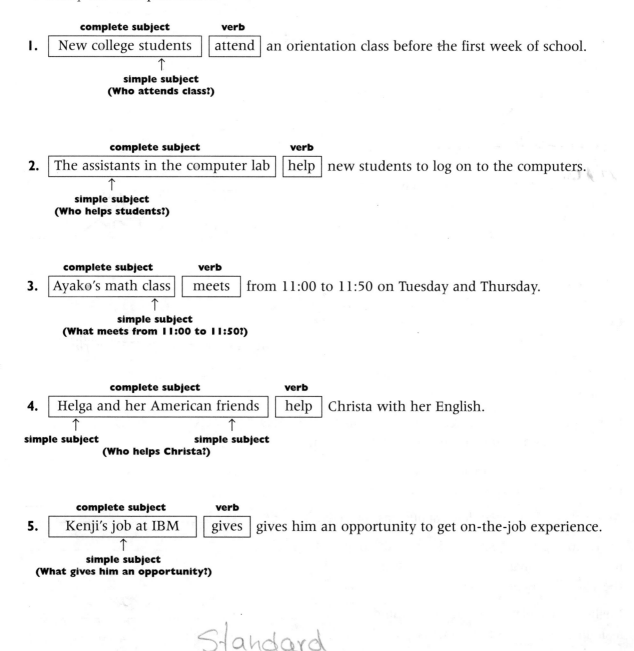

1.
complete subject | verb
New college students | attend | an orientation class before the first week of school.
↑
simple subject
(Who attends class?)

2.
complete subject | verb
The assistants in the computer lab | help | new students to log on to the computers.
↑
simple subject
(Who helps students?)

3.
complete subject | verb
Ayako's math class | meets | from 11:00 to 11:50 on Tuesday and Thursday.
↑
simple subject
(What meets from 11:00 to 11:50?)

4.
complete subject | verb
Helga and her American friends | help | Christa with her English.
↑ ↑
simple subject   simple subject
(Who helps Christa?)

5.
complete subject | verb
Kenji's job at IBM | gives | gives him an opportunity to get on-the-job experience.
↑
simple subject
(What gives him an opportunity?)

Standard

SIMPLE SUBJECTS AND COMPLETE SUBJECTS

▶ **Exercise 4** Underline the <u>complete</u> subject in each sentence. Then write the <u>simple</u> subject and the verb on the lines. Compare your answers with a classmate.

> Remember: First find the verb. Then, to find the subject, ask **who** or **what** did the action.

		simple subject(s)	verb(s)
1.	New students and counselors meet before the first day of class.	students, counselors	meet
2.	Vocational classes prepare students for many kinds of jobs.	classes	prepare
3.	The city busses stop near the bookstore every 30 minutes.	busses	stop
4.	The campus police patrol the parking lots and keep the campus safe for everyone.	police	patrol keep
5.	Students without parking permits pay $1.50 a day to park.	students	pay
6.	The teachers in the language lab give students extra assignments to help them with their classes.	teachers	give
7.	Students apply for work-study jobs at the employment office.	students	apply
8.	Evening classes begin at 6:00 and end at 10:00.	classes	begin end

▶ **Exercise 5** Follow the same directions as in Exercise 4.

		simple subject(s)	verb(s)
1.	The Admissions and Records office sends registration packets to all students.	office	sends
2.	Clerks and secretaries in the Financial Aid office answer questions and help students to fill out forms.	clerks secretaries	help
3.	The instructors at most community colleges prepare green sheets for each of their classes.	instructors	prepare
4.	Green sheets inform students about class objectives.	sheets	inform
5.	Instructors' green sheets also identify the required textbooks and materials for each class and explain the school's absence policy.	sheets	identify explain
6.	English teachers usually attach a reading assignment sheet for the students and a list of important dates for tests, mid-terms, and final exams.	teachers	attach

SIMPLE SUBJECTS AND COMPLETE SUBJECTS

▧➡ **Exercise 6** First underline the complete subjects in each paragraph below. Then circle the simple subject(s) and verb(s). Compare your answers with a partner or in a small group.

Paragraph 1 **The Library**

[1]The library at my school offers many benefits and services to all students. [2]For example, computers on every floor help students to find books and materials for their classes. [3]Also, the reference section* of the library contains encyclopedias, dictionaries, magazines, newspaper articles, and many other good sources of information. [4]The school librarians show students how to look for information in the reference section and to use the computers to complete their class assignments. [5]Everyone appreciates the school library.

Paragraph 2 **A Favorite Restaurant on Campus**

[1]Everyone at my school likes the new Taco Rico restaurant on campus. [2]This popular restaurant serves burritos, tacos, enchiladas, and other Mexican dishes. [3]The delicious aroma* of Mexican food attracts students and teachers from all over the campus. [4]Taco Rico's low prices and good food make this restaurant very popular with everyone.

Paragraph 3 **An Interesting Part-time Job**

[1]Carmela has a very interesting job at the **Chicago Tribune** newspaper. [2]She works part-time in the lost-and-found section of the want-ads department. [3]The clerks in this department answer the phone and take ads for lost pets and other lost items such as purses, jewelry, and bicycles. [4]Carmela's supervisor expects everyone to be friendly and courteous to customers on the telephone. [5]However, Carmela and the other employees in this department sometimes laugh at some of the lost items. [6]Yesterday, for example, someone called to put an ad* in the paper for lost dentures.*

Vocabulary Notes   *__section__: area, department   *__ad__: advertisement
  *__aroma__: good smell   *__dentures__: artificial teeth

USING PRONOUNS AS THE SUBJECTS OF SENTENCES

> ▶ **Learning Point**
>
> We can use a subject pronoun as the subject of a sentence.

▶ Study the examples below.

SUBJECT PRONOUNS	
<u>singular</u>	<u>plural</u>
I	we
you	you
he	they
she	
it	

1. Rosa's (brother) gets off work at 4:30. *He* usually stops at the health club to work out for an hour or so on his way home.

2. (People) in my neighborhood take their health seriously. *They* walk or jog first thing in the morning before work or class.

▶ **Exercise 7** Circle the <u>simple</u> subject in the first sentence. Then write the correct subject pronoun in the blank. Compare your answers with a classmate.

Physical Fitness

1. Today's (students) know the value of a healthy body as well as an educated mind. Therefore, __they__ often choose physical education classes at registration time.

2. (Vinh) always takes a course in soccer. Every semester __she__ works hard to build up his skills in this game.

3. Basketball appeals to many (students). __they__ combines a mixture of skills, team organization, and team play. These classes always fill up quickly.

4. Both (men) and (women) enjoy jogging classes. __they__ recognize the value of jogging for cardiovascular fitness.

5. My (sister) usually chooses an aerobics class. __she__ likes to exercise to music.

6. Many people like golf. __they__ enjoy the fresh air and the challenge of the game.

7. My (friends) and (I) always take swimming lessons. __we__ especially enjoy racing and diving.

8. Physical activity is an important part of (everyone's) life. __they__ is necessary for good health.

Vocabulary Note   *__cardiovascular:__ related to the heart*

✓ CHECK YOUR UNDERSTANDING

A. Answer the questions below.

1. A complete sentence must have two parts: a subject and a verb.

   a. What is a subject? _person place or thing_

   b. What is a verb? _help-gives or studies_

2. In an English sentence, what usually comes first, the subject or the verb? _____

_____

3. What is an infinitive? _____

4. The simple subject of a sentence is always a _____ or a _____ .

5. Write the subject pronouns in the box below.

SUBJECT PRONOUNS

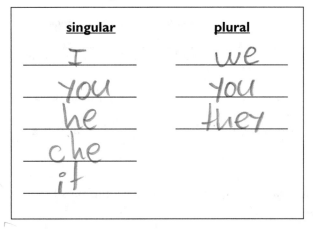

singular	plural
I	we
you	you
he	they
c he	
it	

B. Circle the simple subject in each sentence below. Then rewrite the sentence using a subject pronoun.

1. My sister's (boyfriend) needs a new car.

_____ he _____

2. (His) old car shakes and rattles and makes a lot of noise.

_____ His _____

3. The left side of the (car) has a big dent.

_____ it _____

4. My (sister) and I hate to ride in that old car.

_____ she _____

Part 2
The Complement of a Sentence

THE THIRD PART OF A SENTENCE

➤ You have learned that a complete sentence must have two parts, a subject and a verb.

> ### ▶ Learning Point
>
> Most English sentences have three parts. We call the third part of the sentence **the complement**. The complement of a sentence completes the meaning of the subject and the verb.

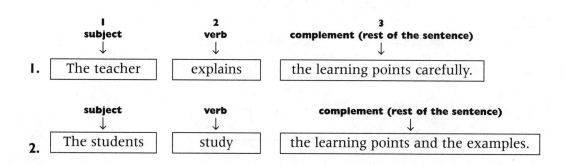

1 subject	**2** verb	**3** complement (rest of the sentence)
1. The teacher	explains	the learning points carefully.
2. The students	study	the learning points and the examples.

➤ A basic English sentence has three parts. Study the examples below.

	1	**2**	**3**
	SUBJECT	**VERB**	**COMPLEMENT** (rest of the sentence)
1.	My English class	begins	at 7:45 on Tuesday and Thursday mornings.
2.	The class	ends	at 9:30.
3.	The students	ask	the teacher a lot of questions.
4.	Everyone	listens	carefully to the teacher's explanations.
5.	We	work	in small groups almost every day.
6.	My classmates	help	one another with their group assignments.
7.	Our teacher	writes	the homework on the board at the end of class.
8.	Our homework	keeps	us busy every night.

THE WORD ORDER OF A BASIC ENGLISH SENTENCE

➡ Although there are many different kinds of sentences in English, most English sentences follow a <u>basic word order</u>: SUBJECT - VERB - COMPLEMENT.

I. The SUBJECT of a sentence is usually <u>first</u>.

2. The VERB is usually <u>second</u>.

3. The COMPLEMENT is usually <u>third</u>.

➡ **Exercise I** The words below are not in the correct order to make a sentence. Put the words in order (s - v - c). Begin each sentence with a capital letter and end each sentence with a period.

I. has - my school - many services and benefits for students

subject	verb	complement
My school	has	many services and benefits for students.

2. the school - child care for students with small children - provides

s	v	c
the school	provides	child care for students with children

3. offers - medical care to all students - the student health center

s	v	c
Medical	offers	Care to all students the students center.

4. offers - the job placement office - students many employment opportunities

s	v	c
The job	offers	placement office students many employment opportunities.

5. students with their resumes - help - employment counselors

s	v	c
students	help	with their resume employment counselors.

6. many interesting activities - student clubs on campus - plan

s	v	c
students clubs	plan	many interesting activities on campus.

7. helps - the computer club - interested students to use the Internet.

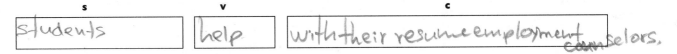

s	v	c
the computer club	helps	interested students to use the Internet.

✓ CHECK YOUR UNDERSTANDING

The paragraph below is difficult to read because the sentences do not begin with a capital letter and end with a period. The reader is confused because it is difficult to know where one sentence ends and the next sentence begins. Remember that a complete sentence in English has a subject and a verb and is a complete thought.

Rewrite the paragraph below. Add capital letters and periods as needed. When you are finished, your paragraph should have 9 sentences. Remember to use correct paragraph form. If you need help, refer to the paragraph rules in Chapter 1, page 4.

a love of books

my father always had a great love of books he used to carry a small book with him at all times he always found at least fifteen minutes a day to read he read the book at every opportunity he read it on the bus, at the doctor's office, and at the barbershop he read the book in line at the bank and in the supermarket he never wasted a spare minute* he always found his fifteen minutes a day to read he read twenty books a year and one thousand books in his lifetime

_____

_____

_____

_____

_____

_____

_____

_____

_____

_____

_____

_____

_____

Vocabulary Note   *_a spare minute:_ free time

Part 3
The Direct Object
of Action Verbs

THE DIRECT OBJECT OF A VERB

> ► **Learning Point**
>
> Sometimes an action verb is followed by a **direct object** in the complement of a sentence. The direct object of a verb is a noun or a pronoun. The direct object tells *who* or *what* receives the action of the verb.

➠ The direct object in each sentence below answers the question **who?** or **what?** after the verb.

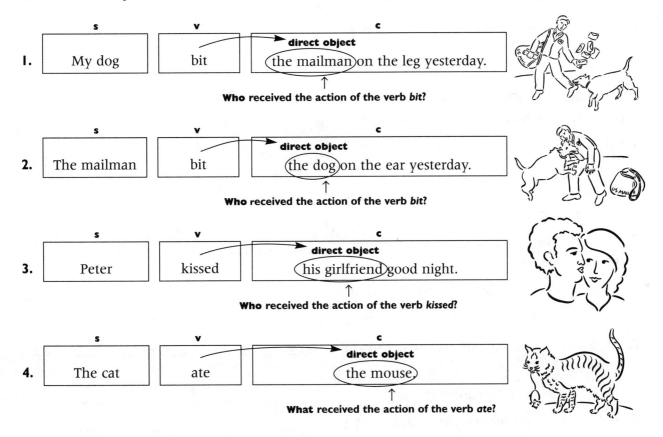

1. | s | v | c |
   | My dog | bit | **direct object** (the mailman) on the leg yesterday. |

   Who received the action of the verb *bit*?

2. | s | v | c |
   | The mailman | bit | **direct object** (the dog) on the ear yesterday. |

   Who received the action of the verb *bit*?

3. | s | v | c |
   | Peter | kissed | **direct object** (his girlfriend) good night. |

   Who received the action of the verb *kissed*?

4. | s | v | c |
   | The cat | ate | **direct object** (the mouse) |

   What received the action of the verb *ate*?

Note: A verb that is followed by a direct object is called a <u>transitive verb</u> (vt. in the dictionary)
   A verb that is <u>not</u> followed by a direct object is an <u>intransitive verb</u> (vi. in the dictionary).

THE DIRECT OBJECT OF ACTION VERBS

➡ **Exercise 1** Write the simple subject, the verb, and the direct object on the lines after each sentence.

> Remember that the direct object answers the question _who?_ or _what?_ after the verb.

		simple subject	verb	direct object
1.	People speak English in most parts of the world.	people	speak	English
2.	Many colleges in the U. S. now offer Japanese and Chinese classes.	Many colleges	now	u.s.
3.	I take twelve units every semester.	I	take	twelve units
4.	My English teacher gives too much homework.	My	gives	English
5.	The teacher reads the students' journals every week.	the teacher	reads	student's
6.	I always write my English compositions on the computer.	I	write	English
7.	My classmates and I often read each other's paragraphs in class.	MY	read	classmates
8.	The students in my class have library cards.	the students	have	class

➡ **Exercise 2** Follow the same directions as in Exercise 1. Then study the sentences for dictation.

1.	Many students attend the nursing program at my school.	Student	attend	nursing
2.	Student nurses take classes at local hospitals to get hands-on experience.	Student	Take	nurses
3.	Nurses in the school clinic advise students on health matters.	nurses	advise	students
4.	Many students get the flu during the winter.	students	get	Flu
5.	I eat fruit and vegetables every day.	I	eat	Fruit
6.	My family takes vitamins every day to supplement their diet.	Family	Takes	vitamins
7.	I ride my bike for exercise every day.	I	ride	bike
8.	I visit the eye doctor and the dentist every year.	I	visit	doctor dentist

WORDS USED AS NOUNS AND VERBS

▪ Sometimes students have trouble finding the direct object in a sentence because some English words can be used as either a noun or a verb.

> **Learning Point**
>
> Sometimes a word is a noun (person, place, or thing), and sometimes a word is a verb (action word). It depends on how the word is used in a sentence.
>
> **1.** When a word **shows action** in a sentence, it is a verb.
>
> **2.** When a word **receives the action** of the verb, it is a noun (direct object).

▪ **Example**   **1.** I <u>cook</u> dinner for my family every night.
                            ↑
                          verb
                        (action)

            2. Our school cafeteria just hired a new <u>cook</u>.
                                                          ↑
                                                        noun
                                                  (direct object)

▪ **Exercise 3** Read each pair of sentences below. Write <u>noun</u> or <u>verb</u> to tell how the underlined word is used in each sentence.

1. I <u>water</u> the plants in my garden every morning.   water - verb (action)

2. Plants need <u>water</u> to survive.   water - noun (direct object)

3. The post office delivers the <u>mail</u> about 9:00 in the morning.   mail - noun direct object

4. I always <u>mail</u> my bills on the first of the month.   mail - verb action

5. I need some <u>change</u> for the coke machine.   change verb action

6. The leaves <u>change</u> from green to brown in the fall.   change noun direction

7. I <u>work</u> at the Lockheed Martin Company in Denver, Colorado.   work - verb action

8. I like my <u>work</u> at Lockheed Martin very much.   work noun

9. My teacher has a nice <u>smile</u>.   smile verb

10. My teacher always <u>smiles</u> at the students.   smile noun

11. I <u>cut</u> my foot on a piece of glass yesterday.   cut verb

12. I cleaned the <u>cut</u> with soap and hot water.   cut noun

13. Everyone in my family <u>helps</u> with the housework on Saturday.   help noun

14. I need <u>help</u> with my math assignment.   help verb

SUBJECT AND OBJECT PRONOUNS

> ## ▶ Learning Point
>
> We use **subject pronouns** as subjects of sentences.
>
> We use **object pronouns** as direct objects of verbs.

➡ Study the chart below.

SUBJECT PRONOUNS		OBJECT PRONOUNS	
singular	**plural**	**singular**	**plural**
1. I	we	1. me	us
2. you	you	2. you	you
3. he		3. him	
she	they	her	them
it		it	

➡ Study the subject and object pronouns in the sentences below.

SUBJECT	VERB	COMPLEMENT (rest of the sentence)
1. Vocational classes ↑ **They**	prepare prepare	direct object students for many different kinds of jobs. ↑ **them** for many different kinds of jobs.
2. Mr. Lozano ↑ **He**	teaches teaches	direct object computer science at the vocational center. ↑ **it** at the vocational center.
3. Van's sister ↑ **She**	takes takes	direct object word processing and math classes three days a week. ↑ **them** three days a week.
4. The vocational center ↑ **It**	helps helps	direct object students to learn new skills and to find jobs. ↑ **them** to learn new skills and to find jobs.

SUBJECT AND OBJECT PRONOUNS

➡ **Exercise 4** Use subject and object pronouns to complete the dialogs below. Then practice the dialogs with a partner. One student is A. One student is B.

1. **A:** Do your parents live in the United States?

   B: No ____they____ don't. __they__ live in Mexico. I visit__them__ during the summer and at Christmas time.

2. **A:** I saw Martha with a good-looking man this morning. Does__she__ have a new boyfriend?

   B: Yes, __she__ does. His name is Nelson Lee. She met __her__ at the school dance last Friday night. __she__ danced together all night, and he called __her__ for a date the next morning.

3. **A:** What's wrong? You look discouraged.

   B: I am. __I__ 'm worried about my math class. All my classmates are worried too.

   A: Why?

   B: The teacher is very strict, and __she__ gives a lot of homework. Last weekend __she__ gave __us__ two chapters to read and 50 problems to solve.

4. **A:** Do you and your husband have any plans for Saturday night?

   B: Yes, __we__ do. Our neighbor, Julia, invited __it__ to her house for dinner on Saturday night.

   A: That sounds like fun.

   B: No, it isn't. Julia's husband likes to barbecue steak and hamburgers in the backyard, but __it__ 's a terrible cook. __he__ always burns the meat, and __he__ always go home hungry!

5. **A:** My brother's phone bills are always very high.

   B: Why?

   A: __he__ lives in Arizona, and his girlfriend lives in New York.

   B: Do __you__ talk a lot on the phone?

   A: Yes, __I__ do. __I__ talk every night. Unfortunately, his girlfriend always calls __him__ collect!

✓ CHECK YOUR UNDERSTANDING

A. Answer the questions below.

1. What is the direct object of a verb? _It is complemeh of a_ _rest sentece._

2. How can you find the direct object in a sentence? _I need to find_ _subjet an verb._

B. Use the verbs in parentheses to write true sentences about your life. Use a direct object after the verb in each sentence. Circle the verb and the direct object.

1. (watched) _My children like watche tv after_ _diner just for 30 minut._

2. (visited) _I visited my unt avery sunday_ _aften nooy._

3. (called) _My sirter Called mi one time_ _a wek._

4. (ate) _____

_____

5. (enjoyed) _____

_____

C. Write the subject pronouns and the object pronouns in the box below.

SUBJECT PRONOUNS		OBJECT PRONOUNS	
singular	**plural**	**singular**	**plural**
_____	_____	_____	_____
_____	_____	_____	_____
_____	_____	_____	_____
_____	_____		

Writing Assignment

➡ Your writing assignment in this chapter is to write a paragraph about why writing is difficult for many ESL students. What do you think? Is writing difficult for you? What are some of the problems that you have when you sit down to write?

▶ What to do ◀

I. Use the topic sentence below to write a paragraph.

> **Topic Sentence:** *Writing is difficult for three reasons.*

2. Write the first draft and the final draft of your paragraph on separate sheets of paper. Do not write in your textbook.

3. Follow the writing steps below. If you need to review the writing steps, go back to Chapter 1, pages 9-14.

STEP 1 *Pre-writing*.

Before you begin to write, take a few minutes to think about the topic sentence. Then write three reasons to explain why writing is often difficult.

STEP 2 Write your *first draft (practice paragraph)*.

Your paragraph should be about 150-200 words long.

STEP 3 *Revise and edit* your practice paragraph.

<u>Revise</u> means to add new sentences or take out sentences. Revise also means to rewrite any sentences that are confusing or unclear. <u>Edit</u> means to correct any mistakes in grammar, spelling, capital letters, or periods.

STEP 4 Write your *final draft (final paragraph)*.

Write your final paragraph in ink. Be sure to use correct paragraph form.

Chapter 3
Writing About Present Time: The Verb <u>Be</u>

To the Student:

In Chapter 2, you learned that most English sentences have three parts: <u>SUBJECT</u> - <u>VERB</u> - <u>COMPLEMENT.</u> You also learned that the verb in a sentence is usually a word that shows action. Action verbs are words like **run, jump, walk, eat.** In this chapter, you will study a verb that does not show action in a sentence: **the verb <u>Be</u>.**

Part I
The Non-Action Verb <u>Be</u>

THE VERB <u>BE</u> - NON-ACTION VERB

➥ You have learned that the verb in a sentence usually shows action. Action verbs are words such as *type, teach, build, study*.

> ▶ **Learning Point**
>
> Some verbs in English do not show action. The most important non-action verb in English is the verb <u>Be</u> (am, is, are).

➥ Study the examples below.

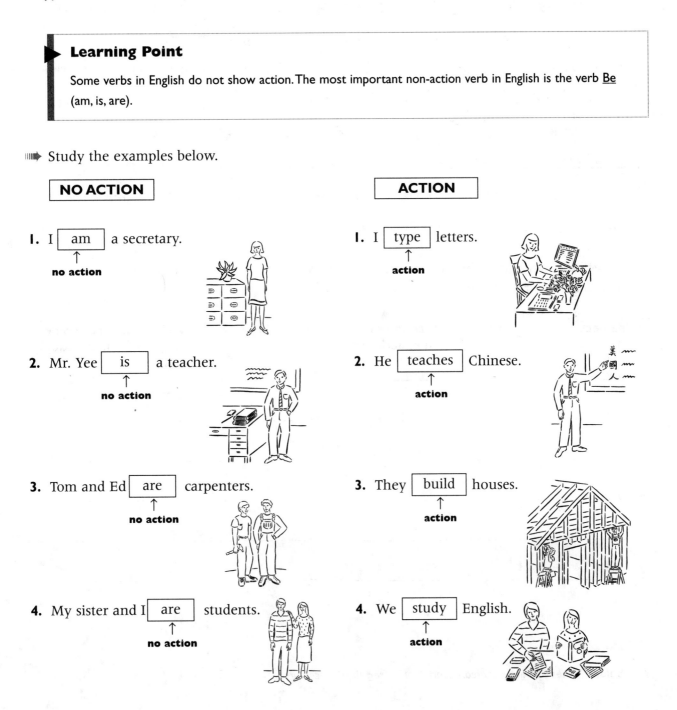

NO ACTION

1. I │ am │ a secretary.
     ↑
   no action

2. Mr. Yee │ is │ a teacher.
            ↑
         no action

3. Tom and Ed │ are │ carpenters.
               ↑
            no action

4. My sister and I │ are │ students.
                    ↑
                 no action

ACTION

1. I │ type │ letters.
     ↑
   action

2. He │ teaches │ Chinese.
       ↑
     action

3. They │ build │ houses.
         ↑
       action

4. We │ study │ English.
       ↑
     action

ACTION AND NON-ACTION VERBS

➡ **Exercise 1** Read the paragraph below. Then circle the subject(s) and verb in each sentence.

Getting Organized

[1]The campus (bookstore) (is) usually one of the most important stops for the well-prepared student at the beginning of a new semester. [2]Most students usually begin in the textbook section*. [3]Students purchase the required* textbooks for all their courses in this section. [4]If possible, they try to buy used textbooks to save money. [5]The school supply section is another busy place in the bookstore. [6]Students buy notebooks, binders, pens, and pencils in this section. [7]Calendars and dictionaries are also available here. [8]Across from the school supply section, the bookstore also sells backpacks, sweatshirts, jackets, and t-shirts. [9]The computer section is the final stop for many students. [10]Students in keyboarding and computer science classes buy diskettes, CDs, plastic containers, and paper for their printers. [11]The bookstore also offers student discounts on personal computers and other computer equipment. [12]The campus bookstore is always a very busy place during the first week of school.

➡ **Exercise 2** Write the subject(s) and verb of each sentence in the paragraph on the lines below. Write *action* or *non-action* after the verb.

subject	verb	action or non-action?		subject	verb	action or non-action?
1. bookstore	is	non-action	7.			
2. students	begin	action	8.			
3.			9.			
4.			10.			
5.			11.			
6.			12.			

Vocabulary Notes   *<u>section</u>: area, department   *<u>required</u>: necessary

THE PRESENT TENSE FORMS OF THE VERB BE

▶ **Learning Point**

The present tense forms of the verb <u>BE</u> are <u>am</u>, <u>is</u>, <u>are</u>.

To form contractions with the verb <u>BE</u>, we combine the subject pronoun and the verb.

(Example: I am → **I'm**   he is→ **he's**   they are → **they're**)

⟫ Present Tense Forms of the Verb <u>Be</u>

	<u>singular</u>		<u>plural</u>	
first person:	**1.** I am	(I'm)	**1.** we are	(we're)
second person:	**2.** you are	(you're)	**2.** you are	(you're)
third person:	**3.** he is	(he's)	**3.** they are	(they're)
	she is	(she's)		
	it is	(it's)		

⟫ Word order of Affirmative Sentences with <u>Be</u>

SUBJECT	VERB <u>BE</u>	COMPLEMENT (rest of the sentence)
1. I	am	a student at Evergreen Valley College.
2. You	are	in one of my ESL classes.
3. He	is	often late for his 8 o'clock class.
4. She	is	an assistant in the language lab.
5. It	is	a beautiful large campus.
6. We	are	all new students in the ESL program.
7. You	are	always attentive in class.
8. They	are	never absent from class.

THE PRESENT TENSE FORMS OF THE VERB <u>BE</u>

▶ **Exercise 3** Complete each sentence below with a subject and the Present Tense of the verb <u>Be</u>.

1. <u>My friends and I are</u> _____ never absent from class.

2. _____ a difficult class for most students.

3. _____ a good school.

4. _____ in my bookbag.

5. _____ my favorite months of the year.

6. _____ large cities in the United States.

7. _____ very expensive.

8. _____ near my house.

9. _____ my days off from work.

10. _____ a discount store.

▶ **Exercise 4** The sentences below contain one or more mistakes. Rewrite each sentence correctly on the lines below.

1. Is the best day of the week.

   _____

2. He my best friend.

   _____

3. Are very nice teachers.

   _____

4. My friends is in the cafeteria.

   _____

5. Tomas he are sick today.

   _____

6. Are good places to shop.

   _____

7. My book it's in my car.

   _____

8. Joe's parents is on vacation in Canada.

   _____

SPECIAL POINT: REVIEW OF NOUNS AND ADJECTIVES

➠ Before you continue to study the verb <u>Be</u>, it is important for you to review *nouns* and *adjectives*.

> ▶ **Learning Point 1**
>
> A **noun** is a word that names a <u>person</u>, <u>place</u>, or <u>thing</u>.

person	place	thing
doctor	school	pencil
teacher	park	desk
Karen	New York	flower
Mr. Carter	Mexico	table

➠ **Exercise 5** Write your own examples of nouns on the lines below.

person	place	thing
1. _____	1. _____	1. _____
2. _____	2. _____	2. _____
3. _____	3. _____	3. _____
4. _____	4. _____	4. _____

> ▶ **Learning Point 2**
>
> An **adjective** is a word that describes a <u>noun</u>.
>
> We never add -s to an adjective (new book / new books, young boy / young boys).

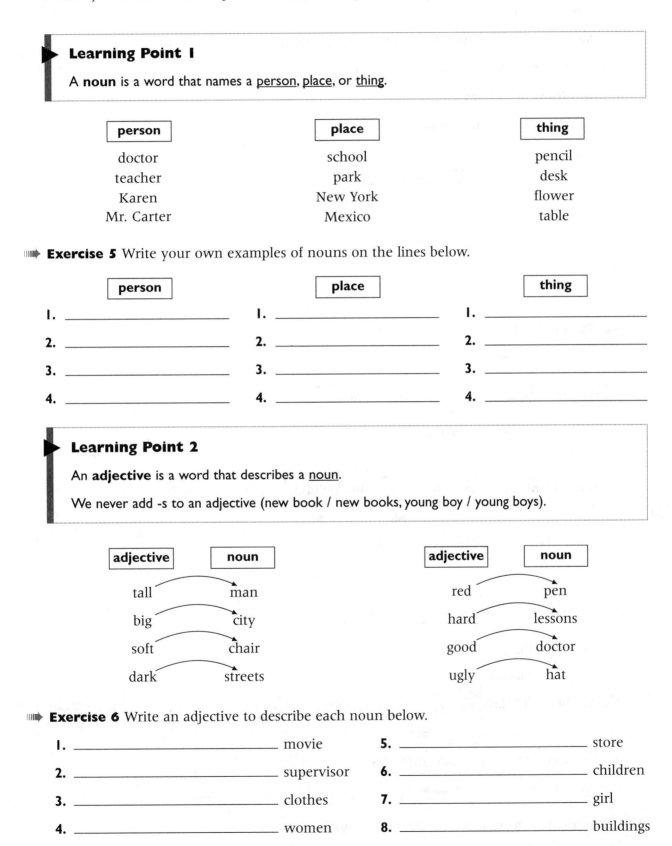

adjective	noun		adjective	noun
tall	man		red	pen
big	city		hard	lessons
soft	chair		good	doctor
dark	streets		ugly	hat

➠ **Exercise 6** Write an adjective to describe each noun below.

1. _____ movie
2. _____ supervisor
3. _____ clothes
4. _____ women

5. _____ store
6. _____ children
7. _____ girl
8. _____ buildings

USING NOUNS, ADJECTIVES, AND LOCATIONS AFTER THE VERB BE

> **Learning Point**
>
> We use the Simple Present Tense of the verb <u>Be</u> in three ways in a sentence:
>
> 1. We use **nouns** after <u>Be</u>.
>
> 2. We use **adjectives** after <u>Be</u>.
>
> 3. We use **locations** after <u>Be</u>.

1. | We use **nouns** after <u>Be</u>.   (Be + noun)

    a. Mr. Lee is an <u>electrician</u>.
                  noun

    b. My favorite flowers are <u>roses</u> and <u>carnations</u>.
                        noun   **noun**

    c. That car is a <u>Ford</u>.
                 noun

2. | We use **adjectives** after <u>Be</u>.   (Be + adjective)

    a. My English class is <u>difficult</u>.
                   adj

    b. The students in my class are <u>friendly</u> and <u>helpful</u>.
                        adj   **adj**

    c. College books and tuition are <u>expensive</u>.
                        adj

3. | We use **locations** after <u>Be</u>.   (Be + location)

    a. Martina is <u>from Russia</u>.
            location

    b. My chemistry class is <u>on the second floor</u>.
                   location

    c. The restrooms are <u>near the elevators</u>.
              location

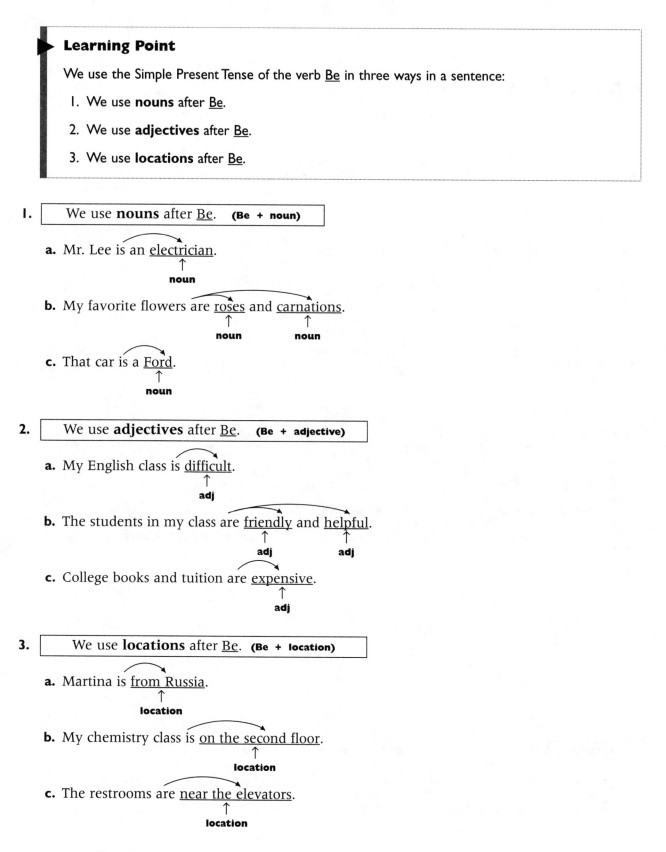

Note: You will study more about <u>Be</u> + location in Part 2.

USING NOUNS, ADJECTIVES, AND LOCATIONS AFTER THE VERB <u>BE</u>

➡ **Exercise 7** Complete each sentence with true statements about your life. Use only the verb <u>Be</u> (*am, is, are*).

1. My house_____ _____
              (be)   **(location)**

2. My favorite store _____ _____
                     (be)   **(noun)**

3. My father _____ _____
               (be)   **(adjective)**

4. My car _____ _____
            (be)   **(adjective)**

5. My favorite food _____ _____
                   (be)   **(noun)**

6. My school _____ _____
               (be)   **(location)**

7. The best month of the year _____ _____
                                (be)   **(noun)**

8. The weather in my city _____ _____
                            (be)   **(adjective)**

➡ **Exercise 8** Write your own sentences with the verb <u>Be</u> (*am, is, are*). Write true sentences about your life. Begin each sentence with a capital letter, and end each sentence with a period.

Be + noun

1. _____

2. _____

Be + adjective

1. _____

2. _____

Be + location

1. _____

2. _____

SENTENCES WITH <u>THERE IS</u> / <u>THERE ARE</u>

▸ Many sentences in English begin with <u>there is</u> or <u>there are</u>. Sometimes students have difficulty finding the subject in a sentence that begins with <u>there</u>.

> ### ▶ Learning Point 1
>
> The word <u>there</u> is **NOT** the subject of the sentence. <u>There</u> is a "dummy" subject. It is not the real subject. In a sentence with <u>there is</u> or <u>there are,</u> the real subject comes after the verb.

Example: 1. There is a **dictionary** on the bookshelf in the back of the room.
     ↑ ↑ ↑
    dummy verb subject
    subject

      2. There are several **students** absent today.
      ↑ ↑   ↑
     dummy verb   subject
     subject

> ### ▶ Learning Point 2
>
> When the subject is singular, the verb must be singular. When the subject is plural, the verb must be plural.

Example: 1. There is a public **telephone** near the bus stop.
      ↑   ↑
     verb subject (singular)

      2. There is an emergency **exit** near the elevator in the library.
      ↑   ↑
     verb   subject (singular)

      3. There are several **people** in line at the admissions office.
      ↑   ↑
     verb subject (plural)

▸ When there is more than one subject in a sentence with <u>there</u>, the verb agrees with the subject closest to the verb.

 1. There is a coffee **machine** and a **microwave** in the room at the end of the hall.
    ↑   ↑   ↑
   verb subject subject

 2. There are two **notebooks** and a **dictionary** on the teacher's desk.
    ↑   ↑   ↑
   verb subject subject

SENTENCES WITH <u>THERE IS</u> / <u>THERE ARE</u>

▶ **Exercise 9** Complete each sentence with <u>there is</u> or <u>there are</u>. Circle the subject in each sentence. Compare your answers with a classmate.

1. <u>There are</u> _____ copy (machines) in the library.

2. _____ several pay phones outside the cafeteria.

3. _____ a fire extinguisher near the elevators on each floor.

4. _____ an electronic classroom in the learning center.

5. _____ tape recorders and VCRs for students in the language lab.

6. _____ a security office near the parking lot.

7. _____ restrooms on the first floor of the physical education building.

8. _____ a beautiful fountain in the middle of our campus.

▶ **Exercise 10** Describe <u>your</u> classroom. Use <u>there is</u> or <u>there are</u> in each sentence. Begin each sentence with a capital letter and end each sentence with a period. Circle the subject and the verb in each sentence.

My Classroom

1. There (is) a (desk) in the front of the room. _____

   _____

2. _____

   _____

3. _____

   _____

4. _____

   _____

5. _____

   _____

6. _____

   _____

7. _____

   _____

8. _____

   _____

PRESENT TENSE OF THE VERB <u>BE</u>

 Exercise 11 Christa Paulick is a foreign student at DeAnza College. She is taking three classes, but she isn't doing very well in her writing class. A recent assignment was to write a paragraph about herself and her school. Christa wrote the paragraph below, but she forgot to begin each sentence with a capital letter and end each sentence with a period.

Rewrite Christa's paragraph on the lines below. Correct her capitalization and punctuation. When you are finished, the paragraph should have 13 sentences. Remember to use correct paragraph form.

A Foreign Student

i am from Berlin, Germany i am a day student at DeAnza College DeAnza is a fairly small school there are only about 800 students in the school everyone is very friendly the instructors at this school are very good they are conscientious and knowledgeable in their subjects my favorite class is English there are students from many different countries and cultures in my class our discussions are always lively and informative my other classes are math and art history these classes are also very interesting i'm happy to be a student at such a good school

_____

_____

_____

_____

_____

_____

_____

_____

_____

_____

_____

_____

_____

PRESENT TENSE OF THE VERB <u>BE</u> - NEGATIVE

> ▶ **Learning Point**
>
> **1.** To form negative sentences with the verb <u>BE</u>, we put *not* after the verb. (Example: He is **not** in my class.)
>
> **2.** There are two ways to form negative contractions with the verb <u>BE</u>:
>
>   **a.** Combine the subject pronoun and the verb <u>BE</u>. (**He's** not in my class.)
>
>   **b.** Combine the verb <u>BE</u> and <u>not</u>. (He **isn't** in my class.)

▥➡ **Negative Forms of the Verb <u>Be</u>**

	<u>singular</u>			<u>plural</u>
1.	I am not	(I'm not / x x x x x)	**1.**	we are not	(we're not / we aren't)
2.	you are not	(you're not / you aren't)	**2.**	you are not	(you're not / you aren't)
3.	he is not	(he's not / he isn't)	**3.**	they are not	(they're not / they aren't)
	she is not	(she's not / she isn't)			
	it is not	(it's not / it isn't)			

▥➡ **Word Order of Negative Sentences with <u>Be</u>**

	SUBJECT	VERB BE + NOT	COMPLEMENT
1	I	am not	usually late for class.
2.	You	are not	always careful with your verb tenses.
3	He	is not	a counselor.
4.	She	is not	a very conscientious student.
5.	It	is not	a difficult English assignment.
6.	We	are not	in a chemistry class this year.
7.	You	are not	in the right classroom.
8.	They	are not	happy with their class schedules this semester.

PRESENT TENSE OF THE VERB <u>BE</u> - AFFIRMATIVE AND NEGATIVE

➡ **Exercise 12** Salvador Ramirez is in the U. S. on a student visa from Panama, and this is his first experience away from home. He lives in an apartment off-campus. Read Salvador's description of his first apartment. Then complete the sentences with the correct Present Tense form of the verb <u>BE</u>. Circle the subjects.

My Apartment

¹My (apartment) ___is___ very satisfactory. ²The living room _____ a good size. ³There _____ enough space for a sofa, end tables, lamps, and a comfortable chair for reading. ⁴There _____ a place to put my TV, stereo, and CD player. ⁵To the left of the living room, the kitchen _____ adequate. ⁶It _____ large enough for a table and four chairs. ⁷The refrigerator _____ big enough to store food and milk for the week. ⁸To the right of the living room, the small bathroom _____ well-ventilated for the shower, and there _____ a bathtub. ⁹The location of my apartment _____ good. ¹⁰I _____ able to walk to school, and the bus stop _____ convenient to get to work. ¹¹All in all, I _____ very happy here.

➡ **Exercise 13** In the paragraph above, Salvador is happy with his apartment. Now pretend that he is not happy with his apartment. Change the whole paragraph to negative. Be careful with capital letters and periods.

My Apartment

_____ My apartment is not very satisfactory.

_____

_____

_____

_____

_____

_____

_____

_____

_____

_____

PRESENT TENSE OF THE VERB <u>BE</u> - YES-NO QUESTIONS

> ### ▶ Learning Point
>
> **Yes-no questions** are questions that we answer with **yes** or **no**.
>
> To form **yes-no questions** with the verb <u>BE</u>, we put the verb <u>Be</u> in front of the subject.
>
> <u>**Example:**</u> Is Robert late for his doctor's appointment?
>
>   Yes, he is. (No, he isn't.)

⟾ Verb <u>Be</u> - Yes-No Questions

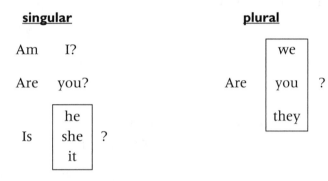

	singular			plural	
Am	I?			we	
Are	you?		Are	you	?
Is	he / she / it ?			they	

⟾ Word Order of Yes-No Questions with <u>Be</u>

VERB <u>BE</u>	SUBJECT	COMPLEMENT	SHORT ANSWERS FOR CONVERSATION
1. Am	I	in the right classroom for English 322?	Yes, you are.
2. Are	you	a student at Silver Creek High School?	No, I'm not.
3. Is	Mario	from Portugal?	Yes, he is.
4. Is	Mario's sister Ana	in your English class?	Yes, she is.
5. Is	your English class	difficult?	No, it isn't.
6. Are	we	late for class?	No, you aren't.
7. Are	you and Ana	good friends?	Yes, we are.
8. Are	Mario and Ana	new students at this school?	No, they aren't.

PRESENT TENSE OF THE VERB <u>BE</u> - YES-NO QUESTIONS

➠ **Exercise 14** Thanh is a new student at City College, and he has several questions about the health services that are available to students. In the dialog below, Thanh is talking to the nurse at the campus health center. Complete the dialog with Thanh's questions.

At the Health Center

1. Thanh: <u>Is the health center open to all students?</u>
   Nurse: Yes, it is. (The health center is open to all students.)

2. Thanh: _____
   Nurse: No, they aren't. (The services are not expensive.)

3. Thanh: _____
   Nurse: No, it isn't.(It is not difficult to get an appointment with a doctor.)

4. Thanh: _____
   Nurse: Yes, it is. (The health center is open at night.)

➠ **Exercise 15** Celia is interested in taking classes at City College. Right now, she is at the Admissions Office to get information about the registration procedures. Complete the dialog below with Celia's questions.

At the Admissions Office

1. Celia: _____
   Clerk: Yes, it is. (Registration is this week.)

2. Celia: _____
   Clerk: Yes, they are. (The placement tests are this week.)

3. Celia: _____
   Clerk: Yes, it is. (The financial aid office is open until 5:00 every day.)

4. Celia: _____
   Clerk: No, they aren't. (The counselors' offices are not in this building.)

REFERENCE CHART: THE VERB <u>BE</u> - NON-ACTION VERB

➡ The verb <u>Be</u> has three forms in the Simple Present Tense: *am, is, are*. Review the forms of the verb <u>Be</u> in the charts below.

<u>Be</u> – Affirmative Sentences

SUBJECT	VERB <u>BE</u>	COMPLEMENT	AFFIRMATIVE CONTRACTIONS
I	am	a student at Carter College.	I'm
You	are	in my computer class.	you're
He	is	a friend of mine.	he's
She	is	in the counselor's office.	she's
It	is	a nice day today.	it's
We	are	in the same English class.	we're
You	are	happy with your class schedules.	you're
They	are	on the teacher's roll.	they're

<u>Be</u> – Negative Sentences

SUBJECT	VERB <u>BE</u> + NOT	COMPLEMENT	NEGATIVE CONTRACTIONS	
I	am not	a student at Carter College.	I'm not	xxxxxxx
You	are not	in my computer class.	you're not	you aren't
He	is not	a friend of mine.	he's not	he isn't
She	is not	in the counselor's office.	she's not	she isn't
It	is not	a nice day today.	it's not	it isn't
We	are not	in the same English class.	we're not	we aren't
You	are not	happy with your class schedules.	you're not	you aren't
They	are not	on the teacher's roll.	they're not	they aren't

<u>Be</u> – Questions

VERB	SUBJECT	COMPLEMENT
Am	I	a student at Carter College?
Are	you	in my computer class?
Is	he	a friend of yours?
Is	she	in the counselor's office?
Is	it	a nice day today?
Are	we	in the same English class?
Are	you	happy with your class schedules?
Are	they	on the teacher's roll?

✓ CHECK YOUR UNDERSTANDING

A. Answer the questions below.

1. Most verbs show action in a sentence. However, the verb <u>Be</u> _____ show action.

2. What are the present tense forms of the verb <u>Be</u>? _____ _____ _____

3. What are three ways that we use the verb <u>Be</u> in the Simple Present Tense?

   a. Be + _____   **b.** Be + _____   **c.** Be + _____

4. Write an example sentence showing each way that we use the verb <u>Be</u>.

   a. _____

   b. _____

   c. _____

5. In a sentence that begins with <u>there</u>, the subject comes _____ the verb.

6. How do we form negative sentences with the verb <u>Be</u>?

   _____

7. How do we form yes-no questions with the verb <u>Be</u>?

   _____

B. *EDITING* - There are 7 mistakes in the use of the verb <u>Be</u> in the paragraph below. Find and correct each mistake. The first one is done for you.

A Great Place to Study

                    is
¹The new library at Evergreen Valley College ~~are~~ a great place to study. ²For one thing, there's computers in every area of the library. ³Old newspapers, magazines, and other reference materials are all available on-line, so it is no necessary to use the old microfilm machines to view old documents. ⁴The computers also provide access to the Internet, so students can find information from all over the world. ⁵Second, there be many small conference rooms on every floor of the new library. ⁶These rooms is just the right size for small groups of three or four students. ⁷Students can study together and discuss their assignments without disturbing anyone else in the library. ⁸Finally, the library's hours very convenient. ⁹It is open every evening until 10:00 p.m. and all day on Saturday and Sunday. ¹⁰A good library with convenient hours are very important, and all of the students appreciate our new library.

Part 2
Prepositions of Location (Where)

INTRODUCTION - WHAT ARE PREPOSITIONS?

> ▶ **Learning Point**
>
> Prepositions are small words such as | **in, on, near, under** |. Prepositions are important because they change the meaning of a sentence.

➠ A noun usually follows a preposition.

Example: **1.** The book is (in) the (desk.)
                prep   **noun**

2. The book is (on) the (desk.)
          prep   **noun**

3. The book is (near) the (desk.)
          prep   **noun**

4. The book is (under) the (desk.)
          prep   **noun**

➠**Exercise 1** Circle the prepositions in the sentences below. Also circle the noun that follows each preposition. Draw an arrow from the preposition to the noun.

1. The teacher and students are (in) the (classroom) now.

2. The teacher's briefcase is on the desk near the blackboard.

3. The students' papers are in the teacher's briefcase.

4. There are some roses in a vase on the teacher's desk.

5. There are several textbooks and dictionaries in the bookcase near the window.

6. The students' backpacks are under their desks.

INTRODUCTION – WHAT ARE PREPOSITIONAL PHRASES?

➤ You have learned that a noun usually follows a preposition.

▶ Learning Point

We call the noun that follows a preposition the **object** of the preposition.

We call a preposition and its object a   **prepositional phrase.**   A prepositional phrase is a part of a sentence.

➤ Study the examples below.

1. The children are   **prepositional phrase**

      in   the   swimming   pool.

      ↑   ↑

     prep   obj of prep

2. The man is standing   **prepositional phrase**

      near the garage.

      ↑   ↑

    prep   obj of prep

3. There are some plates   **prepositional phrase**

      on the picnic table.

      ↑   ↑

    prep   obj of prep

4. There is a bench   **prepositional phrase**

      under the tree.

      ↑   ↑

    prep   obj of prep

5. The car is   **prepositional phrase**

      in the garage.

      ↑   ↑

   prep   obj of prep

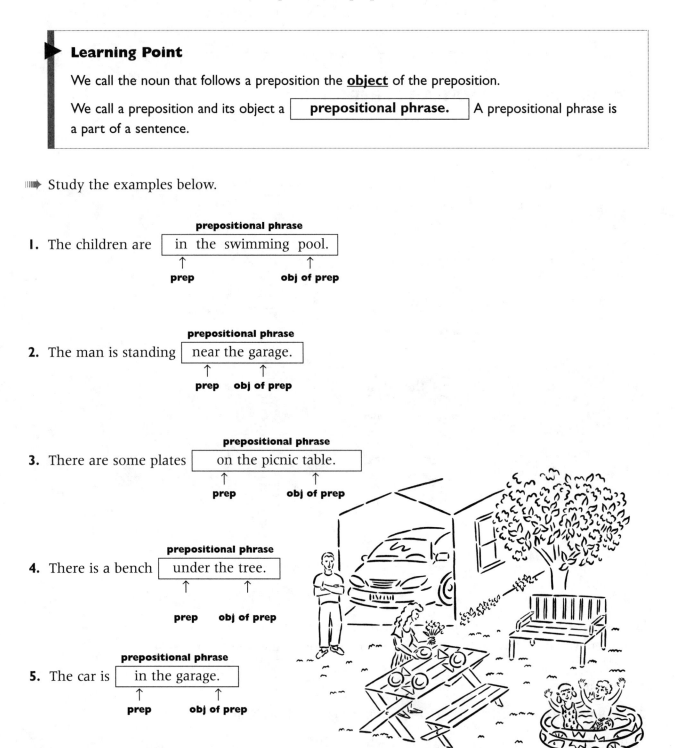

PREPOSITIONS OF LOCATION (WHERE)

▥▶ We often use prepositions in sentences to tell <u>where</u>. Prepositions that tell <u>where</u> are called prepositions of location. Study the meaning of the prepositions in the box below.

prepositions that tell <u>where</u> (location)

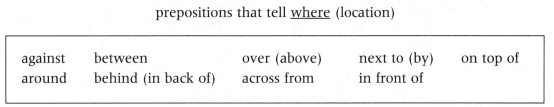

against	between	over (above)	next to (by)	on top of
around	behind (in back of)	across from	in front of	

<u>Note</u>: In English we have one-word prepositions, two-word prepositions, and three-word prepositions.

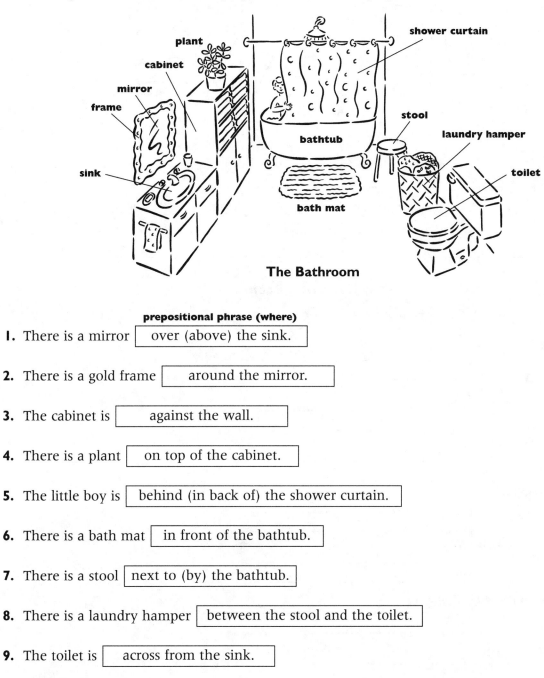

The Bathroom

prepositional phrase (where)

I. There is a mirror │ over (above) the sink.

2. There is a gold frame │ around the mirror.

3. The cabinet is │ against the wall.

4. There is a plant │ on top of the cabinet.

5. The little boy is │ behind (in back of) the shower curtain.

6. There is a bath mat │ in front of the bathtub.

7. There is a stool │ next to (by) the bathtub.

8. There is a laundry hamper │ between the stool and the toilet.

9. The toilet is │ across from the sink.

PREPOSITIONS OF LOCATION (WHERE)

▶ **Exercise 2** Use a preposition from the box to write prepositional phrases about the picture. Some sentences have more than one possible answer. Circle the preposition and the object of the preposition. Your teacher may ask you to write your answers on the board.

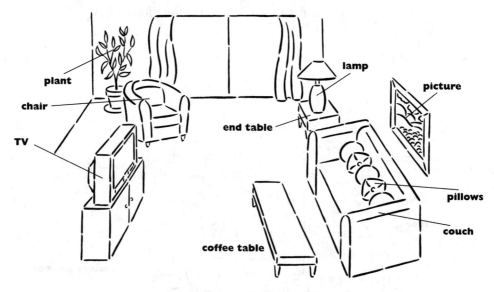

prepositions that tell <u>where</u> (location)

on	over (above)	in front of	behind (in back of)
against	across from	next to (by)	

My New Living Room

prepositional phrase (where)

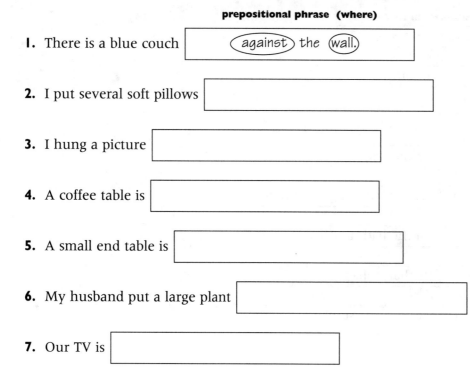

1. There is a blue couch ⟨against⟩ the ⟨wall.⟩

2. I put several soft pillows

3. I hung a picture

4. A coffee table is

5. A small end table is

6. My husband put a large plant

7. Our TV is

PREPOSITIONS OF LOCATION (WHERE)

➡ **Exercise 3** Choose a preposition from the box to write prepositional phrases about the picture. Circle the preposition and the object of the preposition.

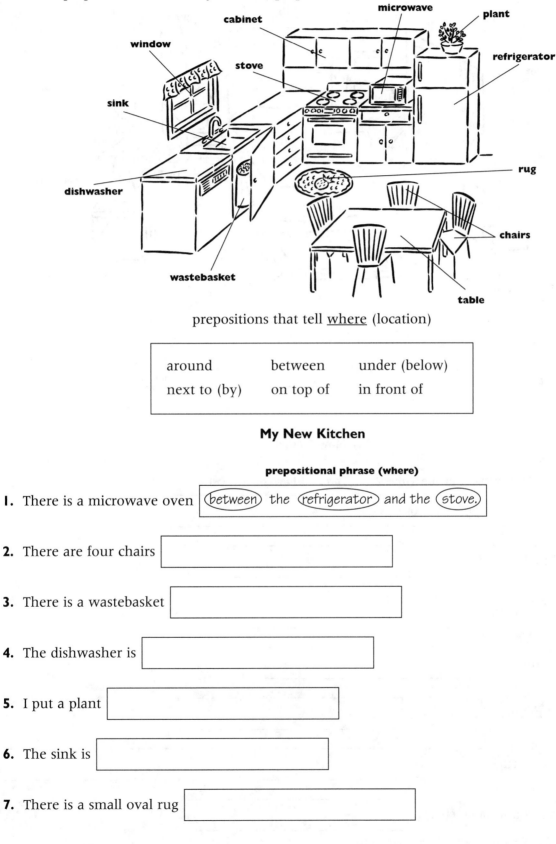

prepositions that tell <u>where</u> (location)

around	between	under (below)
next to (by)	on top of	in front of

My New Kitchen

prepositional phrase (where)

1. There is a microwave oven (between) the (refrigerator) and the (stove.)

2. There are four chairs

3. There is a wastebasket

4. The dishwasher is

5. I put a plant

6. The sink is

7. There is a small oval rug

PREPOSITIONS OF LOCATION (WHERE)

➡ **Exercise 4** Choose a preposition from the box to write prepositional phrases about the picture. Circle the preposition and the object of the preposition.

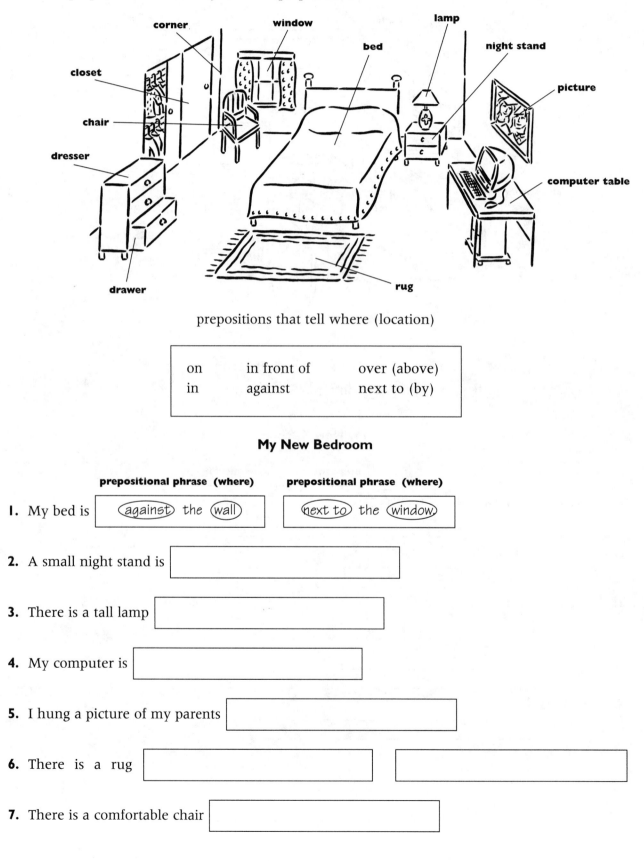

prepositions that tell where (location)

on	in front of	over (above)
in	against	next to (by)

My New Bedroom

	prepositional phrase (where)	prepositional phrase (where)
1. My bed is	(against) the (wall)	(next to) the (window)
2. A small night stand is		
3. There is a tall lamp		
4. My computer is		
5. I hung a picture of my parents		
6. There is a rug		
7. There is a comfortable chair		

☑ CHECK YOUR UNDERSTANDING

A. Use prepositional phrases that tell <u>where</u> to describe <u>your</u> living room, kitchen, and bedroom. Put a period at the end of each sentence. Circle the preposition and the object of the preposition.

My Living Room

1. My couch is _____
   prepositional phrase - where

2. The TV is _____

3. The coffee table is _____

4. My favorite chair is _____

My Kitchen

5. Our kitchen table is_____
   prepositional phrase - where

6. The kitchen chairs are _____

7. The dishes and glasses are _____

8. The silverware is _____

My Bedroom

9. My bed is _____
   prepositional phrase - where

10. There is a night stand _____

11. I hang my clothes _____

12. I keep my socks and underwear _____

B. Underline or highlight 14 prepositional phrases that tell <u>where</u> in the paragraph.

through the window   The Thief   **toward the living room**

¹There was a robbery <u>on Willow Street</u> last night. ²While Mr. and Mrs. Hale were at the movies, a thief entered their house. ³He climbed through an open window in the kitchen. ⁴He walked toward the living room. ⁵He found a gold watch on the coffee table. ⁶He saw a TV, a VCR, and a CD player in a cabinet near the window. ⁷Then he walked up the stairs to the bedrooms on the second floor. ⁸He found $200 and Mrs. Hale's jewelry in the dresser drawers. ⁹Suddenly, he heard voices in the living room. ¹⁰He hid behind the bedroom door and waited.

Part 3
Prepositions of Time (When)

PREPOSITIONS OF TIME - PREPOSITIONS THAT TELL <u>WHEN</u>

▥➡ In Part 2, you used prepositional phrases to tell <u>where</u>. In this part, you will use prepositional phrases to tell | **when.** |

> ▶ **Learning Point**
>
> We often use the prepositions | ***before, during,*** and ***after*** | in prepositional phrases to tell <u>when</u> something happened.

▥➡ Study the examples below.

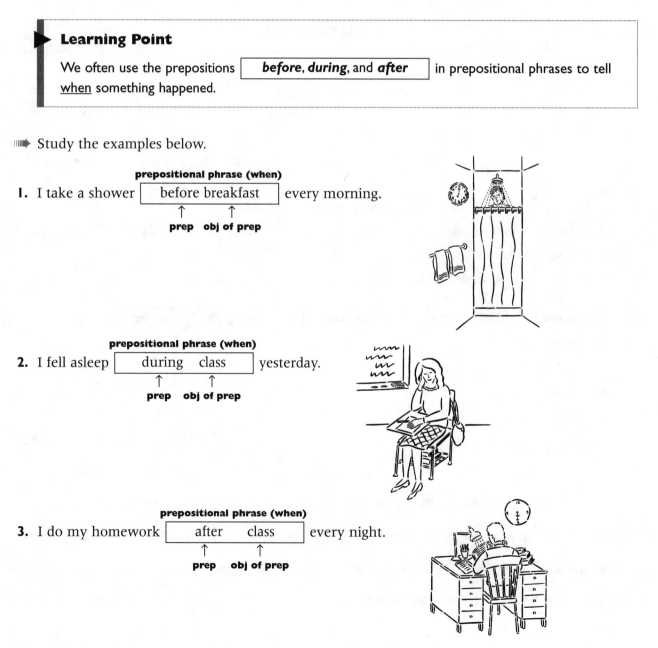

1. I take a shower | before breakfast | every morning.

prepositional phrase (when)
↑   ↑
prep   obj of prep

2. I fell asleep | during   class | yesterday.

prepositional phrase (when)
↑   ↑
prep   obj of prep

3. I do my homework | after   class | every night.

prepositional phrase (when)
↑   ↑
prep   obj of prep

<u>Note</u>: Words such as <u>every morning</u>, <u>yesterday</u>, <u>every night</u>, <u>today</u>, and <u>tomorrow</u> are time words. Time words are not part of a prepositional phrase.

PREPOSITIONS OF TIME (WHEN)

➡ **Exercise I** Choose the correct preposition of time to tell <u>when</u> in each sentence below.

1. Ron likes to go to the beach _____during_____ the summer.
(during - after)

2. Judy always brushes her teeth _____ dinner.
(after - before)

3. Pedro studied hard _____ the test.
(after - before)

4. John ate a big bag of popcorn _____ the movie.
(during - after)

5. Kim wrote a thank-you note to her friends _____ the party.
(before - after)

6. My friends and I always meet for coffee _____ class.
(before - during)

➡ **Exercise 2** Choose <u>*before*</u>, <u>*during*</u>, or <u>*after*</u> to complete each prepositional phrase that tells <u>when</u> in the paragraph below.

A Surprise Birthday Party

[1]We had a good time in class yesterday afternoon. [2]It was our teacher's birthday, so we gave

her a surprise party _____during_____ class. [3]We wanted the party to be special, so

we decorated the classroom with balloons and flowers _____ class. [4]Some of

the students brought karaoke tapes for the television set in the classroom, and we danced and

sang songs _____ the party. [5]One of the students also brought a camera and

took pictures of the teacher and all the students. [6]Then the teacher cut the cake and made a

speech. [7]_____ the party, we carefully cleaned up the room and re-arranged the

desks _____ the next class. [8]The teacher appreciated our thoughtfulness and

wrote a thank-you note to all of the students.

PREPOSITIONS OF TIME (WHEN)

➠ In Part 2, you used prepositional phrases with _at_, _on_, _in_ to tell _where_. We can also use prepositional phrases with [_at, on, in_ to tell _when_.]

➠ Study the following charts carefully. The charts show how we use _at_, _on_, _in_ to tell _when_.

We use **at** to show exact clock time.	We use **on** with exact days.	We use **in** when the time is not exact.
at 8:00 at 10:15 at 2:30 at 6:02 at 9:33 at six o'clock at noon at midnight	* days of the week on Monday on Wednesday * days of the month on January 3 on March 16 * holidays on Christmas Day on Thanksgiving _Note: On the weekend means on Saturday and Sunday_	* parts of the day in the morning in the afternoon in the evening _exception: at night_ * months in January * years in 1995 * seasons in the summer

➠ **Exercise 3** Choose _at_, _on_, or _in_ to complete the prepositional phrases in the sentences below.

prepositional phrase - when

1. The spring semester started | ___on___ January 27. |

2. I have an English class | _____ the morning | and a math class | _____ the afternoon. |

3. I have to meet with my English teacher | _____ 10:00 | tomorrow.

4. We usually have a quiz | _____ Friday. |

5. Our first midterm is | _____ March 3. |

6. We don't have class | _____ Memorial Day. |

7. I'm going to get my AA degree | _____ June. |

8. I plan to transfer to a four-year college | _____ the fall. |

✓ CHECK YOUR UNDERSTANDING

A. Use *at*, *on*, or *in* to complete the dialogs below.

1. A: Where were you last Thursday __*at*__ 2:30 __*in*__ the afternoon?

  B: Let me think. I left home _____ 11:15 _____ the morning and met a friend for lunch _____ noon. After lunch, we went shopping. We were probably at the mall _____ 2:30. Why?

  A: Oh, I thought that I saw you on a TV talk show.

2. A: I never see you at school _____ the morning.

  B: I'm never here _____ the morning. My first class starts _____ noon.

  A: Why do you start school so late?

  B: I hate to get up early _____ the morning!

3. A: Can you give me a ride home after class tonight?

  B: I'm sorry, but I don't have my car. I don't like to drive _____ night, so I take the bus.

4. A: My niece is getting married _____ May. I'm giving her a wedding shower _____ March 8. Would you like to come?

  B: I'd love to come, but my husband and I will be out of town _____ March.

  A: Well, my niece's friends are giving her another shower _____ April 5. Can you come then?

  B: Yes, I'd love to come.

B. Practice your writing. Use a prepositional phrase with *at*, *on*, or *in* to tell <u>when</u> in each sentence. Write true sentences about your life.

  1. My birthday is _____
  prepositional phrase - when

  2. I started classes at this school _____

  3. Our class takes a break _____

  4. We don't have class _____

  5. I usually get up _____

  6. We do the grocery shopping _____

  7. My family likes to go out for dinner _____

  8. We usually take a vacation _____

✎ Writing Assignment

▥➡ Your writing assignment in this chapter is to write a paragraph about your favorite place to study. Some students like to study at the library. Other students prefer to study in their bedroom or at the kitchen table near the refrigerator. Where do you like to study? Why is it a good place to study?

▶ What to do ◀

1. Complete the topic sentence below.

    Topic Sentence: *My favorite place to study is* _____.

2. Write the first draft and the final draft of your paragraph on separate sheets of paper. Do not write in your textbook.

3. Follow the writing steps below.

STEP 1   *Pre-writing*.

    Before you begin to write, take a few minutes to think about your favorite place to study. Then write three reasons to explain why it is a good place to study.

STEP 2   Write your *first draft* (*practice paragraph*).

    Your paragraph should be about 150-200 words long.

STEP 3   *Revise and edit* your practice paragraph.

    <u>Revise</u> means to add new sentences or take out sentences. Revise also means to rewrite any sentences that are confusing or unclear. <u>Edit</u> means to correct any mistakes in grammar, spelling, capital letters, or periods.

STEP 4   Write your *final draft* (*final paragraph*).

    Write your final paragraph in ink. Be sure to use correct paragraph form.

Chapter 4
The Reason and Example Paragraph

To the Student:

In Chapter 1 you wrote a paragraph about why you like your school. In Chapter 2 you wrote a paragraph about why writing is often difficult, and in Chapter 3 you wrote about your favorite place to study. In these paragraphs, you gave reasons to explain and support your topic sentence. In this chapter, you will learn more about this kind of paragraph. We call this kind of paragraph a **Reason and Example** paragraph.

Part I
Prewriting

GETTING READY TO WRITE

➠ You learned in Chapter 1 that it is a good idea to do some kind of prewriting before you start to write a paragraph. You learned that one good way to get ideas is to talk about the topic with your classmates.

➠ In this chapter, your writing assignment will be to write a paragraph about the place where you live. Some people live in an apartment or a house. Other people live in a mobile home or a condominium. Where do you live? Do you like the place where you live? Why or why not? In order to get ready to write your paragraph, follow the prewriting instructions on the next page.

apartment   house

duplex   mobile home

condominium

PREWRITING

▶ What to do ◀

1. Form a group with three or four classmates.

2. In your group, talk about the place where you live. Do you like or dislike it? Why or why not? Is the place where you live large enough for your family, or is it too small? Is your street quiet or noisy? Are your neighbors friendly or unfriendly? What are the reasons that you like or dislike the place where you live?

3. On the lines below, make a list of the things that you like or dislike about the place where you live. Write as many things as you can think of. Do not worry about grammar or spelling. You do not need to write complete sentences. You will use these notes later to help you to write a paragraph.

NOTES

Part 2
Using Reasons and Examples to Support the Topic Sentence

THE REASON AND EXAMPLE PARAGRAPH

▶ In Chapter 1, you learned that the topic sentence of a paragraph gives the main idea of the paragraph and tells the reader what the paragraph is about. All the other sentences in the paragraph explain and support the topic sentence.

▶ In this chapter, you will write a **reason and example** paragraph. When we write a **reason and example** paragraph, we give reasons to explain and support the topic sentence, and we use examples to give additional information about each reason. There is no rule about the number of reasons to use in a paragraph. However, it is common to use two or three reasons to support the topic sentence.

▶ In the paragraph below, Bong Tran began with the topic sentence, **My house is a good place to live for several reasons.** Bong then gave three reasons to explain why he likes his house:

first reason:	First of all, my house is in a convenient location.
second reason:	Second, I live in a very good neighborhood.
third reason:	Finally, we have very nice neighbors.

My House

¹My house is a good place to live for several reasons. ²First of all, my house is in a convenient location. ³For example, it is near the freeway, and it is very close to the main streets of the city. ⁴My house is near the high school, so my children can walk to school every day. ⁵Also, there is a bus stop a block away from my house, so my mother can take the bus to the temple. ⁶Second, I live in a very good neighborhood. ⁷Everyone takes good care of their houses. ⁸They plant flowers and shrubs and mow their lawns every weekend. ⁹In addition, our neighborhood is safe, so we do not have to worry about security. ¹⁰Finally, we have very nice neighbors. ¹¹They are friendly and helpful and always say hello. ¹²They are also very quiet neighbors. ¹³They do not play loud music or have too many parties. ¹⁴For these reasons, my house is a good place to live, and we hope to buy a home in this neighborhood someday.

Bong Tran

PLANNING A REASON AND EXAMPLE PARAGRAPH

▶ Before Bong wrote his paragraph about *My House* on page 66, he made an outline. Just as an architect needs a plan to build a house, Bong needed a plan to write his paragraph. A plan for a paragraph is called an <u>outline</u>. If you write a good outline first, it will be easier for you to write a clear, well-organized paragraph.

▶ In the outline below, Bong wrote the three reasons why his house is a good place to live. Then he gave several examples to support his three reasons. Notice that Bong did not write his reasons and examples in complete sentences. In order to save time, he summarized the reasons and examples in a few words.

<u>Outline</u> - My House

TOPIC SENTENCE: *My house is a good place to live for several reasons.*

REASON 1   *a convenient location*

    examples that   *near the freeway and main streets*
    support Reason 1
        near the school

        bus stop nearby

REASON 2   *a good neighborhood*

    examples that   *neighbors take care of homes*
    support Reason 2
        plant flowers, shrubs and mow their lawns

        neighborhood is safe

REASON 3   *very nice neighbors*

    examples that   *friendly and helpful*
    support Reason 3
        always say hello

        quiet

CONCLUDING SENTENCE: *For these reasons, my house is a good place to live, and we hope to buy a home in this neighborhood someday.*

Part 3
Paragraph Skills

MAKING AN OUTLINE

➠ You have learned that a good way to plan a reason and example paragraph is to make an outline. On the following pages, you will practice working with outlines.

➠ **Activity 1** The student paragraph below is a reason and example paragraph. David Nara began his paragraph with the topic sentence, *My apartment is not a good place to live.* He then supported the topic sentence with two reasons and gave plenty of examples to support each reason. Finally, he finished his paragraph with a concluding sentence.

Read David's paragraph. When you are finished, underline or highlight his topic sentence, his two reasons, and the concluding sentence. Then complete the outline on the next page.

My Apartment

¹My apartment is not a good place to live. ²First of all, my apartment is old and run-down*. ³For example, the kitchen stove and refrigerator are often out of order. ⁴The sink has a leaky faucet, and the linoleum* is old and cracked. ⁵The walls in all the rooms need paint, and the carpets need to be replaced. ⁶Worst of all, there is no air conditioning in the summer, and the furnace does not work in the winter. ⁷As a result, in the summer the rooms are hot, and in the winter the rooms are cold. ⁸For another thing, my apartment building is always noisy. ⁹I live next to a shopping center with stores and restaurants. ¹⁰There is often loud music in the restaurants, and people drink beer and sing songs until 1:00 or 2:00 in the morning. ¹¹My neighbors upstairs are also noisy. ¹²They argue all the time and do not go to bed until 2:00 or 3:00 in the morning. ¹³My family and I are very unhappy in this apartment and want to move as soon as possible.

David Nara

Vocabulary Notes *__run-down__: in bad condition* *__linoleum__: floor covering, usually in the kitchen and bathroom*

MAKING AN OUTLINE

➠ **Activity 2** Here is the outline that David made to help him to plan his paragraph, *My Apartment*. Go back to page 68 and read David's paragraph again. Then complete the outline below to show how he planned his paragraph.

1. Write the two reasons that David used to support his topic sentence.

2. Summarize in a few words the examples that support each reason.

3. Do not write the reasons and examples in complete sentences. Write only the important words to summarize the reasons and examples. This will help you to save time.

Outline - My Apartment

TOPIC SENTENCE: _My apartment is not a good place to live._

    REASON 1 _old and run-down_

        examples that
        support Reason 1 _____

        _____

        _____

        _____

    REASON 2 _____

        examples that
        support Reason 2 _____

        _____

        _____

        _____

CONCLUDING SENTENCE: _____

_____

MAKING AN OUTLINE

➠ **Activity 3** Read Carlo's paragraph below about *A Good Place to Live*. When you are finished, underline or highlight Carlo's topic sentence, three reasons, and the concluding sentence. Then complete the outline on the next page.

A Good Place to Live

¹San Jose is a good place to live. ²First of all, the weather in San Jose is nearly perfect. ³It does not snow in the winter, and there is sunshine most of the year. ⁴The summers are not too hot or humid, and there is usually a pleasant breeze late in the afternoon on even the warmest days. ⁵For another thing, many job opportunities exist in this area. ⁶There are hundreds of computer and other high tech companies such as Intel, Hewlett Packard, and IBM, and these companies all need good employees. ⁷There are also many excellent training centers. ⁸For example, the San Jose Vocational Center, the Adult Education Program, and the local community colleges all provide classes to help a person to learn new job skills. ⁹Finally, San Jose offers many things to see and do. ¹⁰For instance, people can go hiking in the foothills where there are tall pine trees, beautiful wild flowers, and friendly birds. ¹¹On the weekend, they can spend a day at Great America, visit the Japanese Friendship Garden, or attend an ice hockey game at the San Jose Arena. ¹²There are also many cinemas, theaters, museums, and shopping malls. ¹³San Jose has much to offer the people who live there.

Carlo Orsi

www.sj.gov

Welcome to San Jose
and the Silicon Valley!

MAKING AN OUTLINE

➥ **Activity 4** Here is the outline that Carlo made to help him to plan his paragraph, *A Good Place to Live*. Go back to page 70 and read Carlo's paragraph again. Then complete the outline below to show how he planned his paragraph.

1. Write the three reasons that Carlo used to support his topic sentence.

2. Summarize in a few words the examples that support each reason.

3. Do not write the reasons and examples in complete sentences. Write only the important words to summarize the reasons and examples. This will help you to save time.

<u>**Outline - A Good Place to Live**</u>

TOPIC SENTENCE: <u>San Jose is a good place to live.</u>

REASON 1   <u>perfect weather</u>

    examples that
    support Reason 1

_____

_____

_____

REASON 2   _____

    examples that
    support Reason 2

_____

_____

_____

REASON 3   _____

    examples that
    support Reason 3

_____

_____

_____

_____

CONCLUDING SENTENCE: _____

_____

TRANSITION WORDS

➠ When you write a paragraph, it is important to use **transition words**. Transition words help the reader to follow the ideas in your paragraph. Transition words are like road signs or traffic signals that tell you which way to go.

There are many different kinds of transition words in English. As you learn to write different kinds of paragraphs, you will learn to use different kinds of transition words.

transition words to introduce reasons

first,	second,	last,
first of all,	in addition,	last of all,
for one thing,	for another thing,	finally,

➠ We usually put transition words at the beginning of a sentence. We put a comma after the transition word. (First of all, there is a variety of food on the menu.)

↑
comma

➠ **Activity 5** Read Kim Tran's paragraph below. Then underline or highlight the three reasons that Kim used to support her topic sentence, ***Burger House is my favorite restaurant for several reasons***. Circle the transition words that introduce each new reason.

The Best Restaurant in Town

[1]Burger House is my favorite restaurant for several reasons. [2]First of all, there is a variety of food on the menu. [3]For example, the breakfast menu includes scrambled eggs, pancakes, and sweet rolls. [4]For lunch and dinner, the menu includes hamburgers, cheeseburgers, fishburgers, French fries, green salads, and chicken nuggets. [5]For another thing, the prices at Burger House are inexpensive. [6]For example, an entire meal of a hamburger, French fries, and cold drink costs only $2.99. [7]Children's meals cost only $2.09 and always include an attractive toy. [8]Finally, the service at Burger House is fast and convenient. [9]Customers place their order and pay at a counter and always get their food quickly. [10]Then they can either eat at a table in the restaurant or order food-to-go if they are in a hurry. [11]For all these reasons, Burger House is my favorite restaurant.

Kim Tran

TRANSITION WORDS TO INTRODUCE REASONS

➡ **Activity 6** Read the paragraphs below. Then use a transition word from the box on page 72 to introduce each new reason. Be sure to use a comma after each transition word.

Paragraph 1 Television

¹Too much television is bad for children for several reasons. ²_____ it is not healthy. ³For example, when children spend too much time indoors watching TV, they do not get enough exercise. ⁴As a result, their muscles do not develop properly. ⁵Their complexions look pale from lack of sunlight, and they weigh too much from lack of activity. ⁶_____ they miss out on the benefits of group play with other children. ⁷When they spend most of their time in front of the TV, they do not learn how to share with other children. ⁸_____ the commercials on television teach children to want expensive games and toys. ⁹For instance, my four-year-old grandson always says, "I want that! I want that!" during the commercials. ¹⁰Of course, advertisers know this and use the commercials to sell their products to children. ¹¹Television can be a wonderful way to entertain children, but too much television can be harmful.

Dat Nguyen

Paragraph 2 My Favorite Place to Shop

¹One of my favorite places to shop is Home Mart. ²_____ the location is convenient. ³For example, Home Mart is near the freeway and Capital Expressway. ⁴Also, there are several bus lines that you can take to get there. ⁵It is especially convenient for me because I live close by, and I can easily walk there in ten minutes. ⁶_____ the prices at Home Mart are less expensive than at other stores. ⁷For example, a denim shirt for boys costs only $9.99, but Myron's Men's Shop charges $21.99, and the local department stores charge almost $30.00 for the same shirt. ⁸_____ Home Mart has something for everyone in the family. ⁹For instance, they sell household appliances, televisions, telephones, computers, and children's toys. ¹⁰In addition, Home Mart has good buys on chairs and tables for the patio and other garden equipment and supplies. ¹¹They also have a nice coffee shop that sells hot dogs, popcorn, ice cream, and soft drinks. ¹²I like this store for its convenience and great prices.

Amalia Medina

TRANSITION WORDS TO INTRODUCE EXAMPLES

➠ We often use the transition words [for example] and [for instance] to introduce examples.

---

1. For example and for instance have the same meaning.

2. We usually put for example and for instance at the beginning of a sentence. We always use a comma after for example and for instance.

Read the pairs of sentences below. Sentences *a* and *b* have the same meaning.

1. The students at my school come from all over the world.

   a. For example, I have classmates from Spain, China, Vietnam, and Mexico.
   b. For instance, I have classmates from Spain, China, Vietnam, and Mexico. } same meaning

2. My classmates speak many different languages.

   a. For example, they speak Chinese, Vietnamese, French, and Spanish.
   b. For instance, they speak Chinese, Vietnamese, French, and Spanish. } same meaning

➠ We use the transition word [such as] when we want to list several examples in a sentence.

---

1. We put such as in the middle of a sentence.

2. We do not use a comma with such as.

3. We do not use a complete sentence after such as.

---

1. San Francisco has many famous tourist attractions [such as] the Golden Gate Bridge, Chinatown, and Fisherman's Wharf.

2. There are many famous hotels in San Francisco [such as] the St. Francis, the Mark Hopkins, and the Fairmont.

TRANSITION WORDS TO INTRODUCE EXAMPLES

➠ **Activity 7** Read the paragraphs below. Fill each blank with <u>for example</u>, <u>for instance</u>, or <u>such as</u>. Remember to use a comma after <u>for example</u> and <u>for instance</u>. Do not use a comma with <u>such as</u>.

Paragraph 1   A Bad Habit

¹Smoking is a very bad habit. ²First of all, it is bad for your health. ³_____ it often causes lung cancer and heart attacks. ⁴It can also lead to many other diseases _____ high blood pressure, strokes, and emphysema. ⁵Second, smoking is an expensive habit. ⁶_____ a pack of cigarettes costs about $3.50. ⁷If a person smokes a pack a day, he or she spends $24.50 a week. ⁸It also costs the government millions of dollars a year to treat smoke-related diseases. ⁹For another thing, cigarettes can be harmful to other people. ¹⁰People who breathe second-hand smoke can get cancer and other diseases. ¹¹Second-hand smoke is also dangerous for people _____ waiters, waitresses, and bartenders who work in smoky places. ¹²Finally, smoking is unattractive. ¹³_____ smokers often have yellow teeth, smelly hair, and holes in their clothes. ¹⁴I am glad that I do not smoke.

Paragraph 2   Hawaii

¹When I have the time and the money, I want to visit Hawaii. ²For one thing, Hawaii is one of the most beautiful places in the world. ³_____ the oceans are blue and calm and clear as glass. ⁴I love to go snorkeling among the coral and seaweed and the many varieties of exotic fish _____ angel fish and butterfly fish. ⁵Hawaii also has many other natural wonders _____ lush tropical forests, spectacular waterfalls, and magnificent sunsets. ⁶There are also nearly 1,400 species of flowering plants, including orchids, hibiscus, bougainvillea, gardenias, and poinsettias. ⁷For another thing, the climate in Hawaii is mild and pleasant all year, with little difference between the hottest and coolest months. ⁸_____ the average temperature is 72° in January and 80° in July. ⁹Last of all, the tourist attractions make Hawaii an exciting place to visit. ¹⁰_____ most of the hotels have a traditional Hawaiian luau for their guests. ¹¹A luau is an outdoor feast with typical island food _____ roast pig, poi, pineapple, and other tropical fruit. ¹²While the guests eat, entertainers perform hula dances and sing and play Hawaiian music. ¹³For a great vacation, I recommend Hawaii.

OFF-TOPIC SENTENCES

▶ When you write a paragraph, there is another important thing to remember. All of the sentences in the paragraph must support the topic sentence. When a sentence in a paragraph does not support the topic sentence, the sentence is "**off-topic**" and does not belong in the paragraph.

▶ **Activity 8** Three of the sentences in the paragraph below do not support the topic sentence. Draw a line through the off-topic sentences. Then write the numbers of the off-topic sentences on the lines under the paragraph. For example, sentence #5 is an off-topic sentence because it does not support the topic sentence.

Home-Cooking

1

food ads: *newspaper advertisements for special food prices*

produce: *fruit and vegetables*

avoid: *eliminate*

preservatives: *chemicals used to keep food from going bad*

trim: *cut*

reduce: *make less, decrease*

syrup: *sweet liquid to pour over food*

¹I would rather eat at home than in a restaurant for many reasons. ²First of all, it saves money to eat at home. ³For example, I always cut out coupons and check the food ads* in the newspaper to find the lowest prices on groceries. ⁴I also shop at discount grocery stores such as Pack-and-Save and Food for Less to save money. ⁵~~My sister also shops at discount stores.~~ ⁶For another thing, I am always able to have fresh produce* with my meals. ⁷Fresh vegetables such as green beans, broccoli, brussels sprouts, and carrots have more flavor than canned or frozen vegetables. ⁸My children like pizza better than vegetables. ⁹In addition, I can avoid* all of the preservatives* in canned vegetables and fruit. ¹⁰Last of all, home-cooked food is healthier in several other ways. ¹¹For example, I can control the amount of salt in my food because I prepare the food myself. ¹²I also trim* all the fat off meat and chicken, and I use low-fat mayonnaise and salad dressing to reduce* the fat and cholesterol in my diet. ¹³My neighbor down the street wants to lose weight, but she eats a lot of ice cream with chocolate syrup*.¹⁴For these reasons, I prefer to eat at home because it is healthier, less expensive, and the food tastes better.

▶ The numbers of the off-topic sentences are: ___5___   _____   _____

OFF-TOPIC SENTENCES

▶ **Activity 9** Read Orelia Montes's paragraph about *My Favorite Day of the Week*. There are three off-topic sentences in her paragraph. Draw a line through the off-topic sentences. Then write the off-topic sentences on the lines under the paragraph. Compare your answers with a classmate.

My Favorite Day of the Week

[1]Saturday is my favorite day of the week. [2]First of all, I do not have to get up early and go to work on Saturday. [3]A few years ago, Wednesday was my favorite day. [4]During the week, I have to get up at 4:30, so I really like to sleep late on Saturday. [5]Also, this day is special for me because it is the only day that I can enjoy a long, leisurely breakfast with my son and my parents. [6]For another thing, I can spend Saturday with my son and take him to many interesting places. [7]For instance, I often take him to the Children's Story Hour at The Corner Bookstore. [8]I used to work at a bookstore when I was in high school. [9]After the Story Hour, we always go out for an ice cream cone. [10]Other times, we visit the Children's Discovery Museum downtown. [11]The many activities at the museum are both fun and educational for young children. [12]When the weather is nice, I like to take him to the playground near our house or to the beach at Santa Cruz. [13]Last of all, on Saturday evening, my parents babysit my son so that I can go out with my friends. [14]We sometimes go to a party, or we go out for dinner and to a movie. [15]My sister is coming to visit us next weekend. [16]After a hard week at work, I always look forward to Saturday.

Orelia Montes

▶ Off-topic sentences:

_____

_____

_____

_____

_____

_____

_____

✓ CHECK YOUR UNDERSTANDING

A. Answer the questions below.

1. What is a topic sentence? _____

_____

2. In this chapter, you used _____ and _____ to support topic sentences.

3. What is an outline? _____

_____

4. Why is an outline important? _____

_____

5. Why do we use transition words in a paragraph? _____

_____

6. When a transition word comes at the beginning of a sentence, we put a _____ after the transition word.

7. What is an "off-topic" sentence? _____

_____

B.   *EDITING* - The paragraph below contains 5 errors in the use of commas after transition words. Circle each error and write in a comma. The first one is done for you.

Tsugaru Japanese Restaurant

¹Tsugaru Japanese Restaurant is my favorite restaurant. ²For one thing, the food is delicious. ³You will be satisfied with anything on the menu. ⁴For example there are over thirty combinations with beef, fish, or chicken teriyaki. ⁵The restaurant uses all fresh ingredients such as skinless fresh chicken, garden vegetables, and fresh herbs and spices. ⁶For another thing the prices are very reasonable, especially the sushi. ⁷For example one piece of tuna is $1.50, eel is $1.70, and squid is $1.40. ⁸All the combinations cost about $11.00 and come with soup and rice. ⁹Finally it is very convenient to order food-to-go by phone. ¹⁰When I am really tired or lazy, I always call for take-out food. ¹¹The food is ready to pick up within twenty minutes, and I usually send my husband to pick it up. ¹²For all these reasons, my family and I often go to Tsugaru Restaurant to enjoy wonderful Japanese food, and we recommend this restaurant to all our friends.

Etsuko Williamson

Part 4
Getting Ready to Write

GETTING READY TO WRITE A REASON AND EXAMPLE PARAGRAPH

▶ Most good writers do not just sit down and start to write a paragraph. They go through several steps before they are ready to write their final paragraph. On the next few pages, you will study the steps that one student, Trong Nguyen, used when he wrote a paragraph about the place where he lives.

STEP 1 PREWRITING: MAKE A CLUSTER

▶ When you sit down and look at a blank sheet of paper, it is often difficult to think of something to write about. Trong began by thinking about his home and picturing it in his mind. Then he made a **cluster** to get his ideas down on paper as fast as possible.

- First, he wrote the main idea of the paragraph in a circle in the middle of the page.

- Then he wrote down everything that came to his mind about why he likes his home.

- He thought of the reasons why his home is a perfect place to live, and he thought of several examples to explain each reason.

The drawing below is Trong's cluster. Notice that Trong did not use complete sentences in his cluster.

CLUSTER

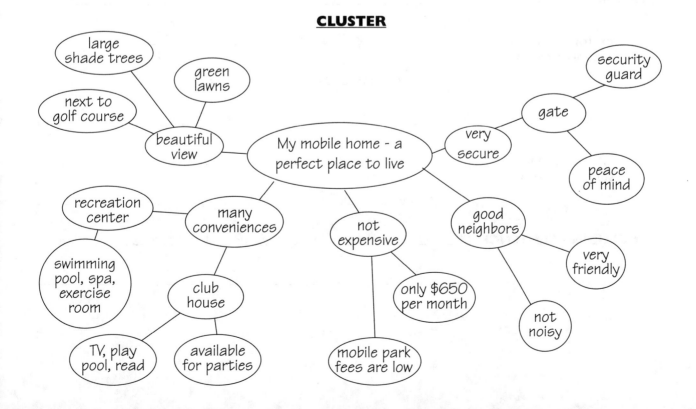

STEP 2 - PLAN YOUR PARAGRAPH - MAKE AN OUTLINE

➠ After Trong finished his cluster of ideas, he needed a plan to help him to organize his paragraph about his mobile home. One of the best ways to write a good paragraph is to make an **outline** first. To make an outline, Trong chose three reasons from his cluster to explain why his mobile home is a good place to live. Then he chose specific examples to explain his reasons. The outline helped Trong to write the ideas for his paragraph clearly and in the right order.

➠ Here is the outline that Trong wrote to support the topic sentence, *My mobile home is a perfect place to live.*

Notice that Trong did not use all of the ideas in his cluster. He picked only the ideas that he wanted to write about.

Outline - My Mobile Home

TOPIC SENTENCE: My mobile home is a perfect place to live.

REASON I   many conveniences

examples that support Reason I
recreation center with swimming pool, spa, exercise room

clubroom to watch TV, play pool, read

clubroom available for parties-refrigerator, microwave, sink

REASON 2   beautiful view

examples that support Reason 2
next to a golf course

green lawns and large shade trees

REASON 3   very secure

examples that support Reason 3
security guard at gate

peace of mind – no robberies

CONCLUDING SENTENCE: My wife and I are very happy in our mobile home, and we plan to stay here a long time.

STEP 3 - WRITE A FIRST DRAFT (PRACTICE PARAGRAPH)

➡ When Trong finished his outline on page 80, he wrote one or more practice paragraphs (drafts) before he wrote his final paragraph.

After Trong wrote the first draft of his paragraph, he read his paragraph carefully to see if he could improve it.

I. First, he **revised** his paragraph. **Revise** means to add new sentences or take out sentences. Revise also means to rewrite any confusing sentences. As Trong read his paragraph, he asked himrself, "Are any of my sentences off-topic? Do I need to add more examples? Did I use transition words? Does the paragraph have a concluding sentence?"

2. Then Trong **edited** his paragraph. **Edit** means to correct any errors in grammar, spelling, and the use of capital letters and periods.

➡ The paragraph below is Trong's practice paragraph. He made all the changes and corrections on his practice paragraph. Look at the changes and corrections that he made.

M   M   H
~~my mobile home~~ ← *capitalize the title*

indent →

My mobile home is a perfect place to live. First of all, the mobile home park offers the residents

conveniences   *and spa*

many convenien(ce) For example, there is a recreation center with a large swimming pool. There is

such as treadmills, weights and bikes.   ^

also an exercise room with all the latest equipment. Every evening before dinner I ~~am~~ go for a

swim or work out in the exercise room. There is also a large clubroom in the recreation center. In

this room, residents watch TV, play pool, read, or talk with their friends. Residents also use the

to (infinitive)

clubroom ˄ give parties. The refrigerator, microwave oven, and sink make it very convenient to have

children's

guests here. In fact, my wife and I always have our (children) birthday parties in the clubroom.

has   *nine-hole*   *off topic*

Second, my mobile home (have) a beautiful view. It is next to a ~~9~~-hole golf course. ~~I like to play golf~~

~~on the weekend.~~ When I look out my living room window, I can see beautiful green lawns and large

looks

shade trees. The golf course (look) like my own back yard. Last of all, the mobile home park is very

is

secure. We have peace of mind because there (are) always a security guard at the gate to the park.

to (infinitive)

Therefore, we do not have ˄ worry about robberies or other crimes. ˄

My wife and I are very happy in our mobile home, and we plan to stay here a long time.

STEP 4 - WRITE THE FINAL DRAFT (FINAL PARAGRAPH)

➡ Here is the final paragraph that Trong wrote after he made all the necessary changes and corrections on his practice paragraph on page 81.

Underline or highlight Trong's topic sentence, his three reasons, and the concluding sentence in his paragraph. Circle the transition words that Trong used to introduce each new reason.

My Mobile Home

My mobile home is a perfect place to live. First of all, the mobile   1
home park offers the residents many conveniences. For example,
there is a recreation center with a large swimming pool and spa*.

spa: a small pool with hot water and steam for relaxing the muscles, hot tub

There is also an exercise room with all the latest exercise equipment
such as treadmills, weights, and stationary bikes. Every evening   5
before dinner I go for a swim or work out* in the exercise room. There

work out: exercise vigorously, especially with weights or other equipment

is also a large clubroom in the recreation center. In this room,
residents watch TV, play pool, read, or talk with their friends.
Residents also use the clubroom to give parties. The refrigerator,

entertain: have guests

microwave oven, and sink make it very convenient to entertain* here.   10
In fact, my wife and I always have our children's birthday parties in
the clubroom. Second, my mobile home has a beautiful view. It is next
to a nine-hole golf course. When I look out my living room window, I can
see beautiful green lawns and large shade trees. The golf course looks
like my own back yard. Last of all, the mobile home park is very   15

secure: safe

secure*. We have peace of mind because there is always a security
guard at the gate to the park. Therefore, we do not have to worry
about robberies or other crimes. My wife and I are very happy in our
mobile home, and we plan to stay here a long time.

Trong Nguyen

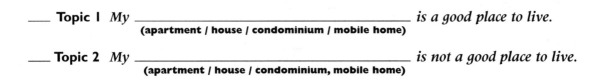 Writing Assignment

▥➡ Your writing assignment in this chapter is to write a reason and example paragraph about the place where you live.

In Part 1, you worked in a group with three or four classmates and talked about the place where you live. Go back and read the notes that you wrote on page 65 of this chapter. Use your notes to help you to write your paragraph.

Choose the topic sentence that is true for you:

_____ **Topic 1** *My* _____ *is a good place to live.*
      (apartment / house / condominium / mobile home)

_____ **Topic 2** *My* _____ *is not a good place to live.*
      (apartment / house / condominium, mobile home)

STEP 1 - MAKE A CLUSTER

▥➡ Take a few minutes to think about your topic. Then make a cluster to get your ideas down on paper as fast as possible. Write your reasons to support your topic sentence. Then write examples to explain each of your reasons. Do not write complete sentences, and do not worry about grammar or spelling in your cluster.

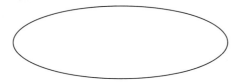

Writing Assignment

STEP 2 - PLAN YOUR PARAGRAPH - MAKE AN OUTLINE

➡ One of the best ways to write a good paragraph is to make an outline first. Write an outline in the space below to organize the ideas in your cluster on page 83. First choose three reasons from your cluster to support your topic sentence. Then choose two or more examples to explain and support each of your reasons. To save time, do not write the reasons and examples in complete sentences.

TOPIC SENTENCE: _____

    REASON 1 _____

        examples that _____
        support Reason 1

        _____

        _____

        _____

    REASON 2 _____

        examples that _____
        support Reason 2

        _____

        _____

        _____

    REASON 3 _____

        examples that _____
        support Reason 3

        _____

        _____

        _____

CONCLUDING SENTENCE: _____

_____

Writing Assignment

STEP 3 - WRITE A FIRST DRAFT (PRACTICE PARAGRAPH)

▶ **What to do** ◀

1. Follow your outline on page 84 to write the first draft of your paragraph.

2. Your paragraph should be about 150 to 200 words long.

3. Give your paragraph a title.

4. Double space your paragraph, and circle the subject(s) and verb(s) in each sentence.

5. Remember that your first draft is only a practice paragraph. You will make all of your changes and corrections on this paragraph before you write your final paragraph.

Writing Assignment

FIRST DRAFT (CONTINUED)

_____

_____

_____

_____

_____

_____

_____

_____

_____

_____

_____

_____

_____

_____

_____

STEP 4 - REVISE AND EDIT YOUR PARAGRAPH

▶ **What to do** ◀

1. When you are finished writing your practice paragraph, read your paragraph to yourself.

2. Revise your paragraph.

   Are all of your sentences clear and easy to understand? Do you want to add new sentences or take out sentences? If you need to make changes, make them on your practice paragraph.

3. Edit your paragraph.

   Are there any mistakes in grammar, spelling, capital letters, or periods? Did you use correct paragraph form? If you need to make corrections, make them on your practice paragraph.

4. When you are finished revising and editing your paragraph, underline or highlight the topic sentence, your reasons, and the concluding sentence.

5. Write your name on the Review Sheet on page 87, and give your book to a partner. Your partner will read and review your paragraph.

Partner Review Sheet

Paragraph written by _____

Paragraph reviewed by _____

➠ **To the Reviewer:** Read your partner's paragraph carefully. Then answer the questions below about your partner's paragraph. Do **not** write on your partner's paper.

1. Does your partner's paragraph have a title?

_____ yes   _____ no

2. Did your partner indent the first sentence of his or her paragraph?

_____ yes   _____ no

3. Write the topic sentence of your partner's paragraph here.

_____

4. Did your partner underline or highlight the topic sentence, reasons, and concluding sentence?

_____ yes   _____ no

5. Which sentence is true about your partner's paragraph?

_____ **a.** All the sentences in my partner's paragraph support the topic sentence.

_____ **b.** My partner's paragraph is not clear because some of the sentences are off-topic.

6. What transition words did your partner use to introduce the reasons in his or her paragraph?

_____   _____   _____

7. Do all of the sentences in the paragraph begin with a capital letter and end with a period?

_____ yes   _____ no

8. Did your partner circle the subject and verb in each sentence?

_____ yes   _____ no

9. Did your partner double space the paragraph?

_____ yes   _____ no

➠ **To the Reviewer:** When you are finished reviewing your partner's paragraph, return your partner's book.

Writing Assignment

STEP 5 - WRITE YOUR FINAL DRAFT (FINAL PARAGRAPH)

▥▶ When your partner returns your book, make any necessary changes or corrections on your practice paragraph. Now you are ready to write the final draft of your paragraph.

▶ What to do ◀

1. Write your final paragraph in ink on a separate sheet of paper. Write as neatly as possible, and use correct paragraph form.

2. Double space your paragraph, and write on only one side of the paper.

3. When you finish your paragraph, underline or highlight the topic sentence, your three reasons, and the concluding sentence.

4. Circle the subject(s) and verb(s) in each sentence.

Additional Writing Topics

Reason and Example Paragraphs

Topic 1: The best time of the year is _____.

What is your favorite time of the year? Is it Christmas? New Year's? Perhaps your favorite time is the summer or fall. What are the reasons for your choice?

Topic 2: My favorite city is _____.

Of all the cities that you have visited or lived in, which is your favorite? Is it in the United States or in another country? What makes it special and interesting? Why is it your favorite city? (Do not write about your home city.)

Topic 3: I would rather live _____.
(**a. in a big city than in a small town.   or**)
  b. in a small town than in a big city.

Some people think that life in a small town is better than life in a big city. There is less crime, and it is a better place to raise children. On the other hand, some people prefer the excitement and opportunities that a big city offers. Where would you prefer to live, in a big city or in a small town? Why?

Chapter 5
Writing About Present Time

To the Student:

Verbs tell us the time that an action in a sentence happened. The time that a verb shows is called <u>tense</u>. The most common tenses in English are present, past, and future. In this chapter, you will use the Simple Present Tense and the Present Progressive Tense to write about present time.

Part I
The Simple (Habitual) Present Tense

coisa que você faz todo dia

habit

THE MEANING OF THE SIMPLE PRESENT TENSE – ACTIONS THAT YOU DO ALL THE TIME

▪➡ The Simple Present Tense is used to describe habitual actions. Habitual actions are actions that we do all the time. In this book, we will call the *Simple Present Tense* the **Habitual *Present Tense***.

> ### Learning Point
>
> We use the Habitual Present Tense to talk about habits or repeated actions – things that we do again and again (every day, every week, every month).

▪➡ Study the examples below. Each sentence talks about a habitual action.

At Home

1. I <u>clean</u> my room every weekend.

2. My husband <u>cooks</u> breakfast for the family every Sunday morning.

3. Our family usually <u>eats</u> dinner at 5:30 or 6:00 during the week.

At Work

1. I always <u>get</u> to work at 7:00.

2. I usually <u>eat</u> lunch from 12:00 to 12:45 in the employee cafeteria.

3. I <u>work</u> on the computer every afternoon.

At School

1. The students in my class always <u>study</u> hard for their tests.

2. We always <u>listen</u> carefully to the teacher's explanations.

3. The teacher usually <u>writes</u> the homework assignment on the board at the end of class.

Leisure Time

1. My family and I <u>visit</u> our relatives in Washington every summer.

2. I usually <u>read</u> or <u>watch</u> TV after dinner.

3. I <u>play</u> cards with my friends every Friday night.

HABITUAL PRESENT TENSE - TIME WORDS (ADVERBS OF FREQUENCY)

➠ We often use time words in sentences when we talk about habitual actions. Time words tell how often an action happens.

➠ Study the Habitual Present Tense time words in the chart below.

TIME WORDS

always	——	100%	——	all of the time
usually	——	95%	——	most of the time
often	——	80%	——	frequently
sometimes	——	40%	——	occasionally
seldom	——	5%	——	almost never, rarely
never	——	0%	——	none of the time

every day, every week, every month, every year

➠ We usually put time words in front of the verb in Habitual Present Tense sentences. We usually put time words with **every** (every day, every week, etc.) at the end of the sentence.

➠ Compare the different meanings of the sentences below.

SUBJECT	TIME WORD	VERB	COMPLEMENT
1. Van	**always**	studies	in the library after class.
2. Ana	**usually**	studies	in the library after class.
3. Roberto	**often**	studies	in the library after class.
4. Kim	**sometimes**	studies	in the library after class.
5. Sarah	**seldom**	studies	in the library after class.
6. Vinh	**never**	studies	in the library after class.
7. Carlos		studies	in the library after class **every day**.

Note: It is also common to put the time word *sometimes* at the beginning of a sentence.
      Example: I <u>sometimes</u> eat lunch in the cafeteria. (correct)
             <u>Sometimes</u> I eat lunch in the cafeteria. (correct)

HABITUAL PRESENT TENSE - TIME WORDS (ADVERBS OF FREQUENCY)

➠ **Exercise 1** What do you do to improve your English? Read the list below. Check the time word that describes how often you do each activity.

How often do you...	always	usually	often (frequently)	sometimes (occasionally)	seldom (rarely)	never
1. watch American TV programs?	____	✔	____	____	____	____
2. read English magazines and books?	____	____	____	____	____	____
3. go to American movies?	____	____	____	____	____	____
4. talk to American students at school?	____	____	____	____	____	____
5. speak English at work?	____	____	____	____	____	____
6. speak English at home?	____	____	____	____	____	____
7. borrow books from the public library?	____	____	____	____	____	____
8. listen to English language tapes?	____	____	____	____	____	____
9. use an American dictionary?	____	____	____	____	____	____
10. listen to English programs on the radio?	____	____	____	____	____	____

➠ **Exercise 2** Now write complete sentences with the time words you chose in Exercise 1. Circle each time word.

1. I (usually) watch American TV programs. _____

2. _____

3. _____

4. _____

5. _____

6. _____

7. _____

8. _____

9. _____

10. _____

THE FIVE FORMS OF ACTION VERBS

➠ Before you continue to study the Habitual Present Tense, take a few minutes to review the five forms of action verbs.

> ▶ **Learning Point**
>
> **Action Verbs** have five forms. Each form has a name. You will use the first two forms of action verbs, the <u>root form</u> and the <u>-s form</u>, in the Habitual Present Tense. You will use forms 3, 4, and 5 when you study other verb tenses.

	↓ 1 ROOT FORM (SIMPLE FORM)	↓ 2 -S FORM	3 PAST FORM	4 PRESENT PARTICIPLE (ing)	5 PAST PARTICIPLE
regular verbs	wait	waits	waited	waiting	waited
	paint	paints	painted	painting	painted
	attend	attends	attended	attending	attended
	mend	mends	mended	mending	mended
	wash	washes	washed	washing	washed
	fix	fixes	fixed	fixing	fixed
	help	helps	helped	helping	helped
	laugh	laughs	laughed	laughing	laughed
	play	plays	played	playing	played
	live	lives	lived	living	lived
irregular verbs	drive	drives	drove	driving	driven
	eat	eats	ate	eating	eaten
	go	goes	went	going	gone
	write	writes	wrote	writing	written
	drink	drinks	drank	drinking	drunk
	sing	sings	sang	singing	sung
	buy	buys	bought	buying	bought
	meet	meets	met	meeting	met
	pay	pays	paid	paying	paid
	sell	sells	sold	selling	sold
	tell	tells	told	telling	told

Note: 1. Regular verbs end in <u>-ed</u> in the past form and past participle (walk-walk<u>ed</u>, dance-dan<u>ced</u>).
2. Irregular verbs do not end in <u>-ed</u>. They usually change spelling (run - ran, give - gave).

➠ There is a more complete verb list in the Appendix on page 410.

USING THE <u>ROOT FORM</u> AND THE <u>-S FORM</u> OF A VERB IN THE HABITUAL PRESENT TENSE

> ### ▶ Learning Point
>
> We use the <u>root form</u> and the <u>-s form</u> of a verb in the Habitual Present Tense to talk about habitual actions in present time.
>
> We use the **root form** of the verb with the subjects <u>I</u>, <u>you</u>, <u>we</u>, <u>they</u>.
>
> We use the **-s form** with the subjects <u>he</u>, <u>she</u>, <u>it</u> (third person singular).

Example: 1. I work at Intel Corporation in Santa Clara, California.
                   ↑
                root form

2. My co-workers and I work very hard every day.
                        ↑
                   root form

3. Our supervisor sometimes ask**s** us to work overtime.
                              ↑
                           -s form

4. Our company make**s** millions of computer chips every year.
                   ↑
              -s form

⟫ Habitual Present Tense Forms of Action Verbs

	<u>singular</u>		<u>plural</u>	
first person:	I	work	we	work
second person:	you	work	you	work
third person:	he she it	work<u>s</u>	they	work

⟫ Word Order of a Simple Affirmative Sentence

SUBJECT	TIME WORD	VERB	COMPLEMENT (rest of the sentence)
1. I	never	have	any spare time during my busy week.
2. You	usually	get	to work early.
3. He	often	ha**s**	a cup of coffee with me during our break.
4. She	sometimes	work**s**	overtime on weekends.
5. It	usually	take**s**	about a half hour to get to work.
6. We	seldom	watch	TV during the week.
7. You	always	finish	your jobs on time.
8. They		make	newer and faster computer chips every year.

THE HABITUAL PRESENT TENSE

➠ **Exercise 3** Dr. Lin is a busy cardiologist in San Jose, California. Complete the sentences about Dr. Lin's busy day. Use the Habitual Present Tense or the Present Tense of the verb <u>Be</u> (*am, is, are*). Circle the subject in each sentence.

Dr. Lin's Typical Day

1. A typical (day) in Dr. Lin's life ____is____ always very busy.

   a. be   **b.** is   **c.** is be

2. Early each morning, Dr. Lin _____ to the hospital to see patients.

   a. go   **b.** is go   **c.** goes

3. He always looks at his patients' medical charts and _____ to the nurses about their progress.

   a. speaks   **b.** speak   **c.** is speaks

4. After that, he _____ to his office a short distance from the hospital.

   a. is   **b.** walk   **c.** walks

5. There _____ always several patients in the waiting room of his office.

   a. have   **b.** is   **c.** are

6. The nurses _____ the patients ready to see Dr. Lin.

   a. gets   **b.** get   **c.** are get

7. They _____ the patients and take their temperature and blood pressure.

   a. weigh   **b.** are weigh   **c.** weighs

➠ **Exercise 4** Follow the same directions as in Exercise 3.

1. Dr. Lin's office _____ from twelve to two in the afternoon.

   a. close   **b.** closes   **c.** is closes

2. During this time, Dr. Lin and the nurses usually _____ paperwork and return patients' telephone calls.

   a. are do   **b.** does   **c.** do

3. The office _____ at two o'clock.

   a. reopens   **b.** is reopen   **c.** reopen

4. Dr. Lin usually _____ about eight more patients in the afternoon.

   a. sees   **b.** is sees   **c.** see

5. The doctor and the nurses seldom _____ the office before six o'clock in the evening.

   a. leaves   **b.** are leave   **c.** leave

THE HABITUAL PRESENT TENSE

▶ **Exercise 5** Five of the sentences in the paragraph below contain verb errors. Circle the errors, and rewrite the sentences correctly on the lines under the paragraph.

An Interesting Job on Campus

work-study: *a college program that provides students with jobs while they are studying*

update: *add or make changes*

placement test: *a test to help a school to put students into the correct class*

sort: *put in the correct order*

variety: *diversity*

¹Amy, Joe, and I enjoy our work-study* jobs in the testing office at Davis College. ²For one thing, there (is) always many different things to do in the office. ³Amy answers the telephone and updates* students' records in the computer. ⁴Joe usually is run errands and collects mail from the mailbox. ⁵I answer students' questions about the testing service and make appointments for placement testing. ⁶In addition to our many office jobs, we also have the opportunity to assist the testing supervisor with the placement tests*. ⁷Every Monday, large groups of students meets in the auditorium. ⁸Joe passes out the test booklets, and Amy and I usually help students to fill out the answer forms and the student information forms. ⁹Then we are walk around the room during the test to answer students' questions. ¹⁰At the end of the test, Joe collects the test booklets, the answer forms, and the student information forms. ¹¹Back in the office, we sort* all the papers to get them ready for the counselors. ¹²Amy, Joe, and I be very happy with our jobs, and we like the variety* of our busy work-study schedule.

sentence

  2   For one thing, there are always many different things to do in the office.

_____ _____

_____ _____

_____ _____

_____ _____

_____ _____

_____ _____

USING THE HABITUAL PRESENT TENSE TO TALK ABOUT HABITUAL ACTIONS

▶ **Exercise 6** Use the Habitual Present Tense to talk about <u>your</u> habitual actions in present time. Write true sentences about yourself, your family, your friends, or your classmates. Circle the subject and verb in each sentence. If possible, try to use the time words *always, usually, often, frequently, sometimes, occasionally, seldom, rarely, never, every _____.*

At Home

1. _____

_____

2. _____

_____

3. _____

_____

4 _____

_____

At School

1. _____

_____

2. _____

_____

3. _____

_____

4 _____

_____

In My Leisure Time

1. _____

_____

2. _____

_____

3. _____

_____

4. _____

_____

SPECIAL POINT – PLACEMENT OF TIME WORDS (ADVERBS OF FREQUENCY)

➡ You have learned that we often use **time words** such as *always, usually, often, frequently, sometimes, occasionally, seldom, rarely, never* in Habitual Present Tense sentences. Be careful. The placement of time words in sentences with the non-action verb <u>Be</u> is different from the placement of time words with action verbs.

> ▶ **Learning Point**
>
> 1. We usually put time words <u>after</u> the verb <u>Be</u> (*am, is, are*).
>
>   **Example:** I am often late for my 8:00 math class.
>
> 2. We usually put time words <u>before</u> action verbs in the Habitual Present Tense.
>
>   **Example:** I often go to the library before class.

➡ **Exercise 7** Rewrite the sentences below. Add a time word to each sentence. Be careful where you put the time words.

time words

always	often	sometimes	seldom	never
usually	frequently	occasionally	rarely	

1. I am very busy during the week.

   I am always very busy during the week.

2. I am late for work.

   _____

3. We take a coffee break around 9:30.

   _____

4. I buy my lunch in the employee cafeteria.

   _____

5. My co-workers are friendly and helpful.

   _____

6. My supervisor is impatient with the employees.

   _____

7. I go out with my friends after work.

   _____

8. My company gives bonuses to the employees at Christmas time.

   _____

✓ CHECK YOUR UNDERSTANDING

A. Answer the questions below.

1. In this chapter, you used the Habitual Present Tense to describe habitual actions. What are habitual actions? _____

   _____

2. What are the names of the five forms of action verbs?

   _____ _____ _____ _____ _____

3. What two parts of a verb do we use in the Habitual Present Tense?

   _____ _____

4. Write seven time words that we often use in the Habitual Present Tense.

   _____ _____ _____ _____ _____ _____ _____

5. Where do we put time words in sentences with action verbs?

   _____

6. Where do we put time words in sentences with the non-action verb <u>Be</u>?

   _____

   _____

B. *EDITING* - Each sentence below contains one or more errors. Circle the errors in each sentence. Then write the sentence correctly. If you need help, refer to the Reference Chart on page 110.

1. My neighbor's son and daughter ⟨are attends⟩ class at City College.

   <u>My neighbor's son and daughter attend class at City College.</u>

2. Counselors helps students to choose their classes.

   _____

3. I tries to take 12 units every semester.

   _____

4. Our teacher every day is give us a lot of homework.

   _____

5. My friends and I play often tennis on the weekend.

   _____

NEGATIVE SENTENCES IN THE HABITUAL PRESENT TENSE

> ▶ **Learning Point**
>
>   1. To form negative sentences in the Habitual Present Tense, we put the helping (auxiliary) verb <u>do not</u> or <u>does not</u> in front of the root form of the main verb.
>
>   2. To form negative contractions, we combine <u>do not</u> → don't   <u>does not</u> → doesn't

1. **affirmative:** I like my English and history classes.
   negative: I <u>do not</u> (don't) like my chemistry class.
                    ↑   ↑
                    hv   **main verb**

2. **affirmative:** Lan works part-time on the weekend.
   negative: She <u>does not</u> (doesn't) work during the week.
                    ↑   ↑
                    hv   **main verb**

3. **affirmative:** My brother attends DeAnza College.
   negative: He <u>doesn't</u> (doesn't) attend this school.
                    ↑   ↑
                    hv   **main verb**

➡ Habitual Present Tense - Negative Form

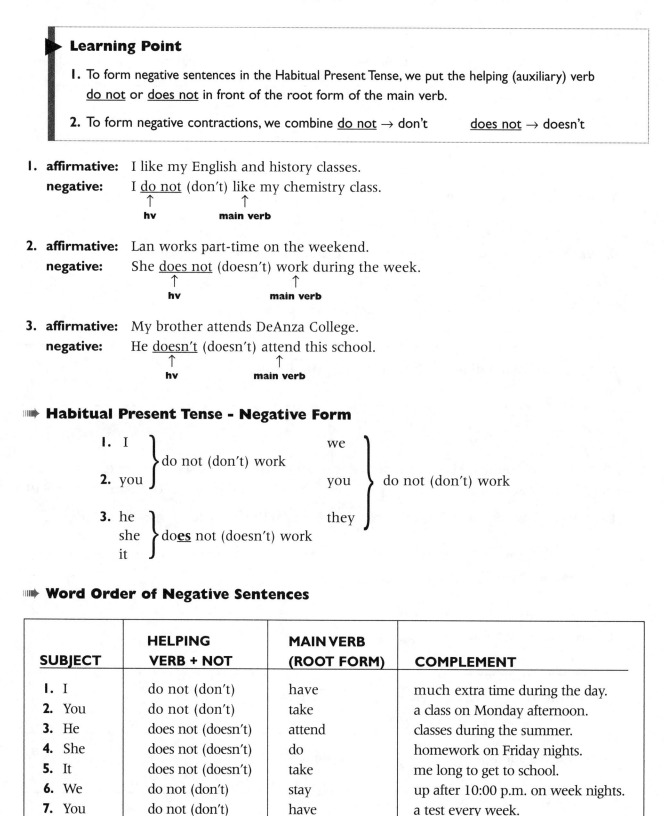

1. I }
       } do not (don't) work
2. you }

          we }
              } do not (don't) work
          you }

3. he   }
   she } do**es** not (doesn't) work
   it   }

          they }

➡ Word Order of Negative Sentences

SUBJECT	HELPING VERB + NOT	MAIN VERB (ROOT FORM)	COMPLEMENT
1. I	do not (don't)	have	much extra time during the day.
2. You	do not (don't)	take	a class on Monday afternoon.
3. He	does not (doesn't)	attend	classes during the summer.
4. She	does not (doesn't)	do	homework on Friday nights.
5. It	does not (doesn't)	take	me long to get to school.
6. We	do not (don't)	stay	up after 10:00 p.m. on week nights.
7. You	do not (don't)	have	a test every week.
8. They	do not (don't)	like	their class schedules.

HABITUAL PRESENT TENSE - NEGATIVE SENTENCES

➠ **Exercise 8** The students at a local school are unhappy about conditions on campus. They prepared a list of complaints and presented it to the school principal. They also posted the list on bulletin boards around the campus. Use the verbs in the chart below to complete their list of complaints. All the sentences will be negative. Use each verb only one time. Read your sentences to a partner.

work	listen	clean	have	is
patrol	serve	✔ give	schedule	are

To: Mr. Neal, Principal
From: Student Body

LIST OF STUDENT COMPLAINTS

1. The bookstore __*doesn't give*__ good refunds on used books.

2. The administrators _____ to the concerns of the students.

3. The school _____ enough parking for the students.

4. The food in the cafeteria _____ very good.

5. The cafeteria _____ hot meals in the evening.

6. The air conditioners in the classrooms _____ very well.

7. The security guards _____ the campus often enough

8. The custodians _____ the classrooms regularly.

9. The administration _____ enough ESL classes.

10. The clerks in the financial aid office _____ helpful to new students.

Do you have any complaints about your school? Write them here.

1. _____

_____

2. _____

_____

3. _____

_____

HABITUAL PRESENT TENSE – NEGATIVE AND AFFIRMATIVE SENTENCES

⮕ **Exercise 9** Think carefully about the meaning of each group of words below. Then write either an affirmative sentence or a negative sentence to describe good students. Use the Habitual Present Tense or the Present Tense of the verb <u>Be</u>. The subject | *good students* | is <u>plural</u>.

Good Students

I. sit in the back of the room and talk to their friends during class

<u>Good students don't sit in the back of the room and talk to their friends during class.</u>

2. do all their own work

_____

3. are late for class

_____

4. wait until the last minute to study for a test

_____

5. ask a lot of questions in class

_____

6. give their work to other students to copy

_____

⮕ **Exercise 10** Follow the same directions as in Exercise 9. Be careful with the verbs. The subject | *a good friend* | is <u>singular</u>.

A Good Friend

I. borrow money and forget to pay you back

<u>A good friend doesn't borrow money and forget to pay you back.</u>

2. laugh at all your jokes and funny stories

_____

3. is always honest with you

_____

4. care about your problems

_____

5. is selfish or unkind

_____

6. talk about you behind your back

_____

HABITUAL PRESENT TENSE - STATEMENTS OF FACT

➡ You have learned that we use the Habitual Present Tense to talk about habitual actions - actions that we do again and again (every day, every week, every month).

> ▶ **Learning Point**
>
> We also use the Habitual Present Tense to talk about <u>statements of fact</u>. A statement of fact is something that is always true and never changes. We do not usually use time words in statements of fact.

➡ Study the sentences below. Each sentence is a statement of fact.

Scientific Facts

1. The sun <u>rises</u> in the East and <u>sets</u> in the West.

2. The earth <u>revolves</u> around the sun.

3. The oceans <u>cover</u> most of the earth's surface.

Health

1. A low-fat diet <u>helps</u> to prevent heart disease.

2. Second-hand smoke <u>causes</u> health problems.

3. People <u>need</u> exercise to stay healthy.

Occupations

1. A hair stylist <u>works</u> in a salon and <u>cuts</u> and <u>colors</u> hair.

2. A plumber <u>fixes</u> pipes, sinks, and toilets.

3. A bank teller <u>takes</u> deposits and <u>cashes</u> checks.

Government

1. The President of the United States <u>lives</u> in the White House in Washington, D.C.

2. The American people <u>elect</u> a President every four years.

3. The U.S. Senate and the House of Representatives <u>make</u> the laws for the country.

HABITUAL PRESENT TENSE - STATEMENTS OF FACT

➡ **Exercise 11** Choose a verb from the box to complete each statement of fact below. Compare your answers with a partner or in a small group.

<u>verbs</u>			
perform	have	contain	speak
pay	treat	cause	celebrate
✔ freeze	grow	boil	

Statements of Fact

1. Water __freezes__ at 32° Fahrenheit and _____ at 212° Fahrenheit.

2. Palm trees _____ in warm climates.

3. Stress _____ high blood pressure and other health problems.

4. A cardiologist _____ patients with heart problems.

5. A surgeon _____ operations.

6. Oranges _____ Vitamin C.

7. The United States _____ fifty states.

8. The American people_____ their independence on the Fourth of July.

9. People in the United States _____ income taxes every year.

10. The people in China _____ Chinese.

➡ **Exercise 12** Write four statements of fact. Use the Habitual Present Tense.

1. _____

_____

2. _____

_____

3. _____

_____

4. _____

_____

HABITUAL PRESENT TENSE - STATEMENTS OF FACT

▸ **Exercise 13** Read each statement of fact below. Then write a negative sentence with the words in parentheses. Use the Habitual Present Tense or the Present Tense of the verb <u>Be</u>.

Facts about the United States

1. The United States has a President. (King and Queen)

   The United States doesn't have a King and Queen.

2. The people in the United States elect a President every four years. (their Senators)

   _____

3. The United States has 50 states. (51)

   _____

4. 48 of the 50 states are in the continental United States. (Alaska and Hawaii)

   _____

5. It snows in Alaska. (Hawaii)

   _____

6. The University of California is a public university. (Stanford University)

   _____

▸ **Exercise 14** Follow the same directions as in Exercise 13.

Facts about English Spelling and Pronunciation

1. The English alphabet has 26 letters. (29 letters)

   The English alphabet doesn't have 29 letters.

2. The letters *a, e, i, o, u* are vowels. (consonants)

   _____

3. We hear the letter *a* in the word <u>cake</u>. (the letter *e*)

   _____

4. The letters *gh* sound like *f* in the word <u>laugh</u>. (the word <u>light</u>)

   _____

5. We add the letter *s* to make nouns plural. (adjectives)

   _____

6. The words <u>wear</u> and <u>where</u> sound the same. (the words <u>fell</u> and <u>felt</u>)

   _____

✓ CHECK YOUR UNDERSTANDING

A. Answer the questions below.

1. How do we form negative sentences in the Habitual Present Tense? _____

_____

2. The negative contractions in the Habitual Present Tense are _____ and _____.

3. We use the _____ form of the main verb in negative sentences in the Habitual Present Tense.

4. Write negative sentences in the Habitual Present Tense. Use the subjects below.

   a. Our teacher _____

   b. The students in my class _____

5. What is a statement of fact?

_____

6. Write two statements of fact.

   a. _____

_____

   b. _____

_____

B. *EDITING* - The paragraph below has 7 verb errors. Find and correct the errors. The first one is done for you. If you need help, refer to the Reference Chart on page 110.

An Unusual Family

do not

[1]Mr. and Mrs. Anderson and their children are an unusual family because they ~~not~~ have a television set in their home. [2]Ed Anderson don't enjoys sports, so he don't like to watch football and basketball games on TV. [3]His wife Jan isn't likes talk shows, game shows, or movies. [4]In addition, they do not want their children to watch television because they not approve of the advertising and violence on TV. [5]In the evening after dinner, the children usually does their homework, and Ed and Jan read the newspaper or a good book. [6]Mr. and Mrs. Anderson and their children are not miss TV at all.

ASKING YES-NO QUESTIONS IN THE HABITUAL PRESENT TENSE

> **Learning Point 1**
>
> **YES-NO QUESTIONS** are questions that we answer with <u>yes</u> or <u>no</u>.

Example: 1. A: Do you have a job?　　　**2. A:** Does he like his job?
　　　　　　B: Yes, I do.　　　　　　　　**B:** No, he doesn't.

　　　　　　A: Do they work with you?　　**A:** Does he want a new job?
　　　　　　B: No, they don't.　　　　　　**B:** Yes, he does.

> **Learning Point 2**
>
> To form **YES-NO QUESTIONS** in the Habitual Present Tense, we put the helping verb <u>do</u> or <u>does</u> in front of the subject. We use the **root form** of the main verb in questions.

　　　　　　　　hv　s　mv　　　　　　　　　　hv　　　　s　　mv
Example: 1. A: Do you work at IBM?　　**2. A:** Does your brother work there too?
　　　　　　B: Yes, I do.　　　　　　　　**B:** No, he doesn't.

▸ Habitual Present Tense - Yes-No Questions

1.	Do	I	work?			
2.	Do	you	work?	Do	we / you / they	work?
3.	Does	he / she / it	work?			

▸ Word Order of Yes-No Questions

	HELPING VERB	SUBJECT	MAIN VERB (ROOT FORM)	COMPLEMENT	SHORT ANSWERS FOR CONVERSATION
1.	Do	you	use	a computer at work?	Yes, I do.
2.	Does	he	want	a new job?	Yes, he does.
3.	Does	she	work	for a good company?	No, she doesn't.
4.	Does	it	offer	good employee benefits?	No, it doesn't.
5.	Do	they	get	a raise every year?	Yes, they do.

HABITUAL PRESENT TENSE - YES-NO QUESTIONS

▶ **Exercise 15** Use the words in parentheses to form yes-no questions in the Habitual Present Tense.

A Visit to San Francisco

1. (you and your husband / like / to go to San Francisco)

   A: <u>   Do   </u> <u> you and your husband </u> <u>   like   </u> <u>   to go to San Francisco ?   </u>
          hv   **s**   **main verb**   **complement**

   B: Yes, we do. My husband and I enjoy San Francisco very much.

2. (you / go / there very often)

   A: _____ _____ _____ _____
          hv   **s**   **main verb**   **complement**

   B: No, we don't. We go to San Francisco about twice a year.

3. (you / ride / the cable cars)

   A: _____ _____ _____ _____
          hv   **s**   **main verb**   **complement**

   B: Yes, we do. We usually park our car and take the cable car to Chinatown.

4. (Chinatown / have / many interesting shops)

   A: _____ _____ _____ _____
          hv   **s**   **main verb**   **complement**

   B: Yes, it does. Chinatown has many different kinds of shops such as clothing and jewelry shops.

5. (you / buy / Oriental food in the grocery stores)

   A: _____ _____ _____ _____
          hv   **s**   **main verb**   **complement**

   B: Yes, I do. I especially like to try different kinds of tea and spices.

6. (you and your husband / go / to Fisherman's Wharf for dinner)

   A: _____ _____ _____ _____
          hv   **s**   **main verb**   **complement**

   B: Yes, we do. Fisherman's Wharf has many wonderful restaurants.

7. (your husband / like / seafood)

   A: _____ _____ _____ _____
          hv   **s**   **main verb**   **complement**

   B: No, he doesn't. He usually orders a pasta dish such as spaghetti or ravioli.

YES-NO QUESTIONS

➠ **Exercise 16** Use the Habitual Present Tense or the Present Tense of the verb <u>Be</u> to complete the conversations below. Then practice the conversations with a partner.

1. *An Employer and a Job Applicant*

    A: We __need__ **(1. need)** someone to work 40 hours a week in our customer service department. _____ **(2. be)** you interested?

    B: No, I'm not. I _____ **(3. not / want)** a full-time job because I go to school three days a week. _____ you _____ **(4. have)** any part-time jobs?

    A: Yes, we do. We _____ **(5. have)** an opening for a part-time clerk in the auto parts department. The hours are 8:00 to 5:00 on Mondays and Fridays. _____ **(6. be)** you available on Mondays and Fridays?

    B: Yes, I am. That would be perfect.

2. *A Receptionist and a Patient*

    A: I _____ **(1. have)** a terrible toothache. I _____ **(2. need)** to see the dentist right away.

    B: _____ you _____ **(3. have)** an appointment?

    A: No, I don't.

    B: Dr. Davis _____ **(4. be)** with a patient right now, but he _____ **(5. have)** an opening in a half hour. You can wait in his office.

    A: Thank you very much.

3. *Boyfriend and Girlfriend*

    A: _____ **(1. be)** you busy tonight? _____ you _____ **(2. want)** to go dancing?

    B: No, I don't. My sister _____ **(3. be)** here on a visit from New York.

    A: Well, _____ she _____ **(4. want)** to go with us?

    B: No, she doesn't. She _____ **(5. not / like)** to dance.

    A: Well, there _____ **(6. be)** other things to do. _____ she _____ **(7. enjoy)** movies?

    B: No, she doesn't. She _____ **(8. hate)** movies.

    A: Well, _____ she _____ **(9. want)** to go out for dinner?

    B: No, she doesn't. She _____ **(10. be)** on a diet.

    A: Well, _____ she _____ **(11. like)** to do anything?

    B: Yes, she does. She _____ **(12. like)** to stay home and study English!

REFERENCE CHART – THE HABITUAL PRESENT TENSE

HABITUAL PRESENT TENSE - AFFIRMATIVE

	singular		plural
first person:	1. I work	1. we
second person:	2. you work	2. you work
third person:	3. he	3. they
	she work**s**	
	it	

HABITUAL PRESENT TENSE - NEGATIVE

	singular		plural
first person:	1. I do not (don't) work	1. we
second person:	2. you do not(don't) work	2. you do not (don't) work
third person:	3. he	3. they
	she does not (doesn't) work	
	it	

HABITUAL PRESENT TENSE - YES-NO QUESTIONS

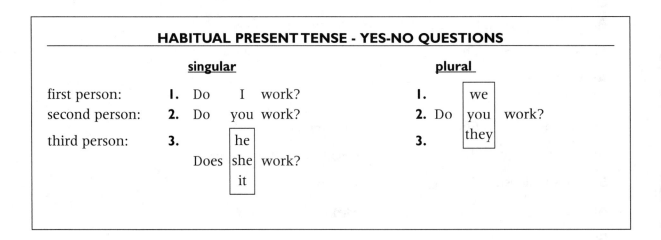

	singular		plural
first person:	1. Do I work?	1. we
second person:	2. Do you work?	2. Do you work?
third person:	3.	3. they
	Does he work?	
	she	
	it	

 **CHECK YOUR UNDERSTANDING**

A. Answer the questions below.

　1. What are yes-no questions?_____

　　_____

　2. How do we form yes-no questions in the Habitual Present Tense? _____

　　_____

　3. We use the_____ form of the main verb in yes-no questions in the Habitual
　　Present Tense.

　4. What is the word order of yes-no questions in the Habitual Present Tense?

　　_____ + _____ + _____ + _____

B. Write a yes-no question for each short answer below. Use only the Habitual Present Tense or the
　Present Tense of the verb <u>Be</u>.

　1. **A:** <u>Do you like all your classes this semester?</u>_____

　　B: Yes, I do.

　2. **A:** _____

　　B: No, he doesn't.

　3. **A:** _____

　　B: Yes, she is.

　4. **A:** _____

　　B: Yes, they are.

　5. **A:** _____

　　B: No, they don't.

　6. **A:** _____

　　B: Yes, it is.

　7. **A:** _____

　　B: Yes, he does.

　8. **A:** _____

　　B: No, I don't

Part 2
The Present Progressive Tense

THE MEANING OF THE PRESENT PROGRESSIVE TENSE - TEMPORARY ACTIONS

➡ In Part 1 of this chapter, you studied the Habitual Present Tense. You learned that we use the Habitual Present Tense to talk about **habitual actions** - things that we do again and again.

You learned that we use the <u>root form</u> and the <u>-s form</u> of verbs to talk about habitual actions.

Habitual Actions: **1.** I always eat dinner at 5:30 or 6:00.
↑
root form

              2. My brother works on his computer every night.
↑
-s form

              3. My friends and I go to the movies every Friday or Saturday night.
↑
root form

➡ In this chapter, you will study a different kind of present tense, the Present Progressive Tense. We use the Present Progressive Tense to talk about **temporary actions**. A temporary action is an action that is happening right now (at the moment of speaking). A temporary action is not permanent and will probably end soon.

We use the verb <u>Be</u> (am, is, are) and the present participle (-ing form) of a verb to talk about temporary actions.

Temporary Actions: **1.** We are reading page 112 right now.
↑   ↑
be   ing

              2. The teacher is explaining the Present Progressive Tense.
↑   ↑
be   ing

              3. Everyone is listening carefully to the teacher.
↑   ↑
be   ing

<u>Note</u>: The Present Progressive Tense is also called the Present Continuous Tense.

THE PRESENT PROGRESSIVE TENSE

> ▶ **Learning Point**
>
> **1.** We use the Present Progressive Tense to talk about actions that are in progress (happening) **right now** at the moment of speaking.
>
> **2.** These actions are **temporary**. The actions will probably end soon.

TIME WORDS
now
right now

We are sitting in class <u>right now</u>.   (The action will end at 3:00 when class is over.)

---------------+---+---------

    right now   **end of action**

⇒ The sentences below talk about temporary actions. These actions are not permanent. The actions will end when class is over.

Example: **1.** We are studying English grammar <u>right now</u>.

        2. We are learning about the Present Progressive Tense.

        3. We are talking about temporary and permanent actions.

        4. The students are reading the example sentences <u>now</u>.

        5. One of the students is asking the teacher a question.

        6. The teacher is telling the students to study all the learning points carefully.

THE PRESENT PROGRESSIVE TENSE: <u>BE</u> + VERB + <u>ING</u>

> ### ▶ Learning Point
>
> We use <u>Be</u> and the <u>-ing form</u> of a verb (present participle) to talk about temporary actions that are in progress (happening) right now. <u>Be</u> is a helping (auxiliary) verb.

Example: **1.** The teacher is explaining the Learning Point on page 114 right now.
             ↑   ↑
            be   **-ing form**
           (hv) **(main verb)**

2. The students are listening carefully to the teacher's explanation.
       ↑   ↑
      be **-ing form**
     (hv) **(main verb)**

⇒ Forms of the Present Progressive Tense

	singular			**plural**	
first person:	I	am	working	we	
second person:	you	are	working	you	are working
third person:	he / she / it	is	working	they	

⇒ **Exercise 1** Look around the classroom. Choose five of the verbs below to describe what you, your classmates, and your teacher are doing at this moment.

smile	talk	laugh	read	write
stand	sit	look	help	explain

1. <u>The teacher is talking to the students right now.</u> _____

   _____

2. _____

   _____

3. _____

   _____

4. _____

   _____

5. _____

THE PRESENT PROGRESSIVE TENSE: <u>BE</u> + VERB + <u>ING</u>

➡ **Exercise 2** Practice using the Present Progressive Tense. Answer the questions below with true answers.

1. What are you doing right now?

_____

2. Where are you sitting in the classroom (in the front, in the middle, or in the back of the room)?

_____

3. Who is sitting on your left?

_____

4. Who is sitting on your right?

_____

5. What are you wearing?

_____

6. What is the teacher wearing?

_____

➡ **Exercise 3** The sentences below contain errors in the use of the Present Progressive Tense. Circle the error in each sentence. Then write the sentence correctly. Use <u>only</u> the Present Progressive Tense.

Class Is Over

1. Our teacher is write the homework assignment on the board now.

   Our teacher is writing the homework assignment on the board now.

2. Some of the students copy the homework assignment in their notebooks right now.

   _____

3. Other students putting their books and papers into their backpacks.

   _____

4. One of the students are erasing the boards for the teacher.

   _____

5. I go to my next class now.

   _____

SENTENCES WITH THIS WEEK, THIS MONTH, THIS SEMESTER, THIS YEAR

➡ You have learned that we use the Present Progressive Tense to talk about temporary actions that are happening right now (at the moment of speaking).

Example: We are studying a new Learning Point right now.

> ### ▶ Learning Point
>
> We can also use the Present Progressive Tense with time words such as ***this week***, ***this month***, ***this semester***, and ***this year*** to talk about temporary actions that are in progress. However, the action may or may not be happening right now (at the moment of speaking).

➡ The sentences below are in the Present Progressive Tense, but the actions are not happening right now.

1. *In the Library*

Peter:　　　Are you taking history this semester?

Carla:　　　Yes, I am. I'm taking history from Prof. Grove.

(Carla is not in her history class right now. She is in the library.)

2. *In the Classroom*

Ana:　　　Are you working at Burger House this month?

Sue:　　　Yes, I am. I'm working there part-time until school is out.

(Sue is not working at Burger House right now. She's in class.)

3. *At a Soccer Game*

Mr. Ryan: Are you attending Kirk High School this year?

Jimmy:　　Yes, I'm attending Kirk High this year. I like it a lot.

(Jimmy isn't attending school right now. He is at a soccer game.)

SENTENCES WITH THIS WEEK, THIS MONTH, THIS SEMESTER, THIS YEAR

▸ We can use the time words in the box below to describe an action that is in progress at the present time but may or may not be happening right now. However, the action is temporary and will probably end in the near future.

time words

this week	this semester
this month	this year

▸ **Exercise 4** Use the time words in the box to write <u>true</u> sentences about something that you are doing temporarily but will end in the near future. Use only the Present Progressive Tense.

1. (this semester) <u>I am taking three classes this semester.</u>

_____

2. (this semester) _____

_____

3. (this week) _____

_____

4. (this week) _____

_____

5. (this month) _____

_____

6. (this month) _____

_____

7. (this year) _____

_____

8. (this year) _____

_____

REFERENCE CHART - THE PRESENT PROGRESSIVE TENSE

PRESENT PROGRESSIVE TENSE - AFFIRMATIVE

		singular			**plural**	
first person:	**I.**	I	am eating	**I.**	we	
second person:	**2.**	you	are eating	**2.**	you	are eating
third person:	**3.**	he / she / it	is eating	**3.**	they	

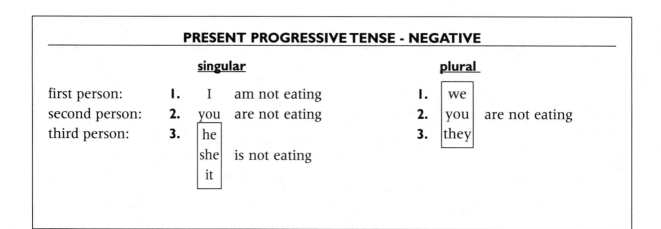

PRESENT PROGRESSIVE TENSE - NEGATIVE

		singular			**plural**	
first person:	**I.**	I	am not eating	**I.**	we	
second person:	**2.**	you	are not eating	**2.**	you	are not eating
third person:	**3.**	he / she / it	is not eating	**3.**	they	

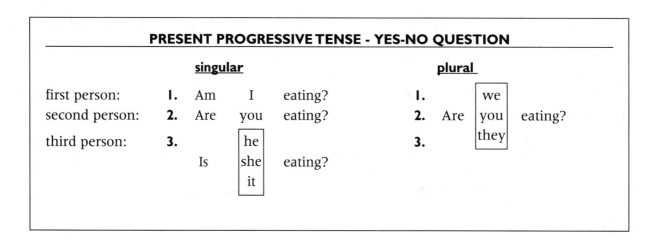

PRESENT PROGRESSIVE TENSE - YES-NO QUESTION

		singular				**plural**		
first person:	**I.**	Am	I	eating?	**I.**		we	
second person:	**2.**	Are	you	eating?	**2.**	Are	you / they	eating?
third person:	**3.**	Is	he / she / it	eating?	**3.**			

Part 3
The Difference Between the Habitual Present and the Present Progressive Tense

HABITUAL ACTIONS AND TEMPORARY ACTIONS

HABITUAL ACTIONS

We use the ***Simple (Habitual) Present Tense*** to talk about actions that we do again and again over a long period of time.

Example: **1.** My friends and I start work at 7:30 every morning.

2. I always eat lunch at 12:00.

3. We get off work at 4:15 every day.

TEMPORARY ACTIONS

We use the ***Present Progressive Tense*** to talk about temporary actions that will probably end soon. The actions are not permanent.

Example: **1.** We are reading page 119 right now.

2. The students are working in small groups now.

3. The teacher is walking around the room and helping the students.

➡ On the following pages, you will practice using the Habitual Present Tense and the Present Progressive Tense. Before you begin the practice exercises, you need to review the forms of the verb that we use in each tense. Complete the charts on page 120. If you need help with the charts, refer to pages 110 and 118.

HABITUAL PRESENT AND PRESENT PROGRESSIVE TENSE

⟱ **Exercise 1** Complete the charts below. Then compare your answers with a partner.

Habitual Present Tense Use the <u>root form</u> and the <u>-s form</u>	**Present Progressive Tense** Use <u>be</u> + <u>-ing</u> (present participle)

affirmative

1. I _____ work _____ hard every day.

2. You _____ hard every day.

3. He/She/It _____ hard every day.

4. We _____ hard every day.

5. You _____ hard every day.

6. They _____ hard every day.

negative

1. I _____ hard every day.

2. You _____ hard every day.

3. He/She/It _____ hard every day.

4. We _____ hard every day.

5. You _____ hard every day.

6. They _____ hard every day.

yes-no questions

1. _____ I _____ hard every day?

2. _____ you _____ hard every day?

3. _____ he/she/it _____ hard every day?

4. _____ we _____ hard every day?

5. _____ you _____ hard every day?

6. _____ they _____ hard every day?

affirmative

1. I _____ am working _____ hard right now.

2. You _____ hard right now.

3. He/She/It _____ hard right now.

4. We _____ hard right now.

5. You _____ hard right now.

6. They _____ hard right now.

negative

1. I _____ hard right now.

2. You _____ hard right now.

3. He/She/It _____ hard right now.

4. We _____ hard right now.

5. You _____ hard right now.

6. They _____ hard right now.

yes-no questions

1. _____ I _____ hard right now?

2. _____ you _____ hard right now?

3. _____ he/she/it _____ hard right now?

4. _____ we _____ hard right now?

5. _____ you _____ hard right now?

6. _____ they _____ hard right now?

⟱ Write two sentences in the Habitual Present Tense.

1. _____

2. _____

⟱ Write two sentences in the Present Progressive Tense.

1. _____

2. _____

HABITUAL ACTIONS AND TEMPORARY ACTIONS

▶ **Exercise 2** Use the Present Progressive Tense, the Habitual Present Tense, or the verb <u>Be</u> to complete the sentences about the picture.

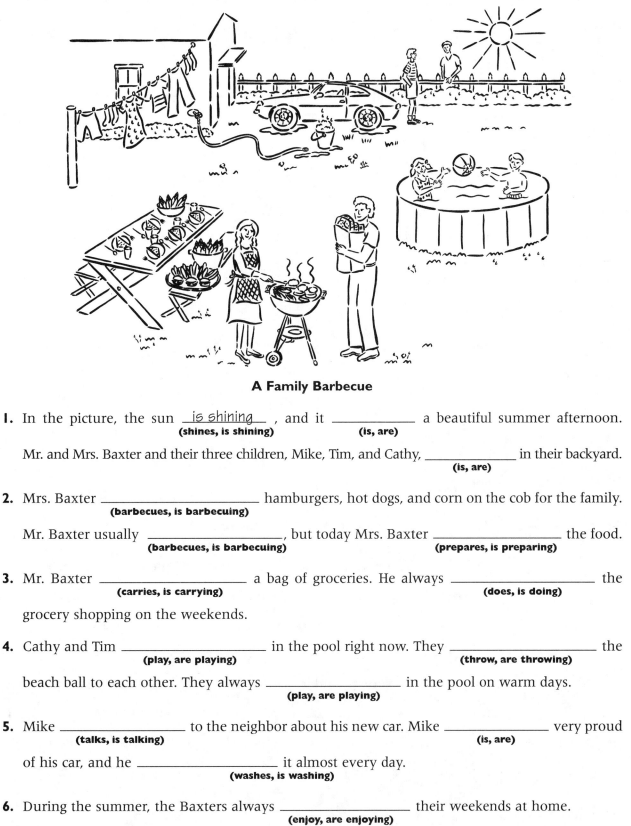

A Family Barbecue

1. In the picture, the sun <u>is shining</u> , and it _____ a beautiful summer afternoon.
                           (shines, is shining)   **(is, are)**

Mr. and Mrs. Baxter and their three children, Mike, Tim, and Cathy, _____ in their backyard.
                                                                      (is, are)

2. Mrs. Baxter _____ hamburgers, hot dogs, and corn on the cob for the family.
                     (barbecues, is barbecuing)

Mr. Baxter usually _____, but today Mrs. Baxter _____ the food.
                          (barbecues, is barbecuing)   **(prepares, is preparing)**

3. Mr. Baxter _____ a bag of groceries. He always _____ the
                 (carries, is carrying)   **(does, is doing)**

grocery shopping on the weekends.

4. Cathy and Tim _____ in the pool right now. They _____ the
                 (play, are playing)   **(throw, are throwing)**

beach ball to each other. They always _____ in the pool on warm days.
                                     (play, are playing)

5. Mike _____ to the neighbor about his new car. Mike _____ very proud
             (talks, is talking)   **(is, are)**

of his car, and he _____ it almost every day.
                   (washes, is washing)

6. During the summer, the Baxters always _____ their weekends at home.
                                   (enjoy, are enjoying)

HABITUAL ACTIONS AND TEMPORARY ACTIONS

➡ **Exercise 3** Choose the Present Progressive Tense, the Habitual Present Tense, or the verb <u>Be</u> to complete the dialogs below. Then practice the dialogs with a partner.

Dialog 1 A Bad Job

A: What **(1. be)** <u>is</u> wrong with Joe?

B: He **(2. be)** _____ very unhappy with his job at Kent Electronics.

A: Why?

B: His company **(3. get)** _____ a lot of new business this year, but they **(4. not / hire)** _____ any new employees. As a result, Joe **(5. have)** _____ to work overtime three or four days every week, and he sometimes **(6. have)** _____ to work on the weekend as well.

A: **(7. try)** _____ Joe _____ to find another job?

B: Yes, he is. He **(8. read)** _____ the want ads in the paper every day, and he **(9. search)** _____ the Internet for job opportunities.

A: I hope that he finds a job soon.

Dialog 2 Drug Prevention

A: Who **(1. be)** _____ that man in Mrs. Hale's classroom?

B: He **(2. be)** _____ Dr. Charles Harris, the director of the new drug abuse clinic. Right now, he **(3. speak)** _____ to Mrs. Hale's students about the dangers of drugs. Every year, thousands of teenagers **(4. begin)** _____ to experiment with drugs, and Mrs. Hale **(5. be)** _____ concerned* about her students. Dr. Harris **(6. be)** _____ very popular with young people, and he **(7. lecture)** _____ and **(8. show)** _____ films at schools all over the city. He always **(9. give)** _____ students the opportunity to ask questions about the new clinic's plans to help people with drug problems.

Vocabulary Note   *<u>concerned</u>: worried*

 **CHECK YOUR UNDERSTANDING**

A. Answer the questions below.

I. What is the difference between the Habitual Present and the Present Progressive Tense?

_____

_____

2. How do we form the Habitual Present Tense? _____

_____

3. How do we form the Present Progressive Tense? _____

_____

4. What time words do we often use with habitual actions (actions that we do again and again)? Give five examples.

_____ _____ _____ _____ _____

5. What time words do we use with temporary actions that are in progress (happening) at the moment of speaking? _____ _____

B. *EDITING* - Each sentence below contains one or more errors in the use of the Habitual Present Tense or the Present Progressive Tense. Re-write each sentence correctly.

I. Is David always ask a lot of questions in class?

_____

2. We are not write a paragraph right now.

_____

3. Are the students often speaking their native language in class?

_____

4. The teacher don't usually giving us a lot of homework.

_____

5. Does Susan going to school now?

_____

6. We are not take the bus to school every day.

_____

7. The students are sit in groups and do their homework now.

_____

8. Do the students take a break right now?

_____

Part 4
Verbs Not Used in the Present Progressive Tense

NON-ACTION VERBS (VERBS THAT DO NOT SHOW ACTION)

⟫ Be careful. We do not usually use **non-action verbs** in the Present Progressive Tense. Non-action verbs are verbs that do not show movement or physical activity. Non-action verbs are also called **non-progressive verbs**.

⟫ Study the verbs in the chart below. We do not usually put -ing on these verbs.

NON-ACTION (NON-PROGRESSIVE) VERBS					
hear	appreciate	hate	be	remember	belong to
see	forgive	need	believe	seem	have (own)
smell	like	prefer	forget	think (believe)	own
taste	love	want	know	understand	possess

⟫ We do not use the Present Progressive Tense with verbs that do not show action. We usually use the Habitual Present Tense with non-action verbs. Study the examples below.

1. <u>not correct</u>: The teacher ~~is wanting~~ everyone to do well in his class. (**no action**)

   <u>correct</u>:   The teacher **wants** everyone to do well in his class.
                                    ↑
                        Habitual Present Tense

2. <u>not correct</u>: All of the students ~~are understanding~~ today's lesson. (**no action**)

   <u>correct</u>:   All of the students **understand** today's lesson.
                                    ↑
                        Habitual Present Tense

⟫ You may hear some of these verbs used in the Present Progressive Tense. In this case, the verb has a special meaning.

   Example: **1.** I <u>am having</u> a party (a test, a good time).

                  2. I <u>am thinking</u> about my family (my job, my homework assignment).

                  3. I <u>am seeing</u> the counselor (the doctor, the dentist) today.

<u>**Note:**</u>   *Non-action (non-progressive) verbs are also called <u>stative verbs</u>.*

ACTION VERBS AND NON-ACTION VERBS

➡ **Exercise I** Complete the dialog below. Choose between the Present Progressive Tense, the Habitual Present Tense, and the verb <u>Be</u>. Be careful. Some of the verbs are non-progressive verbs because they do not show action. We use the Habitual Present Tense with verbs that do not show action.

The New Apartment

➡ Jenny recently left home to start her first year of college. She just moved into a new apartment with two roommates. Complete the telephone conversation between Jenny and her mother.

A: <u>Jenny</u>: Hi, Mom. It's Jenny. I **(1. call)** <u>am calling</u> from my new apartment.

B: <u>Mom</u>: Oh, hi, Jenny. How is everything? How **(2. like)**_____ you _____ your apartment?

A: <u>Jenny</u>: The apartment is great, and I really **(3. like)** _____ my new roommates.

B: <u>Mom</u>: How many roommates **(4. have)** _____ you _____?

A: <u>Jenny</u>: Two, Emily and Kendal. They **(5. be)** _____ both in my English classes.

B: <u>Mom</u>: What time **(6. be)** _____ it in California?

A: <u>Jenny</u>: It's 6:00, and it **(7. begin)** _____ to get dark now. In fact, I can't talk long. We **(8. make)** _____ dinner right now. All of us **(9. have)** _____ a job to do in the kitchen. Emily **(10. prepare)** _____the main dish. Right now she **(11. fry)** _____ garlic, onions, and mushrooms to put in a meat loaf. The kitchen **(12. smell)** _____ wonderful. Kendal **(13. make)** _____ a salad. She **(14. chop)**_____ lettuce, tomatoes, cucumbers, and other vegetables. She **(15. like)** _____ to put lots of fresh vegetables in her salads.

B: <u>Mom</u>: What **(16. be)** _____ your job, Jenny?

A: <u>Jenny</u>: Well, remember, Mom. I **(17. love)** _____ to eat, but I **(18. hate)** _____ to cook. I **(19. have)** _____ the easiest job. Right now, I **(20. peel)** _____ the potatoes!

ACTION VERBS AND NON-ACTION VERBS

➡ **Exercise 2** Right now, it is noon in the school cafeteria. There are a lot of different things going on, and each group of students is talking about something different. Choose between the Present Progressive Tense, the Habitual Present Tense, and the verb <u>Be</u> to complete each dialog below.

Dialog 1 A: My husband and I **(1. save)** <u> are saving </u> money for a new car. I **(2. want)**

_____ a foreign car, but my husband **(3. prefer)** _____ American

cars. What **(4. think)** _____ you _____ ?

B: I **(5. prefer)** _____ American cars because foreign cars **(6. be)**

_____ usually more expensive to maintain. I **(7. own)** _____

a Ford, and it **(8. not/cost)** _____ much to maintain it. The

service and parts **(9. not/be)** _____ too expensive.

Dialog 2 A: I really **(1. need)** _____ a haircut. My hair **(2. be)** _____ too

long. **(3. know)** _____ you _____ a good hairdresser?

B: Yes. I always **(4. go)** _____ to a beauty salon on Bascom Avenue. In

fact, I **(5. go)** _____ there now.

A: (6. be) _____ it hard to get an appointment?

B: No, it **(7. not/be)** _____. They usually **(8. take)** _____ walk-ins.

(9. want) _____ you _____ to come with me?

Dialog 3 A: Excuse me. **(1. belong)** _____ this book _____ to you?

B: No, it doesn't. It **(2. belong)** _____ to Mike, and he probably **(3. need)**

_____ it for his next class.

Dialog 4 A: I **(1. get)** _____ terrible grades in my chemistry class now.

B: What **(2. be)** _____ the problem?

A: I **(3. not/understand)** _____ the lectures because the teacher

always **(4. speak)** _____ too fast.

B: (5. want) _____ you _____ me to tutor you?

A: Oh, thank you. I really **(6. appreciate)**_____ your offer.

✓ CHECK YOUR UNDERSTANDING

A. Answer the questions below.

1. What are non-action verbs? _____

_____

2. Non-action verbs are also called _____.

3. Write six examples of non-action verbs. _____ _____

_____ _____ _____ _____

4. Do we use non-action verbs in the Present Progressive Tense? _____ yes _____ no

5. We usually use non-action verbs in the _____ Tense.

B. Use the non-action verbs below to write <u>true</u> sentences about yourself.

1. (need) _____

_____

2. want) _____

_____

3. (like) _____

_____

4. (forget) _____

_____

5. (hate) _____

_____

6. (understand) _____

_____

7. (own) _____

_____

8. (be) _____

_____

REVIEW OF VERB TENSES

➡ **Direction**: Think carefully about the meaning of the sentences below. Then write *true, false,* or *I don't know* on the line after each sentence.

1. My husband, Bill, is painting our house this month.
   a. Bill finished the house last weekend.   a. _false_____
   b. Bill is painting the house right now.   b. _I don't know.___
   c. Bill paints the house every two years.   c. _I don't know.___

2. Ana takes a computer class every semester.
   a. Ana is taking a computer class this semester.   a. _____
   b. Ana is in her computer class right now.   b. _____
   c. Ana's major is computer science.   c. _____

3. Karen is cooking dinner for her family right now.
   a. Dinner is ready.   a. _____
   b. Karen's family is eating dinner.   b. _____
   c. Karen always cooks dinner for her family.   c. _____

4. Tim is getting good grades in all his classes this semester.
   a. Tim is getting good grades in his history class.   a. _____
   b. Tim usually gets good grades in all his classes.   b. _____
   c. Tim is having trouble in his chemistry class this semester. c. _____

5. Joe wants to find a new job.
   a. Joe searches the Internet for job opportunities every day. a. _____
   b. Joe is reading the want ads in the newspaper right now. b. _____
   c. Joe likes his present job very much.   c. _____

6. Lan never forgets to bring her dictionary to class.
   a. She often has to borrow a dictionary from one of her classmates. a. _____
   b. She doesn't own a dictionary.   b. _____
   c. She's using her dictionary to look up a new word right now. c. _____

7. The class frequently has a party on the last day of school.
   a. The class is having a party right now.   a. _____
   b. The class always has a party on the last day of school. b. _____
   c. The teacher gives everyone a present on the last day of school. c. _____

Writing Assignment

➠ Your writing assignment in this chapter is to write a personal letter to a friend or family member about your typical day.

► What to do ◄

1. First read the sample letter below. In the letter, Phuong is writing to a friend about his typical day.

2. Study the form of Phuong's letter. A personal letter includes: (1) the date you are writing, (2) a greeting, and (3) a closing.

3. On a separate sheet of paper, write your own letter to a friend or family member about your typical day. Be sure to use the correct form for a personal letter.

---

greeting   date

May 20, 200_

Dear Tran,

  In your letter last month, you asked me about my typical day here in the United States. Well, my typical day is usually very busy. I wake up at 4:30 every morning. I get up right away and exercise for about a half hour. Then I watch the morning news on TV and have some toast with a glass of milk. I usually leave my house at 6:30 to avoid heavy traffic on the freeway. The freeways are always very congested here in Silicon Valley. It takes me about forty-five minutes to get to work. I have a good job at Alco Electronics in Sunnyvale. I maintain the hard drives in all of the computer work stations in the company. Sometimes it takes me a long time to find the problem with a drive. As a result, I am very busy all day. After work, I go home, take a shower, and cook dinner. I'm a vegetarian, so I prepare only vegetables and tofu. I never eat meat or fish. Before bedtime, I always do some exercises in order to sleep well. I never go to bed before 10:00 p.m. As you can see, my life is very busy! I hope to hear from you soon. Say hello to your mom and dad for me.

Sincerely,

Phuong

closing

Chapter 6
Sentence Structure: Compound Sentences

Part 1: Combining Simple Sentences to Make Compound Sentences

Part 2: Avoiding Comma Splices and Run-on Sentences

 Writing Assignment

To the Student:

In this chapter, you will learn how to connect your ideas to write longer, more interesting sentences. Although it is possible to use only simple sentences when you write, too many short, simple sentences sound choppy and boring. A good way to improve your writing is to use different kinds of sentences in your paragraphs.

Part I
Combining Simple Sentences
to Make Compound Sentences

COMPOUND SENTENCES

> ▶ **Learning Point**
>
> Sometimes we combine two or more simple sentences to make a longer, more interesting sentence (**S - V - C** + **S - V - C**).
>
> When we combine two or more simple sentences, the new sentence is called a **compound sentence**. (Compound means more than one.)

Study the examples below.

1. *simple sentence*:   John works thirty hours a week.

   simple sentence: He goes to school at night.

                                 S   V   C   S   V   C

   new sentence: John works thirty hours a week, and he goes to school at night.
   (compound sentence)

2. *simple sentence*:   He has class every night.

   simple sentence: He goes to the computer lab on Saturday.

                                 S   V   C   S   V   C

   new sentence: He has class every night, and he goes to the computer lab on Saturday.
   (compound sentence)

3. *simple sentence*:   He wants to get a job as a programmer.

   simple sentence: He still has several courses to take.

                                 S   V   C   S   V   C

   new sentence: He wants to get a job as a programmer, but he still has several courses to take.
   (compound sentence)

4. *simple sentence*:   John wants to be a full-time student.

   simple sentence: He has to work to support his family.

                                 S   V   C   S   V   C

   new sentence: John wants to be a full-time student, but he has to work to support his family.
   (compound sentence)

COMBINING SIMPLE SENTENCES

➠ Many ESL students lead busy lives. They attend day or night classes to improve their English and learn useful skills to help them to get a job as quickly as possible.

➠ **Exercise 1** Read the paragraphs below about stress in students' lives. Identify the sentences in each paragraph as **simple** or **compound**. Circle the subject(s) and verb(s) in each sentence. Then write "S" or "C" in the parentheses.

Stress in Students' Lives

I

stressful: *full of pressure, tension, or strain*

expectations: *anticipation, especially of future success or gain*

¹Many (students) (lead) stressful* lives. (**S**) ²For example, Mai wants to meet her parents' high expectations* for her future, so she works very hard in school. (   ) ³Every semester, she takes 18 units in order to graduate as quickly as possible. (   ) ⁴Her parents want her to be a doctor, so they expect her to get all "A's" in order to get into medical school. (   ) ⁵As a result, she has little free time during this period in her life. (   )

II

motivated: *anxious to succeed*

maintain: *keep, retain*

⁶Vinh is another example of a highly motivated* student. (   ) ⁷He takes 15 units each semester, and he maintains* a "B" average. (   ) ⁸During the week, he works as a waiter at a restaurant, and on Saturday mornings, he works as a math tutor in the learning center at school. (   ) ⁹Vinh plans to major in computer science. (   ) ¹⁰In addition, he sends money home every month to help his parents in Vietnam. (   )

III

manage: *be in charge of, supervise*

¹¹Carlos and Ana are also very hard-working students. (   ) ¹²During the day, Carlos manages* a landscaping business, and he attends business classes at a community college in the evening. (   ) ¹³His wife, Ana, attends cosmetology school during the day, and she also takes night classes at a nearby adult education center. (   ) ¹⁴Carlos and Ana have busy, stressful lives, but they are working hard now to have a good future for themselves and their family. (   )

CONNECTING SENTENCES WITH <u>AND</u> AND <u>BUT</u>

> **Learning Point**
>
> 1. We use the words **_and_** or **_but_** to combine (connect) two or more simple sentences to make compound sentences.
>
> 2. **_And_** and **_but_** are <u>connecting words</u>. Connecting words such as **_and_** and **_but_** are called <u>coordinating conjunctions</u>.

➡ When we write a compound sentence, we put a **comma** before <u>and</u> or <u>but</u>.

<u>AND</u> means <u>IN ADDITION</u>

<u>AND</u> gives additional information.

1. The teacher is explaining compound sentences today, and the students are listening carefully.
↑
additional information

2. The explanation is clear, and everyone understands it.
↑
additional information

3. Some of the students are writing in their notebooks, and other students are working in groups.
↑
additional information

<u>BUT</u> shows <u>CONTRAST</u>

<u>BUT</u> gives contrasting or opposite information. The second idea is sometimes unexpected.

1. My sister never studies for her tests, but she always gets an "A" or a "B".
↑
contrasting information

2. My math teacher gives us a lot of homework, but she never corrects it.
↑
contrasting information

3. My brother works fifty hours a week, but he never has any money.
↑
contrasting information

CONNECTING SENTENCES WITH <u>AND</u> AND <u>BUT</u>

▐▶ **Exercise 2** Choose **_and_** or **_but_** to connect the simple sentences below. When we connect two simple sentences, we put a comma before <u>and</u> or <u>but</u>. When you are finished, take turns reading the new sentences out loud with a partner.

Getting Ready for College

1. I'm in my last year of high school.
   I'm looking forward to college next year.

   I'm in my last year of high school, and I'm looking forward to college next year.

   _____

2. I attend Willow Glen High School.
   I'm also taking an advanced placement class in Japanese at City College.

   _____

   _____

3. My English, calculus, and history classes at Willow Glen High are easy for me.
   I'm having trouble with my Japanese class at City College.

   _____

   _____

4. I usually get good grades on my Japanese homework assignments.
   The oral presentations in class are difficult for me.

   _____

   _____

5. I want to improve my Japanese speaking skills.
   I don't have any Japanese friends to practice with.

   _____

   _____

6. A college education is important to me.
   I'm working very hard to be ready for college next year.

   _____

   _____

CONNECTING SENTENCES WITH <u>OR</u>

➽ You have learned that we often use the connecting words *and* or *but* to connect two simple sentences to make a compound sentence.

▶ **Learning Point**

We can also use the connecting word <u>**or**</u> to make a compound sentence.

We put a comma before the connecting word <u>**or**</u>.

| <u>OR</u> gives a <u>CHOICE</u> |

We use <u>OR</u> when there are two possibilities to choose from.

1. My friends and I usually go to a party on Friday night, or we go to the movies.
        ↑   ↑
  one possibility   **another possibility**

2. I study in the library on week nights, or I go to the language lab to listen to tapes.
    ↑   ↑
 one possibility   **another possibility**

➽ **Exercise 3** Use *or* and the information in parentheses to answer each question below. Remember to use a comma before *or*. Ask and answer the questions with a partner.

1. A: What does John usually do on Friday night?
   B: (watch TV / go to the movies with his friends)

   <u>He usually watches TV, or he goes to the movies with his friends.</u>

2. A: What do you and your husband do to relax on the weekend?
   B: (work in the garden / take a picnic lunch to the park)

   _____

   _____

3. A: What do you do to keep physically fit?
   B: (walk thirty minutes in the morning / stop at the health club on my way home from work)

   _____

   _____

4. A: What do you usually do on your birthday?
   B: (go out for dinner / have a party at home)

   _____

   _____

CONNECTING SENTENCES WITH <u>SO</u>

> ▶ **Learning Point**
>
> We can also use the connecting word <u>*so*</u> to connect two or more simple sentences to make a compound sentence.
>
> We put a comma before the connecting word <u>*so*</u>.

<u>SO</u> shows a <u>RESULT</u>

Students sometimes have trouble with the meaning of <u>SO</u>. We use <u>SO</u> to show a result.

What is the result?

1. My sister studies very hard,   so   she always gets good grades.

2. I have a very busy schedule,   so   I don't have much time to study.

3. I'm failing my English class,   so   I have to get a tutor.

⇒ **Exercise 4** Use the connecting word <u>*so*</u> to make compound sentences.

What is the result?

1. My car is in the shop, <u>so I have to take the bus to school.</u>

2. My TV isn't working, so _____

_____

3. My English midterm is tomorrow at 10:00, so _____

_____

4. Several of my friends are coming for dinner tonight, so _____

_____

5. I have a terrible toothache, so _____

_____

6. My teacher doesn't explain the lessons clearly, so _____

_____

THE CONNECTING WORDS <u>AND</u>, <u>BUT</u>, <u>OR</u>, <u>SO</u>

▶ **Exercise 5** Choose the best connecting word (*and, but, or, so*) to complete each compound sentence below. Compare your answers with a classmate. Take turns reading the sentences out loud.

How To Teach ESL Quickly and Successfully

1. I am a famous teacher, ___and___ I care about my students.

      a. or   (**b.** and)   **c.** so

2. I know how to teach English quickly and successfully, _____ my classes are always full.

      a. but   **b.** or   **c.** so

3. I never give homework, _____ my students are able to enjoy their free time.

      a. so   **b.** but   **c.** or

4. I give a test every week, _____ my students can use their books to find the answers.

      a. or   **b.** but   **c.** so

5. My students are often late for class, _____ I never get angry with them.

      a. and   **b.** so   **c.** but

6. I don't want my students to get too tired, _____ I give them a twenty-minute break every hour.

      a. but   **b.** so   **c.** or

7. We never study on a student's birthday, _____ we always have cake and ice cream to celebrate.

      a. so   **b.** but   **c.** and

8. I usually allow my students to take their final examination at home, _____ I give them a final exam in class.

      a. or   **b.** so   **c.** but

9. I don't want my students to feel bad, _____ everyone gets an "A" in my class.

      a. so   **b.** or   **c.** but

10. For all these reasons, I am the most popular teacher in the school, _____ my students always give me an excellent evaluation.

      a. but   **b.** and   **c.** or

Adapted from a student paragraph
by Hanh Pham

COMBINING SENTENCES

▐► The foreign exchange program is very popular with students all over the world. This program gives both high school and college students the opportunity to live and study in a foreign country. They also have the opportunity to experience the country's customs and culture.

Kieko Watanabe is a foreign exchange student from Japan at San Jose State University. Her goal is to return to Japan and teach high school mathematics. To prepare for this goal, she will study math and science during her two-year program in the United States.

▐► **Exercise 6** Connect the simple sentences about Kieko to make compound sentences. Use the connecting word that makes the best sense (*and, but, or, so*). Use a comma before <u>and</u>, <u>but</u>, <u>or</u>, <u>so</u>.

A Typical Foreign Exchange Student

1. Kieko enjoys college life in the U.S.
She is adapting well to the language and culture of a new country.

<u>Kieko enjoys college life in the U. S., and she is adapting well to the language and culture of</u>

<u>a new country.</u>

2. She is naturally shy.
It is not difficult for her to make new friends.

_____

_____

3. Kieko finds time in her busy schedule to tutor a small group of classmates in math and science.
She also helps her new American friends with their Japanese assignments.

_____

_____

_____

4. Kieko's friends want to show their appreciation for her help.
They often take her on trips to interesting places in northern California.

_____

_____

_____

5. Sometimes they go south to the beautiful beaches and parks in Monterey County.
They go north to visit the theaters, museums, and famous restaurants in and around San Francisco.

_____

_____

SENTENCES WITH RELATED IDEAS

➡ In the previous exercises, you practiced connecting two or more simple sentences to make a compound sentence.

> ▶ **Learning Point**
>
> When you connect two or more simple sentences, you must be careful. The ideas in the two simple sentences must be <u>closely related in thought</u>. If the two ideas are not closely related in thought, the new sentence is **not correct**.

➡ Study the pairs of sentences below.

1. Kieko studies hard, and she likes McDonald's hamburgers. **(not correct - unrelated ideas)**

2. Kieko studies hard, and she does well in all her classes. **(correct - related ideas)**

3. Kieko enjoys shopping, so she studies in the library every night. **(not correct - unrelated ideas)**

4. Kieko enjoys shopping, so she often goes to the Stanford Shopping Center. **(correct - related ideas)**

➡ **Exercise 7** Some of the sentences below are not correct because the two ideas are not closely related in thought. Write "related ideas" after the sentences that are correct and "unrelated ideas" after the sentences that are not correct. Compare your answers with a partner.

1. Kieko's parents call her once a week, and her brother attends   <u>unrelated ideas</u>
   college in New York.

2. Kieko's father often travels to the U.S. on business, so he is   _____
   able to visit his daughter every few months.

3. Several Japanese-American families are active in the foreign   _____
   exchange program, and they often invite the exchange students
   to their homes.

4. There are many good Japanese restaurants in San Jose, but San   _____
   Jose State University does not offer Japanese classes during
   the summer.

5. Kieko loves American music, so she is always happy to go with   _____
   her classmates to a football game on the weekend.

6. One of Kieko's American friends is from Colorado, and Kieko   _____
   plans to spend the Christmas holidays with her at her home
   in Denver.

SENTENCES WITH RELATED IDEAS

▶ **Exercise 8** Draw a line between the simple sentences that are related in thought.

Think About Your Health

column 1	column 2
1. My father has to watch his diet carefully.	**a.** Many people drink decaffeinated coffee.
2. Tim has a terrible smoker's cough.	**b.** She doesn't want to give up desserts.
3. I exercise for 15 minutes every morning.	**c.** A friend always drives him home.
4. My sister wants to lose 20 pounds.	**d.** I also run after dinner every night.
5. Too much caffeine is not healthy.	**e.** His blood pressure goes up.
6. Rob drinks too much at parties.	**f.** He continues to smoke two packs a day.

▶ **Exercise 9** Use the simple sentences in columns 1 and 2 above to make compound sentences. Use *and, but, or, so* in each new sentence.

1. _e_ _____ My father has to watch his diet carefully, or his blood pressure goes up._____

2. ____ _____

    _____

3. ____ _____

    _____

4. ____ _____

    _____

5. ____ _____

    _____

6. ____ _____

    _____

SENTENCES WITH RELATED IDEAS

▶ **Exercise 10** Add an idea that is closely related in thought to complete each compound sentence below. Circle the subject(s) and verb(s).

Learning English

1. My English pronunciation isn't very good, so_____

    _____

2. To improve my English, I watch American TV every day, and _____

    _____

3. I often listen to tapes in the library, or _____

    _____

4. I would like to practice my English outside of class, but _____

    _____

Leisure Time

1. I work hard all week, so _____

    _____

2. It's important to relax in my free time, so _____

    _____

3. My friends and I often go to the movies on Friday night, or _____

    _____

4. I like to travel, but _____

    _____

Good Health

1 Good health is very important, so _____

    _____

2. I eat a lot of fruit and vegetables, and _____

    _____

3. I usually walk for exercise, or _____

    _____

4. I always try to go to bed early, but _____

    _____

✓ CHECK YOUR UNDERSTANDING

A. Answer the following questions.

1. What is a compound sentence? _____

_____

2. What is the meaning of the connecting words that we studied in this chapter?

    a. <u>and</u> _____

    b. <u>but</u> _____

    c. <u>or</u> _____

    d. <u>so</u> _____

3. Where do we put the comma in a compound sentence? _____

_____

4. When we connect simple sentences, the ideas in the simple sentences must be _____

_____

B. Answer the questions below with a compound sentence. Use the connecting word in parentheses in your answer.

1. What kind of job do you want after graduation?

    (so)   <u>I want to work for a software company, so I'm majoring in computer science.</u>

2. What do you want to do this weekend?

    (or) _____

_____

3. Do you want to go to the movies tonight?

    (but) _____

_____

4. What do you usually do on Saturday morning?

    (and) _____

_____

Part 2
Avoiding Comma Splices and Run-on Sentences

COMMA SPLICES

▸ It is a very serious mistake if you put a comma at the end of a sentence instead of a period. This kind of mistake is confusing to your readers because they do not know where one sentence ends and the next sentence begins.

> ▸ **Learning Point**
>
> We cannot put a comma at the end of a sentence. We call this kind of mistake a **comma splice**. We must put a period at the end of a sentence.

not correct: My husband and I are having a lot of trouble with our car, the car is always in the shop.
comma splice

correct: My husband and I are having a lot of trouble with our car. The car is always in the shop.
period and capital letter

PERIOD AND CAPITAL LETTER

One way to correct a comma splice is to use a period and a capital letter to make two simple sentences.

1. not correct: We are trying to save $200 a month for a new car, we already have $2000 in our savings account.
comma splice

correct: We are trying to save $200 a month for a new car. We already have $2000 in our savings account.
period and capital letter

2. not correct: I want a large van with plenty of room for the family, my husband wants a sports car such as a BMW or a Porcshe.
comma splice

correct: I want a large van with plenty of room for the family. My husband wants a sports car such as a BMW or a Porcshe.
period and capital letter

CORRECTING <u>COMMA SPLICES</u> WITH A PERIOD AND A CAPITAL LETTER

➡ **Exercise 1** The sentences below are not correct because they contain comma splices.

1. Re-write each sentence.

2. Use a period and a capital letter to correct the comma splices.

A Good Place to Work

1. Syntex Electronics is a large company in Palo Alto, California, the company employs over 2000 people.

Syntex Electronics is a large company in Palo Alto, California. The company employs over 2000 people.

2. Many of the employees at Syntex come from foreign countries, these employees want to improve their English skills in order to advance in their jobs.

3. The company offers ESL classes in speaking and writing, the classes are free to all employees.

4. The classes meet twice a week for six weeks, the instructors come from community colleges and adult education programs in the area.

5. Students learn work-related vocabulary and other job skills in their classes, each student receives a certificate of achievement at the end of the course.

6. The classes are very popular with everyone, the company plans to continue the program.

ANOTHER WAY TO CORRECT <u>COMMA SPLICES</u>

▥➡ You have learned that one way to correct a comma splice is to use a period and a capital letter to make two simple sentences. There is another way to correct comma splices.

COMMA AND CONNECTING WORD

Another way to correct a comma splice is to use a comma and a connecting word (*and, but, or, so*) to make a compound sentence.

1. not correct: I just turned 16 last month, I want to get my driver's license as soon as possible.
↑
comma splice

   correct: I just turned 16 last month, **so** I want to get my driver's license as soon as possible.
↑
comma and connecting word

2. not correct: My brother takes me out on the freeway after dinner every night, my sister is helping me to study the driver's manual.
↑
comma splice

   correct: My brother takes me out on the freeway after dinner every night, **and** my sister is helping me to study the driver's manual.
↑
comma and connecting word

3. not correct: I don't have enough money to buy a car now, I work at a gas station on weekends to earn money.
↑
comma splice

   correct: I don't have enough money to buy a car now, **but** I work at a gas station on weekends to earn money.
↑
comma and connecting word

CORRECTING <u>COMMA SPLICES</u> WITH A COMMA AND CONNECTING WORD

▮➡ **Exercise 2** The sentences below are not correct because they contain comma splices.

I. Re-write each sentence.

2. Use a comma and a connecting word (*and, but, or, so*) to correct the comma splices. (In some of the sentences, more than one connecting word may be correct.)

A Happy Employee

I. My friend Loc Tran works as a lab technician for Syntex, he is very happy with his job.

   My friend Loc Tran works as a lab technician for Syntex, and he is very happy with his job.

   _____

2. Loc's job is interesting, he likes his supervisor and co-workers very much.

   _____

   _____

3. The company offers a flexible work week, employees do not have to work eight hours every day.

   _____

   _____

4. Loc works ten hours a day Monday through Thursday, he has Friday off to attend class.

   _____

   _____

5. Loc isn't eligible for the company retirement plan yet, he has full medical and dental insurance.

   _____

   _____

6. Syntex is a very good company to work for, Loc hopes to work for this company for a long time.

   _____

   _____

RUN-ON SENTENCES

➠ There is another serious mistake that students sometimes make in their writing. They often "run" two sentences together without a period. This is a serious mistake because the reader does not know where one sentence ends and a new sentence begins.

> ### ▶ Learning Point
>
> Do not "run" two sentences together. We call this kind of mistake a ***run-on sentence***. We must put a period at the end of a sentence.

not correct: There are only two weeks left in the semester everyone is preparing for final exams.
↑
run-on sentence

correct: There are only two weeks left in the semester. Everyone is preparing for final exams.
↑
period and capital letter

PERIOD AND CAPITAL LETTER

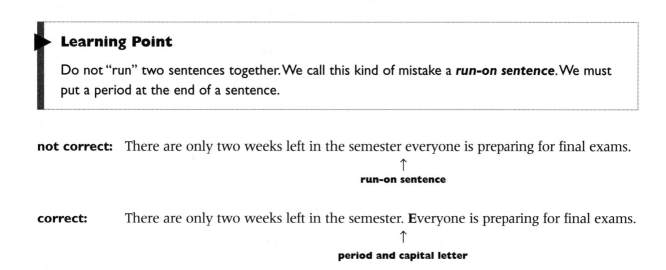

One way to correct a run-on sentence is to use a period and a capital letter to make two simple sentences.

1. not correct: The final exams are always difficult all the students are studying very hard.
↑
run-on sentence

  correct: The final exams are always difficult. All the students are studying very hard.
↑
period and capital letter

2. not correct: Everyone has a party after the final exams we say goodbye to our teachers and classmates until the next semester.   ↑
run-on sentence

  correct: Everyone has a party after the final exams. We say goodbye to our teachers and classmates until the next semester.   ↑
period and capital letter

CORRECTING <u>RUN-ON SENTENCES</u> WITH A PERIOD AND CAPITAL LETTER

▸ **Exercise 3** There are three run-on sentences in the paragraph below. Write the three sentences correctly on the lines under the paragraph. Use a period and a capital letter to correct the run-on sentences. Compare your answers with a partner.

The Movies

¹My family does not go to the movies very often because it is very expensive. ²For one thing, the tickets are expensive. ³An adult ticket costs more than $8.00 children's tickets are about $4.50. ⁴A family of six spends over $30.00 just for the tickets. ⁵For another thing, the prices at the refreshment stand are also very expensive. ⁶For example, a small Coke or a small glass of lemonade costs $2.75 two small bags of popcorn cost over $5.00. ⁷Of course, some people can afford to buy jumbo-sized boxes of popcorn, hot dogs, candy bars, and giant drinks. ⁸However, they are probably single or rich! ⁹These days many families do not go to the movies they prefer to rent a movie at the video store and make their own popcorn at home.

sentence _____ _____

_____

_____

sentence _____ _____

_____

_____

sentence _____ _____

_____

_____

ANOTHER WAY TO CORRECT <u>RUN-ON SENTENCES</u>

▶ You have learned that one way to correct a run-on sentence is to use a period and a capital letter to make two simple sentences. There is another way to correct run-on sentences.

COMMA AND CONNECTING WORD

Another way to correct a run-on sentence is to use a comma and a connecting word (*and, but, or, so*) to make a compound sentence.

1. not correct: My mother-in-law was born on the mainland of China in 1940 she came to the United States three years ago.
↑
run-on sentence

  correct: My mother-in-law was born on the mainland of China in 1940, **and** she came to the United States three years ago.
↑
comma and connecting word

2. not correct: She wanted to become a U.S. citizen she attended citizenship classes three hours a week for eight weeks.
↑
run-on sentence

  correct: She wanted to become a U.S. citizen, **so** she attended citizenship classes three hours a week for eight weeks.
↑
comma and connecting word

3. not correct: She was nervous about the citizenship test she passed the test with a nearly perfect score.
↑
run-on sentence

  correct: She was nervous about the citizenship test, **but** she passed the test with a nearly perfect score.
↑
comma and connecting word

CORRECTING <u>RUN-ON SENTENCES</u> WITH A COMMA AND CONNECTING WORD

➡ **Exercise 4** The sentences below are from students' compositions. Their assignment was to write about good money management. Some of the sentences are correct, but some sentences are run-on sentences. If the sentence is correct, write **C** on the line. If the sentence is a run-on, write **RO** on the line. Then correct the run-on sentence with a comma and a connecting word (*and, but, or, so*).

Ideas on Good Money Management

1. My husband and I always make a monthly budget we try hard to follow it.   <u>**RO**</u>
   <u>My husband and I always make a monthly budget, and we try hard to</u>
   <u>follow it.</u>

2. We pay our credit cards in full every month, so there isn't an interest charge.   _____

3. I check the food ads for sale items every week I also cut out coupons to   _____
   get discounts.

4. I always buy aspirins, vitamins, and other drugs at discount drugstores   _____
   to save money.

5. I make most of my children's clothes my husband gives them their haircuts.   _____

6. My husband takes our car in for regular maintenance we seldom have large   _____
   car repair bills.

7. We keep our thermostat at 65 degrees in the winter in order to avoid high   _____
   utility bills.

8. My family likes to eat out we never go to expensive restaurants.   _____

9. I make long distance calls after 8:00 p.m., or I wait until Sunday to make   _____
   my phone calls.

REVIEW - COMMA SPLICES AND RUN-ON SENTENCES

▐➡ **Exercise 5** Three sentences in the paragraph below are not correct. Circle each error, and write <u>RO</u> (run-on) or <u>CS</u> (comma splice) above the error. The first one is done for you.

The Thrifty* Student

thrifty: *careful with money, economical*

tight budget: *a limited amount of money*

economize: *save money*

quantity: *a certain number of things*

[1]Most students live on a tight budget*, so they have to economize* whenever possible. [2]One of the best places for thrifty students to save money is at the grocery store. [3]First of all, they cut out coupons from the newspaper, then they make a shopping list. [4]At the grocery store, they buy only those items on their list they do not buy any unnecessary items. [5]They also buy food in large quantities* at discount stores such as Food-For-Less and Costco. [6]Finally, non-food items such as toothpaste, aspirin, cosmetics, and cooking utensils are less expensive at other stores, good shoppers do not buy non-food items at the grocery store. [7]In short, thrifty students find many ways to save money at the grocery store.

▐➡ **Exercise 6** In this exercise, use a comma and a connecting word (*and, but, so, or*) to correct the comma splices and run-on sentences that you found in the paragraph. Write the number of the incorrect sentence in the box. Compare your answers with a partner.

sentence [3] <u>First of all, they cut out coupons from the newspaper, and then they</u>
<u>make a shopping list.</u>

sentence [ ] _____

_____

_____

sentence [ ] _____

_____

_____

OMITTING REPEATED WORDS AFTER **AND**

> ### ▶ Learning Point
>
> 1. When we use the connecting word **and** to connect simple sentences, we often omit repeated words in the second sentence such as subjects, verbs, and helping verbs.
>
> 2. When we omit repeated words such as subjects, verbs, and helping verbs, the new sentence is a <u>simple sentence</u>, not a compound sentence. For this reason, we do not use a comma before <u>and.</u>

OMIT REPEATED SUBJECT

1. Many students participate in work-study programs, and they earn money towards their tuition.

   Many students participate in work-study programs and earn money towards their tuition.

2. The students earn money, and they gain job experience at the same time.

   The students earn money and gain job experience at the same time.

OMIT REPEATED SUBJECT AND HELPING (AUXILIARY) VERB

1. I am working in the library on Monday nights, and I am tutoring math on Thursday nights.

   I am working in the library on Monday nights and tutoring math on Thursday nights.

2. My sister is taking classes during the day, and she is working as a lab assistant in the evening.

   My sister is taking classes during the day and working as a lab assistant in the evening.

OMIT REPEATED SUBJECT AND VERB

1. Mr. Harris coaches soccer on Tuesday afternoons, and he coaches tennis on Saturday morning.

   Mr. Harris coaches soccer on Tuesday afternoons and tennis on Saturday morning.

2. Van and Hong assist in the disabled students program, and they assist in the child care center.

   Van and Hong assist in the disabled students program and in the child care center.

OMITTING REPEATED WORDS AFTER <u>AND</u>

➡ **Exercise 7** Rewrite the sentences below. Omit repeated subjects, verbs, and helping verbs. Remember to omit the comma because the new sentence is not a compound sentence.

Sports for Exercise and Fun

1. The physical education program at my school is very extensive, and it offers everyone a chance to participate.
   The physical education program at my school is very extensive and offers everyone a chance to participate.

2. The PE classes are very popular, and they always fill up fast.

3. Team sports such as basketball and soccer teach teamwork, and they teach good sportsmanship.

4. Many students enroll in tennis classes, and they learn the rules of singles and doubles tennis.

5. The golf classes at our school are new this year, and they are already very popular.

6. My friends and I are taking an aerobics class, and we're enjoying it very much.

7. Exercise with music is healthy, and it's a lot of fun.

8. Some of my classmates are taking a self-defense class, and they are learning to defend themselves in a variety of situations.

9. Sports offer plenty of exercise, and they offer a chance to meet other people.

10. Participation in sports also relieves stress, and it promotes good physical fitness.

✔ CHECK YOUR UNDERSTANDING

A. Answer the following questions.

1. What is a comma splice? _____

_____

2. What is one way to correct a comma splice? _____

_____

3. What is another way to correct a comma splice? _____

_____

4. What is a run-on sentence? _____

_____

5. What is one way to correct a run-on sentence? _____

_____

6. What is another way to correct a run-on sentence? _____

_____

7. When we use the word <u>and</u> to connect two simple sentences, we can omit repeated words

such as _____, _____, and _____.

B. Circle the letter that describes each sentence.

1. We take our final exams in May, we don't get our grades until the end of June.

    a. comma splice   **b.** run-on sentence   **c.** correct sentence

2. I work ten hours a day, but I get every Friday off.

    a. comma splice   **b.** run-on sentence   **c.** correct sentence

3. I'm learning how to use my new Macintosh computer my brother is helping me.

    a. comma splice   **b.** run-on sentence   **c.** correct sentence

4. The Internet is a world-wide network of computers, and people use it to get information from all over the world.

    a. comma splice   **b.** run-on sentence   **c.** correct sentence

5. E-mail allows everyone to communicate quickly and easily, many people don't write letters anymore.

    a. comma splice   **b.** run-on sentence   **c.** correct sentence

✎ Writing Assignment

➠ Your writing assignment in this chapter is to write a reason and example paragraph. What do you think is the best age for a man and a woman to get married? Marriage is an important decision and a big responsibility. In fact, it takes a lot of hard work to make a successful marriage and to build a happy family. What do you think is a good age for a man and a woman to get married? Why? (If you need to review the reason and example paragraph, refer to Chapter 4.)

▶ **What to do** ◀

1. Use the topic sentence below to write a reason and example paragraph.

> **Topic sentence:** *A good age for a man and a woman to get married is _____.*

2. Write the first draft and the final draft of your paragraph on separate sheets of paper. Do not write in your textbooks.

3. Try to use compound sentences in your paragraph.

4. Follow the writing steps below.

STEP 1	Before you begin to write, take a few minutes to think about your topic. Then make a *cluster* of your ideas.
STEP 2	Write an *outline* to help you to plan your paragraph.
STEP 3	Follow your outline to write a *first draft (practice paragraph)*.
STEP 4	*Revise and edit* your practice paragraph.
STEP 5	Write your *final draft (final paragraph)*.

Chapter 7
The Descriptive Paragraph

To the Student:

In this book you will learn to write different kinds of paragraphs. In Chapter 4, you studied the Reason and Example paragraph, and you used reasons and examples to support the topic sentence. In this chapter, you will study another kind of paragraph, the **Descriptive** paragraph. We write a Descriptive paragraph when we want to tell the reader what a person, place, or thing looks like such as a good friend, a comfortable room, or an interesting place to visit. In this kind of paragraph, we support the topic sentence with a description.

Part I
Prewriting

GETTING READY TO WRITE

⮕ In this chapter, you will learn how to write a Descriptive paragraph. We write this kind of paragraph when we want to tell the reader what a person, a place, or a thing looks like. For example, look at the pictures below. Then read the description of each picture. The description tells what the picture looks like.

1.

Ana is a very stylish young woman. She looks very nice today. She is wearing a long-sleeved black blouse, a short black and white skirt, and a white leather belt.

2.

My friend Bob bought an expensive new car. It's a bright red sports car with black leather seats and a sunroof.

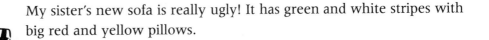

3.

My sister's new sofa is really ugly! It has green and white stripes with big red and yellow pillows.

⮕ In this chapter, you will describe persons, places, and things. To help you to prepare for your writing assignments, follow the prewriting instructions on the next page.

PREWRITING

⟹ First read the example description below. Then do Activity 1.

Example Description:

1. This person is about 5' 10" tall.

2. He has light brown hair and brown eyes.

3. He wears glasses and has a beard.

4. He is in his early twenties.

5. Today he is wearing a blue and red jacket and jeans.

6. He is friendly, and he always tries to help the other students in his group.

7. He has a good sense of humor and likes to tell funny stories.

Activity 1

▶ **What to do** ◀

1. Work by yourself. Look around your classroom. Choose someone in your class to describe. Do not tell anyone who the person is.

2. Write your description on the lines below.

Description of Your Classmate

_____

_____

_____

_____

_____

_____

_____

_____

_____

_____

_____

PREWRITING

➠ On the previous page, you described a classmate. Now, you will describe a common everyday object such as a spoon, a lemon, an egg, a rose, or a pillow. Look at the example below.

Example:

1. <u>This object is soft.</u>
2. <u>You can usually find it in bedrooms, living rooms, and family rooms.</u>
3. <u>It comes in different shapes, colors, and sizes.</u>
4. <u>It sometimes has feathers inside.</u>
5. <u>We can use it 24 hours a day, but we especially use it at night.</u>

What is it? <u>It's a pillow.</u>

Activity 2

▶ What to do ◀

1. Work by yourself. Think of a common object. You can choose anything that you want to describe. Write your sentences on the lines below. You can describe how the object looks, smells, feels, tastes, or sounds, but **do not** tell what the object is used for.

2. Write your description on the lines below.

Description

_____

_____

_____

_____

_____

Activity 3

▶ What to do ◀

1. Now form a group with three or four classmates and take turns reading your descriptions.
2. First go back to Activity 1 on page 158. Can the other students guess <u>who</u> you described?
3. Then read your description in Activity 2 on this page. Can the other students guess <u>what</u> you described?

Part 2
Using Description to Support the Topic Sentence

THE DESCRIPTIVE PARAGRAPH

➡ You have learned that every paragraph must have a topic sentence that gives the main idea of the paragraph. All the other sentences in the paragraph explain and support the topic sentence. In Chapter 4, you used reasons and examples to support the topic sentence. In this chapter, you will use description to support the topic sentence.

➡ When you write a descriptive paragraph, you are like an artist painting a picture, but you do not use a brush and paint. You use <u>words</u> to paint the picture. Like an artist, you want your readers to "see" what you see and to "feel" what you feel. You use words that appeal to your reader's five senses: sight, hearing, touch, smell, and taste.

➡ Read the descriptive paragraph below. Try to find the words that the writer used to help you to picture the beach at sunset. Then answer the questions on page 161.

MODEL PARAGRAPH I

An Ocean Panorama*

panorama: *view, scene*

patch: *a small area or section*

ablaze: *on fire, bright with color*

squish: *squeeze*

surf: *waves*

inhale: *breathe in*

chill: *cool, make cold*

[1]Santa Cruz, California is a perfect place to enjoy an early sunset on the beach. [2]A patch* of pink appears in the sky, and within an hour, the whole sky is ablaze* in vibrant* shades of pink. [3]Honking seagulls fly overhead, wet seaweed squishes* under my bare feet, and the crashing surf* rises and falls like the changing rhythms of a symphony. [4]I sit down on an old log and inhale* the salty sea air. [5]A small sailboat floats on the waves to my left, and farther out, there is a large oil tanker. [6]Close up, a couple of surfers are still riding the waves. [7]Then a sea breeze stings my face and chills* my bones, so I gather my belongings together and head back to the car. [8]Truly, the seaside is a good place to become re-acquainted with your senses.

THE DESCRIPTIVE PARAGRAPH - MODEL PARAGRAPH I

➤ **Activity I** Answer the questions below about the paragraph, *An Ocean Panorama*, on page 160.

I. What is the topic sentence of the paragraph?

_____

_____

2. What color does the setting sun "paint" the sky?

_____

3. Several words in sentence 3 of the paragraph appeal to your sense of hearing. Write two sounds that you "hear" in this sentence.

_____

_____

4. Which one of the senses do the following words appeal to?

seaweed squishes under my bare feet . . .

sight hearing touch smell taste

5. When the writer sits down on an old log and looks out at the ocean, what does she see?

_____

_____

_____

6. What does the writer mean when she says, ". . . a sea breeze stings my face and chills my bones"?

_____

_____

_____

7. Does the writer's description of the beach support the topic sentence? Does the writer's description paint a picture of the beach at sunset?

_____

_____

_____

THE DESCRIPTIVE PARAGRAPH - MODEL PARAGRAPH 2

⇒ **Activity 2** Read the descriptive paragraph below. In this paragraph, Dung Le is describing his country home on the island province of Ben-Tre in Vietnam. After you read the paragraph, answer the questions on page 163.

MODEL PARAGRAPH 2

A Childhood Memory

Saigon: *Now called Ho Chi Minh City*

immense: *very big, huge*

lush: *having rich plants and vegetation*

moored: *anchored*

criss-crossed: *covered in many directions*

sampan: *a flat-bottomed Asian boat*

soothing: *calm, peaceful*

weary: *tired*

¹The memory of my country home, Ben-Tre, is crystal clear in my mind. ²Ben-Tre is an island province about 120 miles from Saigon*. ³To get there, I have to cross the Tien-Giang River on a ferry boat from My-Tho. ⁴The beautiful scenery along this river is unforgettable. ⁵Forty-five minutes of travel on this immense* body of water gives me a sweeping view of my homeland with its lush* green coconut orchards. ⁶After the ferryboat is moored*, I set foot on my homeland. ⁷It is criss-crossed* with thousands of canals of many sorts. ⁸Sampans* and other kinds of boats are the main means of transport. ⁹The chugging sound of motorboats and the soothing* sound of waves under oars can be heard along the canals from dawn to dusk. ¹⁰At the end of the day, the beauty of the setting sun behind the mountains, the gently blowing breezes, and the flocks of birds on the way to their nests fill my heart with emotion. ¹¹Weary* ploughmen walk home from the fields with their tired beasts, and buffalo boys lead their animals home, too. ¹²In the cool of the evening, smoke rises from the cottages, and the hungry families know that dinner will be ready soon. ¹³These are my memories of my childhood home in the countryside of Vietnam. ¹⁴Truly, Ben-Tre holds a very special place in my heart.

Dung Le

THE DESCRIPTIVE PARAGRAPH - MODEL PARAGRAPH 2

▶ **Activity 3** Answer the questions below about the paragraph, *A Childhood Memory*, on page 162.

1. What is the topic sentence of the paragraph?

_____

_____

2. What is the name of Dung Le's homeland?

_____

3. What sight does Dung Le see after forty-five minutes of travel on the Tien Giang River?

_____

_____

4. Read the following sentence from the paragraph:

> *The chugging sound of motorboats and the soothing sound of waves under oars can be heard along the canals from dawn to dusk.*

Which one of the senses does this sentence appeal to?

                 sight   hearing   touch   smell   taste

5. What sights always fill the writer's heart with emotion?

_____

_____

_____

6. How do the hungry families know that dinner will soon be ready?

_____

_____

7. How does Dung Le feel about his homeland?

_____

_____

_____

8. Does Dung Le's description of his homeland support the topic sentence of his paragraph?

_____

_____

Part 3
Paragraph Skills

USING SPECIFIC DESCRIPTIVE DETAILS

▥➡ You have learned that when we write a descriptive paragraph, we support the topic sentence with words that appeal to the reader's sense of sight, hearing, touch, taste, and smell. We call these words **descriptive details**.

Descriptive details are words that "paint" a picture for the reader. In order to paint a clear picture, the descriptive details must be as **specific** as possible. Descriptive details that are vague (not clear) will not give the reader a good picture of what you are describing.

▥➡ Study the examples below. Which description is clearer and more vivid?

not specific: The kitchen is a mess.

specific: An inch or two of greasy water covers the dirty plates in the kitchen sink. The counters are covered with bits of food, and the floor is sticky with spilled orange juice.

not specific: The cafeteria is always noisy.

specific: Trays, plates, and silverware clang* on the counters and tables, and loud music blares* from the speakers. Shouts of greeting and the sound of hundreds of conversations fill the crowded room.

not specific: My bed is comfortable.

specific: On cold nights, I love to climb into bed. My electric blanket is warm, and my head sinks into my soft, down-filled* pillow.

not specific: The house smells good on Thanksgiving morning.

specific: The delicious smell of roasting turkey fills the house early on Thanksgiving morning. Later, the pumpkin pies and mince pies baking in the oven add the spicy fragrance of cinnamon, nutmeg, raisins, and apples.

not specific: I want a dish of ice cream.

specific: I want a banana split with three large scoops of vanilla, chocolate, and strawberry ice cream on two halves of a banana. Cover the ice cream with chocolate and strawberry syrup, and add whipped cream, nuts, and two cherries on top.

Vocabulary Notes   *__clang__: *make the loud sound of metal hitting metal*   *__blare__: *make a loud, unpleasant sound*
*__down-filled__: *full of small, soft feathers*

USING SPECIFIC DESCRIPTIVE DETAILS

▥➡ **Activity 1** Work with a partner or in a small group. Make the vague descriptions below clear and interesting. Write two or three sentences with specific descriptive details.

1. not specific: The freeway is congested.

   specific: There is bumper to bumper traffic for twenty miles. A stalled car is blocking the left lane of the freeway, and two exits are closed because of highway construction.

2. not specific: The food at Pete's Diner is terrible.

   specific: _____

_____

_____

3. not specific: My neighbor's front yard is a mess.

   specific: _____

_____

_____

4. not specific: My apartment is noisy.

   specific: _____

_____

_____

5. not specific: It's a nice day today.

   specific: _____

_____

_____

6. not specific: My garden looks and smells beautiful in the spring.

   specific: _____

_____

_____

DESCRIPTIVE DETAILS

⫸ **Activity 2** In the paragraph below, the mother did not paint a vivid picture of her daughter's messy bedroom because she did not use specific descriptive details. Read the paragraph. Then do Activity 3 on the next page.

A Messy Bedroom

twin bed: *a bed for one person*

unmade: *not arranged*

debris: *rubbish*

trash: *garbage, rubbish*

[1]My teenage daughter's bedroom is always messy. [2]The twin bed* on the left side of the room is always unmade*. [3]Next to the bed, the bedside table is full of debris*. [4]There is a glass and a plate on the table. [5]The floor is also a mess. [6]It is covered with shoes and clothes. [7]There is usually trash* on the floor around the wastebasket in the corner. [8]Opposite the bed, the closet is the final area of disorder. [9]The shelves are full of my daughter's old possessions. [10]Also, there are more clothes on the floor than on the hangers. [11]A teenager's life is not easy. [12]However, it is not easy for the teenager's parents either!

DESCRIPTIVE DETAILS

➡ **Activity 3** The paragraph, *A Messy Bedroom*, on page 166 needs specific descriptive details in order to paint a clear picture of the daughter's bedroom. Rewrite sentences 1, 2, 4, 6, 7, and 9 from the paragraph on the lines below. Change the underlined words from each sentence to add specific details.

Sentence 1: Change <u>messy</u> to <u>a disaster area</u>.

       My teenage daughter's bedroom is always a disaster area.

Sentence 2: Change <u>unmade</u> to <u>a jumble of twisted sheets and blankets</u>.

    _____

    _____

Sentence 4: Change <u>a glass and a plate</u> to <u>a half-empty glass of sour milk and a plate with the last bite of a sandwich</u>.

    _____

    _____

Sentence 6: Change <u>shoes and clothes</u> to <u>tennis shoes, dirty socks, jeans, shirts, and sweaters</u>.

    _____

    _____

Sentence 7: Change <u>trash</u> to <u>Kleenex, crumpled paper, and gum wrappers</u>.

    _____

    _____

Sentence 9: Change <u>old possessions</u> to <u>old games, stuffed animals, boxes of loose photographs, and stacks of magazines</u>.

    _____

    _____

➡ **Activity 4** Think about <u>your</u> bedroom at home. What picture comes to mind? How do you feel about your bedroom? Is it messy? Is it crowded? Is it the most comfortable room in your house? On a separate sheet of paper, write a descriptive paragraph about your bedroom. Use plenty of specific descriptive details so that the reader can visualize your room in his or her mind. Your paragraph should not be longer than 150 to 200 words.

THE ORGANIZATION OF A DESCRIPTIVE PARAGRAPH

How do you organize a descriptive paragraph? Where should you begin your description? For example, if you want to describe a room, should you begin on the right side of the room or the left side of the room? In a descriptive paragraph, there is no one way to begin, and it doesn't really matter what you describe first. However, once you begin, it is important that you arrange your ideas so that the reader can follow your description from one thing to another.

SPACE ORDER

The most common way to organize the details in a descriptive paragraph is to use space order. When we use space order, we arrange our sentences and details according to the location of the objects we are describing. We can begin our description from left to right, from top to bottom, from far to near, and so on.

In the paragraph below, the space order is from right to left. The description moves from the sofa bed on the right side of the cabin to the windows on the left side of the cabin.

A Big Disappointment

¹Every summer we rent a small cabin at Lake Tahoe for a week's vacation. ²Usually, we are satisfied with our cabin, but this year we are very disappointed. ³Our cabin this year is a dim, dark, musty-smelling room. ⁴Against the wall on the right, there is a small, lumpy, uncomfortable-looking sofa bed. ⁵There is a tarnished lamp on a table in the corner next to the sofa bed. ⁶The lamp and the table both look like they came from a garage sale many years ago. ⁷The kitchen area on the far wall is tiny and cramped. ⁸In the kitchen, there is an electric stove covered with grease, an old yellow refrigerator, and a sink with a dripping faucet. ⁹There are two dark brown cabinets on the wall over the sink. ¹⁰Finally, on the wall to the left, two small, dirty windows offer a view of a beat-up old wooden shed and a dead tree. ¹¹What a horrible place to spend a vacation!

THE ORGANIZATION OF A DESCRIPTIVE PARAGRAPH - SPACE ORDER

➡ **Activity 5** Read the descriptive paragraph below. Can you identify the space order?

Springtime at Evergreen Valley College

[1]Evergreen Valley College is a beautiful school at any time of the year, but the view from my classroom window is especially beautiful in the spring. [2]Against the sky in the background, the foothills of Mt. Hamilton rise to about 4,500 feet. [3]Both the foothills and the fields behind the campus are covered with a thick carpet of emerald green grass, and bright yellow mustard flowers peek up here and there in the grass. [4]Closer to the school, rows of cherry trees bloom with hundreds of deep pink blossoms, and the hedges outside the window of my classroom are alive with new growth. [5]Inside the classroom, I can almost smell the sweet fragrance of the grass, flowers, trees, and shrubs, and I long* to be outside. [6]Sometimes it is very hard to pay attention on a beautiful spring day at Evergreen Valley College!

➡ What space order did the writer of the paragraph use?

_____ **right to left**   _____ **top to bottom**

_____ **left to right**   _____ **far to near**

Vocabulary Note   *__long__: want very much

THE ORGANIZATION OF A DESCRIPTIVE PARAGRAPH - SPACE ORDER

▰▸ **Activity 6** Read the descriptive paragraph below. Can you identify the space order?

My Lived-in Family Room

¹My family room is a very comfortable place to relax. ²One of my favorite things about the room is the old-fashioned red brick fireplace against the far wall. ³Almost every evening in the late fall and winter, we have dinner in front of a blazing fire. ⁴On each side of the fireplace, there are floor-to-ceiling mahogany bookcases and cabinets with a television, a VCR, and stereo equipment. ⁵After dinner, we sit on the brown leather couch to the left of the fireplace or on the matching loveseat in front of the fireplace and watch TV, read, or listen to music. ⁶There are also two over-stuffed chairs on the right side of the room. ⁷One chair is green velvet, and the other is cream, tan, and red plaid. ⁸There is a convenient reading lamp on an end table between the chairs. ⁹Framed family pictures cover the wall behind the chairs and lamp. ¹⁰Some of these pictures go back several generations. ¹¹Altogether, there is a feeling of warmth, roominess, and solid comfort about this room. ¹²It is a wonderful place to relax after a hard day's work.

▰▸ What space order did the writer of the paragraph use?

_____ **right to left**   _____ **top to bottom**

_____ **left to right**   _____ **far to near**

✓ CHECK YOUR UNDERSTANDING

Answer the questions below.

1. In this chapter, you used _____ to support the topic sentence.

2. A good descriptive paragraph appeals to the reader's five senses. What are the five senses?

_____ _____ _____ _____ _____

3. What are descriptive details? _____

_____

4. Change the vague descriptions below to specific descriptive details:

        vague   **specific**

a. an expensive car   _____

b. a special dessert   _____

c. nice jewelry   _____

d. sports equipment   _____

e. some new clothes   _____

5. What is the most common way to organize a descriptive paragraph?

_____

_____

6. When we use space order, how do we arrange our sentences and details?

_____

_____

7. What are some examples of space order?

_____

_____

DESCRIBING A PERSON

▶ On previous pages, you studied descriptive paragraphs that described places. We can also use a descriptive paragraph to describe a person.

There are several ways to describe a person's appearance. For example, you can describe a person's physical appearance such as his or her height, weight, hair, eyes, and facial shape. You can also describe the person's personality or the person's hobbies and activities. The most important thing to remember, however, is that you must use specific descriptive details in order to make your description of the person vivid and clear.

▶ Read the following descriptive paragraph, and see if you get a good picture of what rock star, Ricky Moreno, looks like.

Rock Idol

sensation: exciting star

Latino: person of Hispanic descent

ballad: love song

seductive: attractive, especially in a sexual way

emphasize: call attention to

key ingredients: important parts

[1]To most teenage girls, the Puerto Rican singing sensation*, Ricky Moreno, is the most handsome Latino* in the world! [2]Tall, dark, and handsome, the 28-year-old singer performs to screaming young audiences all over Latin America, Europe, and the United States. [3]Ricky appeals to his young fans not only because of his music but also because of the way he communicates to them through his facial expressions and body movements. [4]During a romantic ballad*, his dark, expressive eyes are gentle and seductive*, but the same eyes flash with joy during one of his fast Latin songs. [5]Also, depending on the music, his expression can be serious and sad, or his sparkling smile and brilliant white teeth can light up the theater. [6]Dressed all in black or white with his shirt open at the collar, his costumes emphasize* his broad shoulders, narrow waist, and long legs. [7]Lights, sound, and music are key ingredients* in Ricky Moreno's concerts. [8]However, his own great looks and exciting personality make his shows spectacular performances.

Carla Solano

DESCRIBING A PERSON

Activity 7 Answer the questions below about the paragraph, *Rock Idol*, on page 172.

1. Who is Ricky Moreno?

_____

_____

2. What does Ricky Moreno look like?

_____

_____

3. How does he communicate with his young fans?

_____

_____

4. Describe Ricky's eyes when he sings a romantic ballad.

_____

_____

5. Describe Ricky's eyes when he sings one of his fast Latin songs.

_____

_____

6. What does Ricky wear when he performs?

_____

_____

7. What are the key ingredients in Ricky Moreno's concerts?

_____

_____

8. What makes Ricky's shows spectacular performances?

_____

_____

VOCABULARY LIST TO DESCRIBE A PERSON

▐▶ Here is some common vocabulary that we use to describe people. Use this list to help you do Activity 8 below.

PHYSICAL APPEARANCE

general	hair	eyes	face	body shape	style of clothing
attractive	straight	brown	thin face	tall	well-dressed
unattractive	wavy	blue	round face	short	elegant
good-looking	curly	hazel	pointed chin	5'10"	casual
handsome	long	intelligent	mustache	slim	sloppy
young	short	alert	beard	plump	latest fashion
middle-aged	bald	large	wrinkles	fat	jeans
	blond	sad	attractive smile	a little overweight	slacks
	brown		glasses	145 pounds	sweatshirt
	gray				

PERSONALITY

happy	- sad	energetic	- lazy	responsible	- irresponsible
friendly	- unfriendly	generous	- selfish	hard-working	- unambitious
shy	- outgoing	cheerful	- grouchy	dependable	- undependable
kind	- unkind	loyal	- disloyal	interesting	- boring

HOBBIES

like sports (baseball, golf, tennis)	play a musical instrument (piano, guitar, drums)
play games on the computer	work in the garden
surf the Internet	like to go shopping
collect (stamps, coins)	like to play cards (bridge, poker)
like to read	like to cook

Vocabulary Note: Be careful when you describe a person's physical appearance. Some words such as skinny and fat are not polite.

▐▶ **Activity 8** Pretend that you have a pen pal in a foreign country or someone you exchange E-mail with over the Internet. You and your friend have never met in person. On a separate sheet of paper, write a paragraph to send to this person. Describe your physical appearance and your personality. You may also want to describe your favorite hobbies. You do not need to describe every detail. Just describe the things that are important about yourself.

Part 4

Getting Ready to Write

GETTING READY TO WRITE A DESCRIPTIVE PARAGRAPH

➠ Your first writing assignment in this chapter will be to write a descriptive paragraph about a tourist attraction in your city or country. Before you begin, study the steps that Judy Wong used when she wrote a descriptive paragraph about Fisherman's Wharf, a famous tourist attraction in San Francisco.

STEP 1 - PRE-WRITING: BRAINSTORMING

When you write a descriptive paragraph, brainstorming is a good way to get your ideas down on paper quickly. When you brainstorm, you make a list of every idea that comes into your mind. Think about the place that you are going to describe. What picture comes to your mind? What do you see? What do you hear? What do you feel? What do you taste? What do you smell?

Below is the brainstorming list that Judy made to get ideas for her descriptive paragraph about Fisherman's Wharf. Notice that Judy did not write complete sentences.

BRAINSTORMING LIST

Name of the place: Fisherman's Wharf in San Francisco, California

beautiful San Francisco Bay	street performers
brisk sea breeze off the bay	music - singers, trumpets, guitars
clanging cable car bells	famous Italian restaurants
waterfront - Fish Alley	smell of fish and garlic
old wooden piers	bay cruises
fishing boats, nets, ropes	Alcatraz – prison
people fishing	picnicking, hiking on Angel Island
noisy seagulls	Pier 39 - souvenir shops
Maritime Museum	underwater aquarium
historic sailing ships	the loud barking of sea lions
sidewalk vendors selling seafood	bay cruises
crab, shrimp, clam chowder	in the distance Golden Gate Bridge
sourdough bread	

STEP 2 – WRITE A FIRST DRAFT (PRACTICE PARAGRAPH)

➡ When Judy finished brainstorming and making a list of ideas about Fisherman's Wharf, she chose ideas from her brainstorming list to help her to write her first draft (practice paragraph).

After Judy wrote the first draft of her paragraph, she read the paragraph carefully to see if she could improve it.

1. First, she **revised** her paragraph. **Revise** means to add, move, or take out sentences. Revise also means to rewrite any confusing sentences. As Judy read her paragraph, she asked herself, "Did I use plenty of specific descriptive details to paint a clear, vivid picture of Fisherman's Wharf? Did I use space order to arrange the sentences and details according to the location of the objects I described?"

2. Then Judy **edited** her paragraph. **Edit** means to correct any errors in grammar, spelling, and the use of capital letters and periods.

➡ The paragraph below is Judy's practice paragraph. Look at the changes and corrections that she made. She made all the changes and corrections on her practice paragraph.

indent→

F   W
~~Fisherman's wharf~~ ← capitalize the title

A tourist to San Francisco, California should not miss a visit to San Francisco's Fisherman's

                  sightseeing   to (infinitive)
Wharf and its many restaurants, markets, and ^attractions. One of the best ways ^begin a visit to

Fisherman's Wharf is to ride a crowded, clanging cable car up and down the steep hills to the

                               visitors
wharf. A short walk from the cable car stop takes ~~you~~ to the waterfront and "Fish Alley". Fish

                         colorful   raucous
Alley is the home of the San Francisco fishing fleet with its ^fishing boats and hungry, ^seagulls.

Visitors to Fish Alley are soon attracted by the delicious smells of fresh seafood and sourdough

                   Dungeness   cauldrons   shrimp and crab
bread. Sidewalk vendors along the street sell ^crabs from steaming ~~pots~~, paper cups of ~~seafood~~

cocktails, and clam chowder in sourdough bread bowls. Adding to the excitement, the music of folk

     electric   jazz   small
singers, ^guitars, and ^trumpets fill the air. Magicians pull coins from behind the ears of ~~the~~ children,

                long, skinny
a clown makes toy animals from ^balloons, and other street performers entertain the crowd. After

enjoying these sights and sounds, visitors can spend the rest of the day taking a bay cruise to

             underwater World
the former prison on Alcatraz, visiting the ^aquarium at Pier 39, or shopping in the many shops

and art galleries in the area. ↑

With so many things to see and do there, it is easy to see why Fisherman's Wharf is San Francisco's number one tourist attraction!

STEP 3 - WRITE THE FINAL DRAFT (FINAL PARAGRAPH)

➡ After Judy **revised** and **edited** (changed and corrected) her practice paragraph on page 176, she was ready to write her final paragraph. Read Judy's final paragraph below.

Fisherman's Wharf

A tourist to San Francisco, California should not miss a visit to Fisherman's Wharf and its many restaurants, markets, and sightseeing attractions. One of the best ways to begin a visit to Fisherman's Wharf is to ride a crowded, clanging* cable car up and down San Francisco's steep hills to the wharf. A short walk from the cable car stop takes visitors to the waterfront and "Fish Alley"*. Fish Alley is the home of the San Francisco fishing fleet with its colorful fishing boats and hungry, raucous* seagulls. Visitors to Fish Alley are soon attracted by the delicious smells of fresh seafood and sourdough bread. Sidewalk vendors along the street sell Dungeness* crab from steaming cauldrons*, paper cups of shrimp and crab cocktails, and clam chowder* in sourdough bread bowls. Adding to the excitement, the music of folk singers, electric guitars, and jazz trumpets fills the air. Magicians pull coins from behind the ears of small children, a clown makes toy animals from long, skinny balloons, and other street performers entertain the crowd. After enjoying these sights and sounds, visitors can spend the rest of the day taking a bay cruise to Alcatraz*, visiting the Underwater World aquarium at Pier 39, or browsing in the many shops and art galleries in the area. With so many things to see and do, it is easy to see why Fisherman's Wharf is San Francisco's number one tourist attraction!

Judy Wong

clanging: the noisy sound of a streetcar bell

alley: a narrow street or walkway

raucous: loud, making an unpleasant noise

Dungeness: a kind of crab

cauldron: large metal cooking pot

chowder: seafood soup

Alcatraz: an island in San Francisco Bay, the former site of a maximum-security prison

Writing Assignment

▶ Your writing assignment in this chapter is to write a descriptive paragraph about a famous tourist attraction in your city or country. Use the topic sentence below:

Topic sentence:

A tourist to _____ *should not miss a visit to* _____.
(name of your city or country)   (tourist attraction)

STEP 1 - PREWRITING: BRAINSTORMING

Now that you have chosen a place to write about, make a brainstorming list to help you to get your ideas down on paper quickly. Think about the place you are going to describe. What picture comes to your mind? What do you see? What do you hear? What do you feel? What do you taste? What do you smell? Do not write complete sentences, and do not worry about grammar or spelling in your list.

BRAINSTORMING LIST

_____   _____

_____   _____

_____   _____

_____   _____

_____   _____

_____   _____

_____   _____

_____   _____

_____   _____

_____   _____

_____   _____

_____   _____

_____   _____

_____   _____

_____   _____

Writing Assignment

STEP 2 - WRITE A FIRST DRAFT (PRACTICE PARAGRAPH)

► What to do ◄

1. Now that you have written the details of your paragraph on your brainstorming list on page 178, you are ready to write the first draft of your paragraph. Remember that you do not need to use all the details on your list.

2. Make your descriptive details vivid and specific so that the reader can easily visualize what you are describing.

3. Double space your paragraph, and circle the subject(s) and verb(s) in each sentence. Be sure to give your paragraph a title.

Writing Assignment

FIRST DRAFT (CONTINUED)

_____

_____

_____

_____

_____

_____

_____

_____

_____

_____

_____

_____

_____

_____

STEP 3 – REVISE AND EDIT YOUR PARAGRAPH

▶ **What to do** ◀

1. When you are finished writing your practice paragraph, read your paragraph to yourself.

2. Revise your paragraph.

   Are all of your sentences clear and easy to understand? Do you want to add, move, or take out sentences? If you need to make changes, make them on your practice paragraph.

3. Edit your paragraph.

   Are there any mistakes in grammar, spelling, capital letters, or periods? Did you use correct paragraph form? If you need to make corrections, make them on your practice paragraph.

4. When you are finished revising and editing your paragraph, write your name on the Review Sheet on page 181, and give your book to a partner. Your partner will read and review your paragraph.

Partner Review Sheet

Paragraph written by _____

Paragraph reviewed by _____

➤ **To the Reviewer:** Read your partner's paragraph carefully. Then answer the questions below about your partner's paragraph. Do **not** write on your partner's paper.

1. Does your partner's descriptive paragraph have a title?

_____ yes   _____ no

2. Write the title here:

_____

3. Write the topic sentence of your partner's paragraph here:

_____

_____

_____

4. Did your partner use plenty of specific descriptive details to support the topic sentence?

_____ yes   _____ no

5. Which sentence is true about your partner's paragraph?

_____ **a.** The reader can easily visualize the place my partner is describing.

_____ **b.** The reader cannot visualize the place because the details are not specific.

6. Do all of the sentences in the paragraph begin with a capital letter and end with a period?

_____ yes   _____ no

7. Did your partner circle the subject(s) and verb(s) in each sentence?

_____ yes   _____ no

➤ **To the Reviewer:** When you are finished reviewing your partner's paragraph, return your partner's book.

Writing Assignment

STEP 4 - WRITE YOUR FINAL DRAFT (FINAL PARAGRAPH)

When your partner returns your book, make any necessary changes or corrections on your practice paragraph. Now you are ready to write the final draft of your paragraph.

▶ **What to do** ◀

1. Write your final paragraph in ink on a separate sheet of paper. Write as neatly as possible, and use correct paragraph form.

2. Double space your paragraph, and write on only one side of the paper.

3. When you finish your paragraph, underline or highlight the topic sentence and the concluding sentence.

4. Circle the subject(s) and verb(s) in each sentence.

Additional Writing Topics

Descriptive Paragraphs

Topic 1: _____ is the most beautiful place I know.

Describe the most beautiful place you know. What place comes to mind? Is it a crystal-blue lake? A snow-covered mountain? A bamboo forest? Use plenty of descriptive details to paint a vivid picture of this beautiful place.

Topic 2: A peaceful place to spend a Sunday afternoon is _____

Describe the place to your reader. What does it look like? Use lots of specific descriptive details so that your reader can visualize your peaceful place.

Topic 3: The most comfortable room in my house is _____

Think about your house. Which room is the most comfortable? Use plenty of details to show what makes the room so comfortable.

Chapter 8
Writing About Past Time

Part 1: The Simple Past Tense of the Verb <u>Be</u>

Part 2: The Simple Past Tense of Action Verbs

Part 3: The Past Progressive Tense

Writing Assignment

To the Student:

In Chapter 5, you used the Simple (Habitual) Present Tense and the Present Progressive Tense to write about present time. In this chapter, you will use two common verb tenses, the Simple Past Tense and the Past Progressive Tense, to write about past time.

Part I
The Simple Past Tense of the Verb <u>Be</u>

THE PAST FORMS OF THE NON-ACTION VERB <u>BE</u>

> ▶ **Learning Point**
>
> You have learned that the verb <u>Be</u> has three forms in the Simple Present Tense: *am, is, are*.
>
> The verb <u>Be</u> has only two forms in the Simple Past Tense: *was* and *were*.

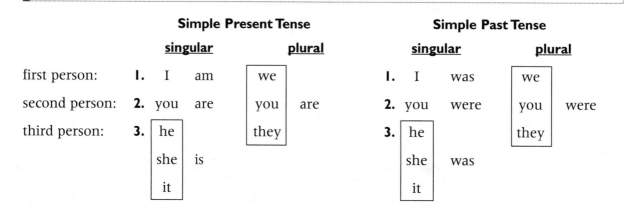

	Simple Present Tense				Simple Past Tense			
	singular		**plural**		**singular**		**plural**	
first person:	**1.** I	am	we		**1.** I	was	we	
second person:	**2.** you	are	you	are	**2.** you	were	you	were
third person:	**3.** he / she / it	is	they		**3.** he / she / it	was	they	

▥▶ **Word Order of Past Tense Affirmative Sentences with <u>Be</u>**

SUBJECT	VERB <u>BE</u> PAST	COMPLEMENT (rest of the sentence)
1. I	was	at school yesterday.
2. You	were	absent last Monday and Wednesday.
3 He	was	a teacher at this school last year.
4. She	was	in the office a few minutes ago.
5. It	was	a difficult assignment.
6. We	were	nervous about the last test.
7. You	were	late for class yesterday.
8. They	were	in Prof. Martin's chemistry class last semester.

PRESENT AND PAST TENSE OF THE VERB <u>BE</u>

➡ **Exercise 1** In the student paragraph below, Rahid Sethna is describing his supervisor, Dan Miller. Circle the subject(s) in the paragraph. Then complete each sentence with the correct <u>Present</u> Tense form of the verb <u>Be</u> (*am, is, are*).

A Good Boss

(¹Dan Miller) __is__ the best supervisor I ever had. ²First of all, he _____ very considerate of all his employees. ³For example, he _____ always available to talk with an employee when there _____ a problem. ⁴Also, employees _____ able to take time off from the job when there _____ a family emergency. ⁵For another thing, Dan _____ always fair to everyone. ⁶He _____ not partial to any individual or group of employees, and his performance appraisals of his employees _____ always fair and accurate. ⁷Finally, he _____ knowledgeable about all aspects of the job. ⁸His instructions to the employees _____ always complete and easy to understand, and the work assignments _____ clear. ⁹The employees in my department _____ happy to work for this supervisor.

Rahid Sethna

➡ **Exercise 2** Now pretend that it is several years later, and Rahid does not work for Dan Miller anymore. Rewrite Rahid's paragraph in the Simple <u>Past</u> Tense of the verb <u>Be</u> (*was, were*).

A Good Boss

Dan Miller was the best supervisor I ever had. _____

_____

_____

_____

_____

_____

_____

_____

_____

_____

_____

USING NOUNS, ADJECTIVES, AND LOCATIONS AFTER <u>BE</u>

> ▶ **Learning Point**
>
> In Chapter 3, you learned that we use the verb <u>Be</u> in three ways in a sentence:
>
> **1.** We use **nouns** after <u>Be</u>.
>
> **2.** We use **adjectives** after <u>Be</u>.
>
> **3.** We use **locations** after <u>Be</u>.

▐➡ Study the examples below.

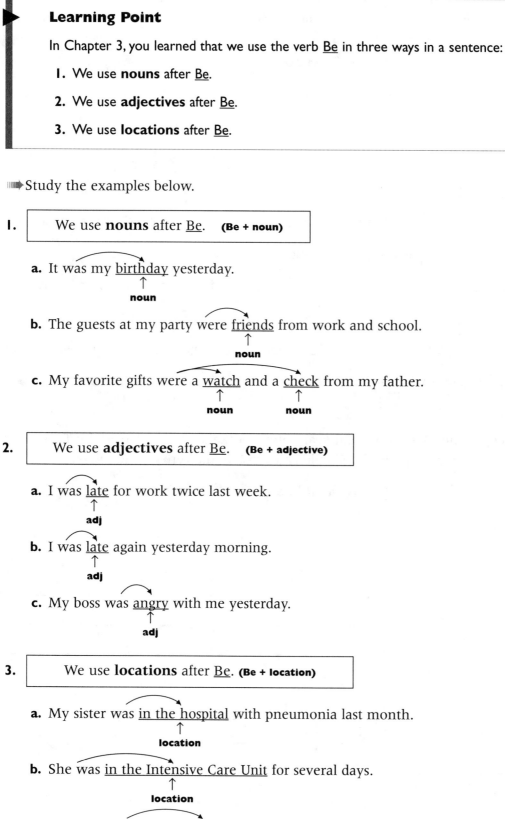

1. | We use **nouns** after <u>Be</u>. **(Be + noun)**

    a. It was my <u>birthday</u> yesterday.
        noun

    b. The guests at my party were <u>friends</u> from work and school.
        noun

    c. My favorite gifts were a <u>watch</u> and a <u>check</u> from my father.
        noun   **noun**

2. | We use **adjectives** after <u>Be</u>. **(Be + adjective)**

    a. I was <u>late</u> for work twice last week.
        adj

    b. I was <u>late</u> again yesterday morning.
        adj

    c. My boss was <u>angry</u> with me yesterday.
        adj

3. | We use **locations** after <u>Be</u>. **(Be + location)**

    a. My sister was <u>in the hospital</u> with pneumonia last month.
        location

    b. She was <u>in the Intensive Care Unit</u> for several days.
        location

    c. Her room was <u>near the nurses' station</u>.
        location

USING NOUNS, ADJECTIVES, AND LOCATIONS AFTER <u>BE</u>

➠ **Exercise 3** Drunk driving is a major cause of automobile accidents in the U.S. Drunk drivers seriously injure or kill thousands of people each year. Just recently, a drunk driver caused a tragic accident in my neighborhood. Read the paragraph below. Choose a <u>noun</u>, an <u>adjective</u>, or a <u>location</u> from the box to complete the sentences in the paragraph. Use each adjective, noun, or location only **one** time. Compare your answers with a classmate.

<u>nouns</u>	<u>adjectives</u>	<u>locations</u>
man	hurt	on the scene
victims	upset	there
✔ accident	injured	in the back seat of the car
woman	drunk	on my way home

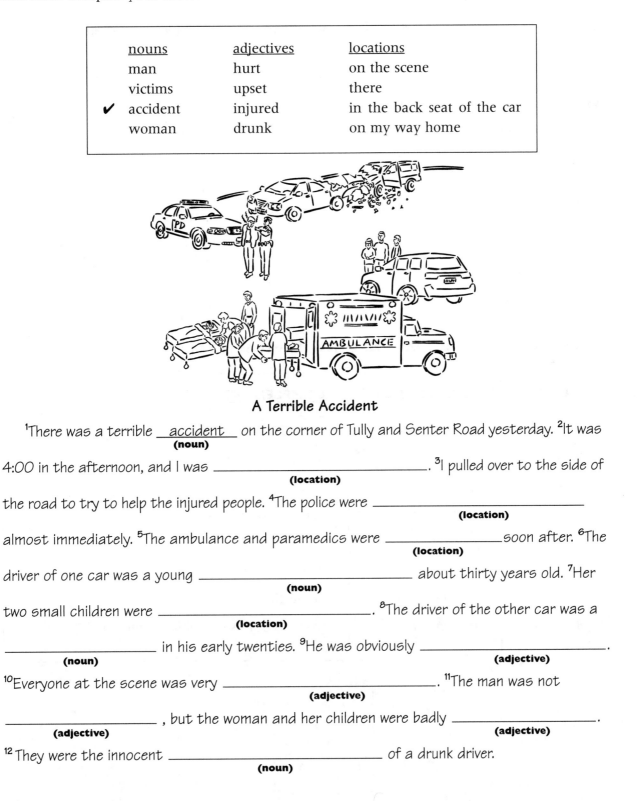

A Terrible Accident

¹There was a terrible ___accident___ on the corner of Tully and Senter Road yesterday. ²It was
(noun)

4:00 in the afternoon, and I was _____. ³I pulled over to the side of
(location)

the road to try to help the injured people. ⁴The police were _____
(location)

almost immediately. ⁵The ambulance and paramedics were _____ soon after. ⁶The
(location)

driver of one car was a young _____ about thirty years old. ⁷Her
(noun)

two small children were _____. ⁸The driver of the other car was a
(location)

_____ in his early twenties. ⁹He was obviously _____.
(noun)   (adjective)

¹⁰Everyone at the scene was very _____. ¹¹The man was not
(adjective)

_____, but the woman and her children were badly _____.
(adjective)   (adjective)

¹²They were the innocent _____ of a drunk driver.
(noun)

PAST TENSE OF THE VERB <u>BE</u> - NEGATIVE

▶ **Learning Point**

1. To form negative sentences with the verb <u>BE</u> in the Simple Past Tense, we put **not** after the verb <u>Be</u> (**was not, were not**).

2. To form negative contractions, we combine the verb <u>BE</u> and not (**wasn't, weren't**).

⟩ Negative Forms of the Verb <u>Be</u> Past

<u>singular</u>		<u>plural</u>	
1. I was not	(I wasn't)	1. we were not	(we weren't)
2. you were not	(you weren't)	2. you were not	(you weren't)
3. he was not	(he wasn't)	3. they were not	(they weren't)
she was not	(she wasn't)		
it was not	(it wasn't)		

⟩ Word Order of Past Tense Negative Sentences with <u>Be</u>

SUBJECT	VERB BE + NOT	COMPLEMENT
1. I	was not	ready for the last test.
2. You	were not	in class last night.
3. He	was not	on time for his appointment.
4. She	was not	happy with her last job.
5. It	was not	cold yesterday.
6. We	were not	hungry at lunch time.
7. You	were not	home all day yesterday.
8. They	were not	students at this school last semester.

PAST TENSE OF THE VERB <u>BE</u> - NEGATIVE AND AFFIRMATIVE

▪➡ **Exercise 4** Read the dialogs below carefully. Then complete the dialogs with either the negative or the affirmative form of the Simple Past Tense of the verb <u>Be</u>.

Dialog 1

Joe: Hi, Mike. How was your trip to San Diego last weekend?

Mike: It was terrible.

Joe: Why was it terrible?

Mike: My room at the hotel __*wasn't*__ comfortable, and the food in the hotel restaurant _____ bad. The weather _____ cloudy, and the beaches _____ clean. Worst of all, the San Diego Zoo _____ open.

Dialog 2

Sue: How was your date with your brother's friend last Saturday?

Emily: It was awful.

Sue: Why?

Emily: He _____ unattractive. His clothes _____ stylish. He _____ a good dancer, and he _____ a terrible conversationalist. All in all, it was a very boring evening.

Dialog 3

Pat: How was the movie last night?

Jan: The movie _____ terrible, and it _____ worth the money. The popcorn _____ stale, and the seats _____ uncomfortable. Also, the other people in the theater _____ noisy, and the sound _____ loud enough.

Dialog 4

Minh: Why did you quit your job?

Loan: The Vortex Company _____ a good place to work. The boss _____ always angry about something. The work _____ hard, the hours _____ long, and the pay _____ bad. The other workers _____ friendly or cooperative. The building _____ old and damp, and the bathrooms _____ always dirty.

PAST TENSE OF THE VERB <u>BE</u> - YES-NO QUESTIONS

> ### ▶ Learning Point
>
> To form YES-NO QUESTIONS with the verb <u>BE</u> in the Simple Past Tense, we put the verb <u>Be</u> in front of the subject.

⫸ **Verb <u>Be</u> Past - Yes-No Questions**

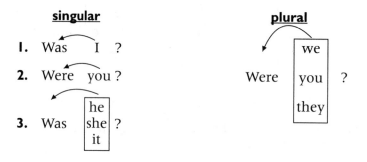

		singular			plural
1.	Was	I ?			
2.	Were	you ?		Were	we / you / they ?
3.	Was	he / she / it ?			

⫸ **Word Order of Yes-No Questions with <u>Be</u> Past**

	VERB <u>BE</u> PAST	SUBJECT	COMPLEMENT	SHORT ANSWERS FOR CONVERSATION
1.	Was	I	in any of your classes last semester?	No, you weren't.
2.	Were	you	a student in the nursing program?	Yes, I was.
3.	Was	he	one of the best students in the program?	Yes, he was.
4.	Was	she	your favorite professor?	No, she wasn't.
5.	Was	it	a difficult program?	Yes, it was.
6.	Were	we	all "A" students?	No, you weren't.
7.	Were	you	in Prof. Jardin's biology class?	Yes, we were.
8.	Were	they	student nurses at St. Mary's Hospital?	Yes, they were.

PAST TENSE OF THE VERB <u>BE</u> - YES-NO QUESTIONS

➠ **Exercise 5** Use the Simple Past Tense of the verb <u>Be</u> to write yes-no questions with the words in parentheses. Answer each question with a short answer (affirmative or negative).

The First Day of Class

1. (you / nervous on the first day of class)

   A: <u>Were you nervous on the first day of class?</u>

   B: <u>Yes, I was.</u>

2. (it / difficult to find a place to park on the first day)

   A: _____

   B: _____

3. (it / easy to register for your classes)

   A: _____

   B: _____

4. (the counselors / helpful)

   A: _____

   B: _____

5. (it / easy to locate your classrooms)

   A: _____

   B: _____

6. (your new classmates / friendly)

   A: _____

   B: _____

7. (your books and tuition / expensive)

   A: _____

   B: _____

8. (your teacher / on time for class)

   A: _____

   B: _____

REFERENCE CHART - PAST TENSE OF THE VERB <u>BE</u>

➠ The verb <u>Be</u> has two forms in the Simple Past Tense: *was* and *were*. Study the past forms of the verb <u>Be</u> in the charts below.

<u>Be</u> – Affirmative Sentences

SUBJECT	VERB BE	COMPLEMENT
I	was	a student at Carter College last year.
You	were	in my computer class last semester.
He	was	a friend of mine in grade school.
She	was	in the counselor's office a few minutes ago.
It	was	a nice day yesterday.
We	were	in the same English class last semester.
You	were	happy with your schedules last year.
They	were	on the teacher's roll.

<u>Be</u> – Negative Sentences

SUBJECT	VERB BE+ NOT	COMPLEMENT
I	was not	a student at Carter College last year.
You	were not	in my computer class last semester.
He	was not	a friend of mine in grade school.
She	was not	in the counselor's office a few minutes ago.
It	was not	a nice day yesterday.
We	were not	in the same English class last semester.
You	were not	happy with your schedules last year.
They	were not	on the teacher's roll.

<u>Be</u> – Questions

VERB BE	SUBJECT	COMPLEMENT
Was	I	a student at Carter College last year?
Were	you	in my computer class last semester?
Was	he	a friend of yours in grade school?
Was	she	in the counselor's office a few minutes ago?
Was	it	a nice day yesterday?
Were	we	in the same English class last semester?
Were	you	happy with your schedules last year?
Were	they	on the teacher's roll?

✓ CHECK YOUR UNDERSTANDING

A. Answer the questions below.

1. Most verbs show action in a sentence. However, the verb <u>Be</u> _____ show action.

2. What are the present tense forms of the verb <u>Be</u>? _____ _____ _____

3. What are the past tense forms of the verb <u>Be</u>? _____ _____

4. What are the three ways that we use the verb <u>Be</u>?

   a. Be + _____ **b.** Be + _____ **c.** Be + _____

5. Write an example sentence in the Simple Past Tense to show each way that we use the verb <u>Be</u>.

   a. _____

   b. _____

   c. _____

6. How do we form negative sentences with the verb <u>Be</u> in the Simple Past Tense?

   _____

7. Write a negative sentence with the verb <u>Be</u> in the Simple Past Tense.

   _____

8. How do we form yes-no questions with the verb <u>Be</u> in the Simple Past Tense?

   _____

9. Write a yes-no question with the verb <u>Be</u> in the Simple Past Tense.

   _____

B. *EDITING* - There are 6 mistakes in the use of the verb <u>Be</u> in the paragraph below. Find and correct each mistake. If you need help, refer to the Reference Chart on page 192.

A Year Abroad

[1]Paul was an American exchange student in Paris last year. [2]He i~~s~~ *was* a guest in the home of the DuBois family. [3]Their home was near the University of Paris where Paul and Yvette DuBois be students. [4]Paul's favorite classes was art and French history, so he was anxious to visit the many historic places in the city. [5]Yvette was his guide around Paris. [6]They are frequent visitors at the famous Louvre Museum, the Eiffel Tower, and Notre Dame Cathedral. [7]The Palace of Versailles, home of the French monarchs, were also one of Paul's favorite places to visit. [8]In the evenings, there was many interesting things to see and do in the cafes, night clubs, and theaters of Paris. [9]Paul's year abroad was exciting and educational and a wonderful experience for a young college student.

Part 2
The Simple Past Tense of Action Verbs

THE MEANING OF THE SIMPLE PAST TENSE - ACTIONS THAT BEGAN AND ENDED IN THE PAST

> ► **Learning Point**
>
> We use the Simple Past Tense to talk about an action that happened at a particular time in the past (for example, *yesterday, last night, last year*). The action began and ended in the past. The action is finished and will never happen again at that particular time.

⟹ Each sentence below talks about a past action.

At Home

1. My husband and I <u>moved</u> into our new house last month.

2. Some of our friends <u>helped</u> us to move.

3. Our new neighbors <u>welcomed</u> us warmly.

TIME WORDS
yesterday
last <u>week</u>
last <u>year</u>
<u>a month</u> ago
<u>two years</u> ago
in <u>1995</u>

At Work

1. I <u>worked</u> ten hours of overtime last weekend.

2. My boss <u>interviewed</u> several people for a job in our department last week.

3. He <u>hired</u> three new people yesterday.

At School

1. I <u>worked</u> for several hours on my homework last night.

2. I <u>typed</u> a paper for my English class and <u>studied</u> for a math test.

3. I finally <u>finished</u> my homework at midnight.

Leisure Time

1. My family and I <u>camped</u> for two weeks in Yosemite National Park last summer.

2. We <u>hiked</u> in the mountains and <u>fished</u> in the beautiful lake near our campsite.

3. Everyone <u>enjoyed</u> our camping trip very much.

THE PAST FORM OF REGULAR VERBS

➠ In Chapter 5, you learned that English verbs have 5 forms:

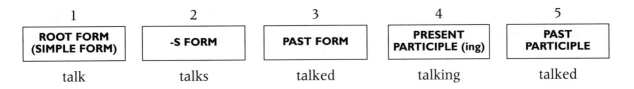

1	2	3	4	5
ROOT FORM (SIMPLE FORM)	-S FORM	PAST FORM	PRESENT PARTICIPLE (ing)	PAST PARTICIPLE
talk	talks	talked	talking	talked

➠ We use the <u>past form</u> of verbs in the Simple Past Tense.

▶ **Learning Point**

Most verbs add **-ed** to the root form to show an action that happened in the past. Verbs that add **-ed** to show past action are called **regular verbs** (talk - talked, play - played, fix - fixed).

➠ **Past Form of Regular Verbs**

<u>Note:</u> We use the same form of the verb for all subjects.

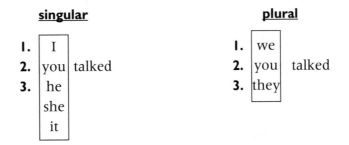

	singular			**plural**	
1.	I		1.	we	
2.	you	talked	2.	you	talked
3.	he		3.	they	
	she				
	it				

➠ **Word Order of Past Tense Affirmative Sentences**

SUBJECT	VERB	COMPLEMENT
1. I	called	the dentist for an appointment yesterday.
2. You	looked	nice at the party last night.
3. He	died	in 1989.
4. She	visited	her relatives in Los Angeles last Christmas.
5. It	rained	all day yesterday.
6. We	played	cards with some friends of ours last night.
7. You	helped	us a lot last weekend.
8. They	earned	$72,000 last year.

THE PAST FORM OF REGULAR VERBS

Exercise 1 Before the invention of computers, students in composition classes spent a lot of time writing and rewriting their assignments. They usually wrote the first draft of their paragraphs in longhand. Then, when they made changes in their paragraph, they had to copy the whole paragraph again. When they were ready to write their final draft, they had to type it on a typewriter. Because it was very difficult to type a paper perfectly without any mistakes, or "typos", students often had to type the final draft several times. The paragraph below explains how today's computers help students to save time when they write a composition.

Use the Simple Past Tense of the regular verbs in the box below to complete the paragraph. Use each verb only once. Compare your answers with a classmate.

check	permit	save
✔ require	learn	complain
consider	include	prove

A Student's Best Friend

When teachers first **(1.)** __required__ students to use computers for their writing assignments, most students **(2.)** ______________. However, they quickly **(3.)** ______________ to appreciate the benefits of the personal computer. First of all, the computer helped students to organize their paragraphs. It **(4.)** ______________ them to add topic sentences and transition words and to move sentences easily for better organization. For another thing, students **(5.)** ______________ a lot of time in the revising and editing steps. The computer allowed them to add, delete, and rewrite sentences. It also allowed them to correct errors in grammar and punctuation. In addition, the computer **(6.)** ______________ a spell-checker and automatically **(7.)** ______________ the paragraph for spelling errors. Finally, students were able to print out a copy of their paragraph at any time. Before long, students **(8.)** ______________ the personal computer their best friend. The PC **(9.)** ______________ to be a big time-saver for them.

REGULAR VERBS: THE PRONUNCIATION OF -ED

➡ Verbs that end in -ed in the past form are called regular verbs.

> ▶ **Learning Point**
>
> **-ed** makes three sounds:
>
>   **1.** wanted /**id**/   **2.** walked /**t**/   **3.** played /**d**/

➡ Learn the three -ed pronunciation rules.

RULE 1: When the root form of a verb ends in a t or d sound, the -ed makes a separate syllable. We hear /**id**/.

root form	-	past form		root form	-	past form
want		want-ed /id/		need		need-ed /id/
wait		wait-ed /id/		attend		attend-ed /id/
start		start-ed /id		remind		remind-ed /id/
invite		invit-ed /id/		decide		decid-ed /id/
permit		permit-ted /id/				

RULE 2: -ed sounds like /t/ when the root form of the verb ends in the sounds p, k, f, x, ss, sh, ch.

root form	-	past form		root form	-	past form
help		helped /t/		miss		missed /t/
talk		talked /t/		wash		washed /t/
look		looked /t/		finish		finished /t/
fix		fixed /t		watch		watched /t/

RULE 3: -ed sounds like /d/ in all other regular verbs.

root form	-	past form		root form	-	past form
call		called /d/		borrow		borrowed /d/
listen		listened /d/		earn		earned /d/
explain		explained /d/		copy		copied /d/
live		lived /d/		study		studied /d/

REGULAR VERBS: THE PRONUNCIATION OF -ED

▐► **Exercise 2** Your teacher will read the root form and the past form of the regular verbs below. Listen carefully for the sound of -ed.

1. If -ed sounds like /**id**/, write id. 2. If -ed sounds like /**t**/, write t. 3. If -ed sounds like /**d**/, write d.

root form		past form			root form		past form		
1. pass	-	passed	/ t /		13. appreciate	-	appreciated	/	/
2. ask	-	asked	/	/	14. apply	-	applied	/	/
3. plan	-	planned	/	/	15. argue	-	argued	/	/
4. save	-	saved	/	/	16. practice	-	practiced	/	/
5. rent	-	rented	/	/	17. learn	-	learned	/	/
6. erase	-	erased	/	/	18. recommend	-	recommended	/	/
7. depend	-	depended	/	/	19. discuss	-	discussed	/	/
8. complain	-	complained	/	/	20. stop	-	stopped	/	/
9. expect	-	expected	/	/	21. connect	-	connected	/	/
10. promise	-	promised	/	/	22. try	-	tried	/	/
11. visit	-	visited	/	/	23. graduate	-	graduated	/	/
12. worry	-	worried	/	/	24. deduct	-	deducted	/	/

▐► **Exercise 3** Listen for the sound of -ed as your teacher reads each sentence. Write t or d or id.

A House in the Country

1. My sister and brother-in-law retired / d / last year and decided /   / to move out of the city.

2. They purchased /   / an old two-story house on three acres of land in the Santa Cruz mountains.

3. The house needed /   / a lot of work, so their friends offered /   / to help them to fix it up.

4. First, everyone worked /   / on the outside of the house.

5. They painted /   / the house gray with white trim.

6. They also pulled /   / the weeds and planted /   / a new lawn in front of the house.

7. Then they started /   / on the inside of the house.

8. They installed /   / new plumbing in the bathrooms and kitchen.

9. They also repaired /   / all the electrical wiring and sanded /   / the hardwood floors.

10. Finally, they painted /   / and wallpapered /   / all the rooms in the house.

11. When they finished /   /, the whole house looked /   / clean and attractive.

THE PAST FORM OF IRREGULAR VERBS

➠ You have learned that we add -ed to most English verbs to show that an action began and ended at a particular time in the past.

However, not all verbs add -ed to show past time. There are about 150 common verbs that do not add -ed to show past time. These verbs are called **irregular verbs.**

▶ **Learning Point**

1. Irregular verbs do not end in -ed to show actions that happened in the past.

2. Irregular verbs usually change spelling in the past form. (example: eat - ate, go - went)

3. A few irregular verbs do not change spelling. (example: quit - quit, put - put)

➠ **Past Form of Irregular Verbs**

Note: We use the same form of the verb for all subjects.

	singular			plural	
1.	I		**1.**	we	
2.	you	ate	**2.**	you	ate
3.	he		**3.**	they	
	she				
	it				

➠ **Word Order of Simple Affirmative Sentences**

SUBJECT	VERB	COMPLEMENT
1. I	wrote	a letter to my parents yesterday.
2. You	did	very well on your last test.
3. He	quit	his job at the post office last week.
4. She	felt	sick after class yesterday.
5. It	took	three hours to drive to Sacramento last Sunday.
6. We	saw	a good movie last Friday night.
7. You	forgot	to pick up your papers after class yesterday.
8. They	bought	a new color printer for their computer.

REFERENCE CHART - THE PAST FORM OF IRREGULAR VERBS

➡ Study the list of irregular verbs below. You must memorize the past forms of irregular verbs. Note: There is also a verb list on page 410 in the Appendix.

root form	past form	past participle	root form	past form	past participle
1. be	was, were	been	44. lend	lent	lent
2. become	became	become	45. let	let	let
3. begin	began	begun	46. lie	lay	lain
4. bite	bit	bitten	47. lose	lost	lost
5. blow	blew	blown	48. make	made	made
6. break	broke	broken	49. mean	meant	meant
7. bring	brought	brought	50. meet	met	met
8. build	built	built	51. pay	paid	paid
9. buy	bought	bought	52. put	put	put
10. catch	caught	caught	53. quit	quit	quit
11. choose	chose	chosen	54. read	read	read
12. come	came	come	55. ride	rode	ridden
13. cost	cost	cost	56. ring	rang	rung
14. cut	cut	cut	57. rise	rose	risen
15. do	did	done	58. run	ran	run
16. draw	drew	drawn	59. say	said	said
17. drink	drank	drunk	60. see	saw	seen
18. drive	drove	driven	61. sell	sold	sold
19. eat	ate	eaten	62. send	sent	sent
20. fall	fell	fallen	63. set	set	set
21. feed	fed	fed	64. shake	shook	shaken
22. feel	felt	felt	65. shoot	shot	shot
23. fight	fought	fought	66. shut	shut	shut
24. find	found	found	67. sing	sang	sung
25. fly	flew	flown	68. sit	sat	sat
26. forget	forgot	forgotten	69. sleep	slept	slept
27. forgive	forgave	forgiven	70. speak	spoke	spoken
28. freeze	froze	frozen	71. spend	spent	spent
29. get	got	gotten	72. stand	stood	stood
30. give	gave	given	73. steal	stole	stolen
31. go	went	gone	74. sweep	swept	swept
32. grow	grew	grown	75. swim	swam	swum
33. hang	hung	hung	76. take	took	taken
34. have	had	had	77. teach	taught	taught
35. hear	heard	heard	78. tear	tore	torn
36. hide	hid	hidden	79. tell	told	told
37. hit	hit	hit	80. think	thought	thought
38. hold	held	held	81. throw	threw	thrown
39. hurt	hurt	hurt	82. understand	understood	understood
40. keep	kept	kept	83. wake	woke	woken
41. know	knew	known	84. wear	wore	worn
42. lay	laid	laid	85. win	won	won
43. leave	left	left	86. write	wrote	written

THE PAST FORM OF IRREGULAR VERBS

⟫ **Exercise 4** Complete each sentence below with the Simple Past Tense of one of the irregular verbs in the box below. Use each verb only <u>once</u>. If you need help with the irregular verbs, refer to the chart on page 200.

teach	build	✔ get
take	buy	cost
think	give	put
make	become	begin

A Computer for the Home

1. Glen Martin and his wife Mary just _____<u>got</u>_____ a personal computer and a laser printer through an ad in the paper, and they are very happy with them.

2. The PC and printer _____ around $900.00.

3. Glen _____ a table for the computer and a cabinet for the printer.

4. Glen and Mary _____ an introductory computer class through the Adult Education program at a high school near their home.

5. They _____ of many ways to use the computer in their home.

6. They _____ the phone numbers and addresses of all their friends into the computer.

7. Glen _____ some software to keep track of their personal finances on the computer.

8. Glen and Mary also _____ their children how to use the computer.

9. Glen's parents _____ the children several games for the computer and some software to make their own greeting cards.

10. The children _____ Christmas and birthday cards for all their friends on the computer.

11. The family also _____ to use the Internet and were soon able to access information from all over the world.

12. The computer _____ an important part of their lives.

THE SIMPLE PAST TENSE OF REGULAR AND IRREGULAR VERBS

▪➡ **Exercise 5** Use the Simple Past Tense of the verbs in parentheses to complete the conversations below. Then practice the conversations with a partner.

I. *Teacher and Student*

Teacher: Congratulations, Thanh. You _____ **(I. do)** very well on your last composition.

Thanh: Thank you. I _____ **(2. take)** your advice and _____ **(3. make)** an outline before I _____ **(4. begin)** to write. The outline really _____ **(5. help)** me to plan my paragraph.

Teacher: I also _____ **(6. like)** your paragraph because you _____ **(7. use)** plenty of examples and specific details to explain your topic sentence. Keep up the good work!

2. *Police Officer and Motorist*

Police officer: You _____ **(I. go)** through a red light at the last intersection.

Motorist: Really? I _____ **(2. think)** that the light _____ **(3. be)** green.

Police officer: No, the light _____ **(4. be)** red. Also, your speed _____ **(5. be)** 60 mph, and the speed limit on this expressway is 45 mph.

Motorist: Really? My speedometer _____ **(6. say)** 45.

Police officer: Show me your driver's license.

Motorist: Here it is, Officer.

Police officer: This license _____ **(7. expire)** on your birthday last year.

Motorist: Yes. I _____ **(8. plan)** to renew it last week, but I _____ **(9. get)** very busy at work.

Police officer: You are a danger to other drivers! I'm taking your driver's license, giving you three tickets, and calling a tow truck to take away your car. I'll see you in court!

THE SIMPLE PAST TENSE

▶ **Exercise 6** Nine of the sentences in the student paragraph below contain verb errors, and five of the sentences are correct. If a sentence is correct, write _correct_ on the line below the paragraph. If a sentence is not correct, write the correct verb on the line. Compare your answers with a classmate.

A Trip to Freedom

[1]Sixteen years ago, my family ⟨was escape⟩ from Vietnam in search of freedom. [2]We left Vietnam in a small boat. [3]The boat was about fifty feet long and twelve feet wide. [4]There was 45 people on the boat, including 15 children. [5]There is hardly* room to move or lie down. [6]The boat was move slowly at about 10 mph. [7]It took us five days and four nights to reach a small island in Malaysia. [8]It was a terrible trip, but we have no choice. [9]We had to leave Vietnam or return to a concentration camp. [10]Each person was have only a quarter of a liter of water and an eighth of a liter of dehydrated rice a day to survive. [11]We literally* had nothing except the clothes on our backs. [12]Finally, we reach the land of freedom. [13]A representative of the United Nations come to interview us and granted* us the status* of refugee and gave us food and clothes. [14]My family were stay on the island for one year before the United States of America offered my family political asylum*.

hardly: almost none, very little

literally: exactly, truly

granted: gave

status: legal position

asylum: protection and shelter

sentence:

1.	_escaped_	8.	
2.	_correct_	9.	
3.		10.	
4.		11.	
5.		12.	
6.		13.	
7.		14.	

MORE PAST TENSE TIME WORDS

➠ Time words tell us when an action happened in the past. Study the chart below.

PAST TENSE TIME WORDS			
yesterday	yesterday	yesterday morning	yesterday evening
	the day before yesterday	yesterday afternoon	
last ____	last night	last summer	last Monday
	last week	last fall	last Tuesday
	last month	last winter	last weekend
	last year	last spring	
____ ago	a few minutes ago	two days ago	a month ago
	an hour ago	a week ago	five years ago
in _____	in 1996	in the 1950s	in the 19th century

➠ **Exercise 7** Use the time words in parentheses to write true sentences about your life. Use only the Simple Past Tense.

I. (yesterday morning) *I got up early yesterday morning.* _____

_____

2. (the day before yesterday) _____

_____

3. (last Tuesday) _____

_____

4. (last spring) _____

_____

5. (a few minutes ago) _____

_____

6. (five years ago) _____

_____

7. (in 2001) _____

_____

8. (in the 1990s) _____

✓ CHECK YOUR UNDERSTANDING

A. Answer the questions below.

1. When do we use the Simple Past Tense? _____

_____

2. What are regular verbs? _____

_____

3. Give three examples of regular verbs.

root form - **past form**	**root form** - **past form**	**root form** - **past form**
_____ _____	_____ _____	_____ _____

4. -ed makes three sounds: / **id** /, / **t** /, and / **d** /. Read each word below. Write the sound of -ed.

   a. called /　/   **b.** decided /　/   **c.** helped /　/   **d.** worked /　/

   e. wanted /　/   **f.** listened /　/   **g.** fixed /　/   **h.** waited /　/

5. What are irregular verbs? _____

_____

6. Give three examples of irregular verbs.

root form - **past form**	**root form** - **past form**	**root form** - **past form**
_____ _____	_____ _____	_____ _____

B. Complete the chart below. Write true information about your life. Begin with the year that you were born. (<u>Example</u>: <u>　1985　</u>   <u>I was born in Mexico City in 1985.　</u>) Write your sentences in chronological order (time order).

year	**Important Events in My Life**
1. _____	_____
2. _____	_____
3. _____	_____
4. _____	_____
5. _____	_____
6. _____	_____
7. _____	_____
8. _____	_____

NEGATIVE SENTENCES IN THE SIMPLE PAST TENSE

> ### Learning Point
>
> **1.** To form negative sentences in the Simple Past Tense, we put the helping (auxiliary) verb <u>did not</u> in front of the **root form** of the main verb.
>
> **2.** To form negative contractions, we combine <u>did not</u> ⟶ **didn't**.

1. affirmative: I got good grades in my computer classes last semester.

    negative: I <u>did not</u> (didn't) get good grades in my history class.
                      ↑   ↑
                    hv   **main verb**

2. affirmative: My brother had enough money to buy a used car a few months ago.

    negative: He <u>did not</u> (didn't) have enough money to buy a new car.
                     ↑   ↑
                   hv   **main verb**

3. affirmative: I finished all my English assignments last night.

    negative: I <u>did not</u> (didn't) finish my math assignment.
                    ↑   ↑
                 hv   **main verb**

➡ Simple Past Tense - Negative Form

1.	I		**1.**	we
2.	you	did not (didn't) eat	**2.**	you	did not (didn't) eat
3.	he		**3.**	they
	she			
	it			

➡ Word Order of Past Tense Negative Sentences

SUBJECT	HELPING VERB + NOT	MAIN VERB (ROOT FORM)	COMPLEMENT
1. I		drive	to school yesterday morning.
2. You		study	much for the last test.
3. He		eat	lunch in the cafeteria yesterday.
4. She	did not	do	her math assignment last night.
5. It	(didn't)	rain	much last winter.
6. We		practice	pronunciation in class yesterday.
7. You		pay	attention to the teacher's explanation.
8. They		prepare	a speech for their conversation class.

SIMPLE PAST TENSE - NEGATIVE SENTENCES

➠ **Exercise 8** Michael is a freshman at Chico State College this semester. It's his first time away from home, and he's really enjoying his freedom. He has a lot of new friends and a very busy social life. He never misses a football game or a party. However, his social life is beginning to interfere with his studies. Read Michael's description of one of the most terrible days of his life.

A Terrible Day

[1]I had a terrible day yesterday. [2]First of all, I forgot to set my alarm clock, so I overslept 45 minutes. [3]I got up, took a shower, and threw on my clothes. [4]Then I ran downstairs and jumped into my car. [5]On the way to school, I ran out of gas and had to wait almost an hour for a tow truck to bring me some gas. [6]When I finally got to school, I quickly parked and ran to class. [7]Of course, I missed my first class, and I was twenty minutes late for my second class. [8]I also got an F on my homework assignment because it was incomplete. [9]Things got worse. [10]I left my wallet at home, so I had no money for lunch. [11]I tried to borrow some money from my friends, but no one had any extra money. [12]I went to my two o'clock class, and I promptly fell asleep in the middle of a lecture. [13]My snoring disturbed the class, so the teacher asked me to leave. [14]Finally, it was time to go home. [15]When I got to my car, I saw a parking ticket on the windshield. [16]My car was in a handicapped zone, and the fine on the ticket was $280.00. [17]Then I had to fight heavy traffic all the way home. [18]After an hour, I finally pulled into my carport. [19]I was home at last! [20]I took out my key, opened the front door, and stepped into a puddle of water. [21]There was water all over the living room floor.

➠ **Exercise 9** Write eight negative sentences in the Simple Past Tense. Explain why Michael had a terrible day. Compare your answers with a classmate.

1. He didn't set his alarm clock. _____

2. _____

3. _____

4. _____

5. _____

6. _____

7. _____

8. _____

SIMPLE PAST TENSE - AFFIRMATIVE AND NEGATIVE SENTENCES

➠ Nowadays, it is very difficult for a young couple to buy their first home. In order to make the dream of owning their own home come true, many young people temporarily move in with their parents, limit their expenses, and work extra jobs in order to save money for a down payment on a house.

Saving for a Home

sacrifice: *give up something, do without*

charge: *ask for payment*

room and board: *a bed and meals*

limit their expenses: *try to spend as little as possible*

give up: *sacrifice, do without something*

[1]When they were first married, my sister and brother-in-law made many sacrifices* to save enough money to buy their first home. [2]First of all, they moved in with my parents instead of renting their own apartment. [3]Fortunately, my parents have a house with a room and bath over the garage. [4]My parents charged* my sister and her husband only $300 a month for room and board*. [5]In addition, my sister and brother-in-law limited all their expenses*. [6]For example, they watched TV instead of going to the movies. [7]They gave up* their tickets to sporting events such as basketball and football, and my sister cut her own hair and gave herself home permanents. [8]Finally, they both worked extra jobs. [9]In addition to his regular job, my brother-in-law worked at night at Fry's Electronics store. [10]My sister worked three nights a week as a clerk at a Barnes & Noble bookstore. [11]Because of all their sacrifices, my sister and brother-in-law were finally able to move into their own home three months ago.

➠ **Exercise 10** Use the Simple Past Tense to complete the following sentences about the paragraph. Be careful. Some of the sentences are affirmative, and some of the sentences are negative.

1. In order to save money, my sister and brother-in-law (move) __*moved*__ in with my parents. They (rent) __*didn't rent*__ an apartment.

2. They (have) _____ their own room and bath over the garage. They (live) _____ in the house with my parents.

3. My sister and brother-in-law (pay) _____ my parents much for rent. They (pay) _____ them only $300 a month.

4. They (go) _____ out very much. They usually (watch) _____ TV at home.

5. My sister (go) _____ to the beauty salon. She (cut) _____ her own hair.

6. They (have) _____ much free time because they both (work) _____ two jobs.

✓ CHECK YOUR UNDERSTANDING

A. Answer the following questions.

   1. How do we form negative sentences in the Simple Past Tense? _____

   _____

   2. The negative contraction in the Simple Past Tense is _____ .

   3. We use the _____ form of the main verb in negative sentences.

   4. Write negative sentences in the Simple Past Tense. Write true sentences about your life. Use a time word in each sentence.

      a. _____

      _____

      b. _____

      _____

      c. _____

      d. _____

      _____

B. *EDITING* - The paragraph below has 7 verb errors. Find and correct the errors. The first one is done for you. If you need help, refer to the Reference Chart on page 214.

A Bad Textbook

did not like

[1]My classmates and I ~~did not liked~~ our last textbook. [2]First of all, we did not found the book interesting. [3]We not enjoy the stories and articles because they were boring, and they not relate to our daily lives. [4]Second, the book was not explained things clearly. [5]Some of the reference charts were difficult to understand, and there was not enough example sentences. [6]Finally, the book used difficult vocabulary, but it did not includes a glossary* to explain the new words. [7]Our teacher decided to use a different textbook in the future.

Vocabulary Note   ***glossary:*** *definitions of words*

ASKING YES-NO QUESTIONS IN THE SIMPLE PAST TENSE

> **Learning Point**
>
> To form YES-NO QUESTIONS in the Simple Past Tense, we put the helping verb **did** in front of the subject. We always use the **root form** of the verb in question sentences.

hv   s   mv

Example: 1. A: Did you go to the movies with your friends last weekend?

   B: Yes, I did.

                hv   s   mv

2. A: Did you like the movie?

   B: No, we didn't.

                hv   s   mv

3. A: Did John apply for the job at Hewlett Packard last week?

   B: Yes, he did.

                hv   s   mv

4. A: Did they call him in for an interview?

   B: No, they didn't.

⟹ Simple Past Tense - Yes-No Questions

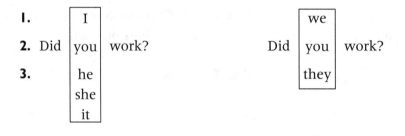

⟹ Word Order of Yes-No Questions in the Simple Past Tense

	HELPING VERB	SUBJECT	MAIN VERB (ROOT FORM)	COMPLEMENT	SHORT ANSWERS FOR CONVERSATION
1.	Did	I	leave	the computer on last night?	Yes, you did.
2.	Did	you	remember	to call your mother yesterday?	No, I didn't.
3.	Did	he	lose	his car keys and wallet?	Yes, he did.
4.	Did	she	pass	her driving test last Friday?	No, she didn't.
5.	Did	it	cost	much to fix your car?	Yes, it did.
6.	Did	we	tell	you about our trip to Alaska?	Yes, you did.
7.	Did	you	have	a good time at Carla's party?	Yes, we did.
8.	Did	they	find	an apartment to rent?	No, they didn't.

SIMPLE PAST TENSE - YES-NO QUESTIONS

➡ **Exercise 11** Use the words in parentheses to form yes-no questions in the Simple Past Tense.

A Beautiful Wedding

1. (you / go / to Susan's wedding last Sunday)

A: ___Did___ ___you___ ___go___ _____to Susan's wedding last Sunday?_____
        hv   s   main verb   complement

B: Yes, I did. It was beautiful.

2. (the bride / wear / a long white dress and veil)

A: _____ _____ _____ _____
        hv   s   main verb   complement

B: Yes, she did. She wore her mother's wedding dress and carried a bouquet of pink roses.

3. (the groom / wear / a tuxedo)

A: _____ _____ _____ _____
        hv   s   main verb   complement

B: No, he didn't. He wore a dark gray suit. He looked very handsome.

4. (they / have / a large reception)

A: _____ _____ _____ _____
        hv   s   main verb   complement

B: Yes, they did. There were almost 200 people at the reception at the Fairmont Hotel.

5. (everyone / toast / the bride and groom)

A: _____ _____ _____ _____
        hv   s   main verb   complement

B: Yes, we did. We toasted the bride and groom with champagne, and then we sat down to a delicious dinner.

6. (they / have / an orchestra)

A: _____ _____ _____ _____
        hv   s   main verb   complement

B: No, they didn't. They had a disk jockey, and the music was really good.

7. (the bride and groom / leave / on their honeymoon right after the reception)

A: _____ _____ _____ _____
        hv   s   main verb   complement

B: No, they didn't. They spent the night at the Fairmont and left early the next morning for Hawaii.

SIMPLE PAST TENSE - YES-NO QUESTIONS

▸ **Exercise 12** Everyone remembers his or her worst job. In the paragraph below, Etsuko describes babysitting as her worst job. Read Etsuko's paragraph.

My Worst Job

¹The worst job I ever had was a babysitting job. ²First, babysitting is very stressful. ³A month ago, I baby-sat for a neighbor's two children at my home. ⁴They were two and four years old. ⁵It was terrible because they left toys all over the house, fought with each other, and ran wild all day long. ⁶When they got tired of playing with each other, they started to bother me. ⁷They wanted me to play with them. ⁸If I refused to play with them, they were totally uncontrollable. ⁹Their energy drove me crazy, and it was very difficult to control my temper. ¹⁰Second, babysitting is a big responsibility. ¹¹I had to protect the children from accidents. ¹²Small children, especially children under two years old, try to eat everything: pins, dish detergent, pills, and so on. ¹³For this reason, I had to watch the children every minute. ¹⁴They were very active and ran all over the house. ¹⁵I was afraid to take my eyes off them. ¹⁶By the end of the day, I was totally exhausted. ¹⁷Last week, when my neighbor asked me to babysit again, I refused. ¹⁸I like children, but I do not like babysitting!

▸ **Exercise 13** Use the words in parentheses to write yes-no questions about the paragraph. Use the Simple Past Tense of the verb Be or the Simple Past Tense of action verbs. Answer each question with a short answer. When you are finished, take turns asking and answering the questions with a partner. (Note that questions 4-12 continue on the next page.)

1. (Etsuko / enjoy her job as a babysitter)

   Q: _Did Etsuko enjoy her job as a babysitter?_____

   A: _No, she didn't._____

2. (the children / make Etsuko angry)

   Q: _____

   A: _____

3. (the children / pick up their toys)

   Q: _____

   A: _____

SIMPLE PAST TENSE - YES-NO QUESTIONS

⟱➤ **Exercise 13** (continued)

4. (the children / easy to take care of)

   Q: _____

   A: _____

5. (the children / get along with each other)

   Q: _____

   A: _____

6. (they / want Etsuko to play with them)

   Q: _____

   A: _____

7. (Etsuko / a conscientious babysitter)

   Q: _____

   A: _____

8. (Etsuko / watch the children carefully)

   Q: _____

   A: _____

9. (the children / take a long nap)

   Q: _____

   A: _____

10. (Etsuko / tired by the end of the day)

   Q: _____

   A: _____

11. (Etsuko's neighbor / ask Etsuko to babysit again)

   Q: _____

   A: _____

12. (Etsuko / agree to take care of her neighbor's children again)

   Q: _____

   A: _____

REFERENCE CHART - THE SIMPLE PAST TENSE

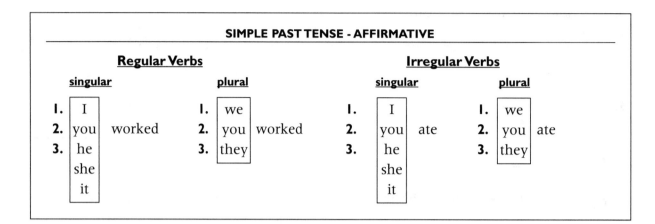

SIMPLE PAST TENSE - AFFIRMATIVE

Regular Verbs

singular		plural	
1. I		**1.** we	
2. you worked		**2.** you worked	
3. he		**3.** they	
she			
it			

Irregular Verbs

singular		plural	
1. I		**1.** we	
2. you ate		**2.** you ate	
3. he		**3.** they	
she			
it			

SIMPLE PAST TENSE - NEGATIVE

Regular Verbs

singular		plural	
1. I		**1.** we	
2. you did not work		**2.** you did not work	
3. he		**3.** they	
she			
it			

Irregular Verbs

singular		plural	
1. I		**1.** we	
2. you did not eat		**2.** you did not eat	
3. he		**3.** they	
she			
it			

SIMPLE PAST TENSE - YES-NO QUESTIONS

Regular Verbs

singular		plural	
1.	I	**1.**	we
2. Did	you work?	**2.** Did	you work?
3.	he	**3.**	they
	she		
	it		

Irregular Verbs

singular		plural	
1.	I	**1.**	we
2. Did	you eat?	**2.** Did	you eat?
3.	he	**3.**	they
	she		
	it		

REVIEW OF VERB TENSES

➠ **Direction**: Think carefully about the meaning of the sentences below. Does the sentence talk about a habitual action, an action that is happening right now, or an action that happened in the past? Then write *true*, *false*, or *I don't know* on the line after each sentence.

1. Ann and Sue are watching a good program on TV.
   a. The program was over an hour ago.   a. _____false_____
   b. The television is on now.   b. _____true_____
   c. Ann and Sue watch TV every day.   c. _I don't know._

2. My father always watches his diet carefully because he doesn't want to gain weight.
   a. My father didn't eat chocolate cake and ice cream for dessert last night.   a. _____
   b. My father is eating a bag of potato chips right now.   b. _____
   c. My father often eats fattening food.   c. _____

3. Karen is having a good time on her vacation in New York.
   a. Karen is in New York now.   a. _____
   b. Karen got back from her trip to New York a few days ago.   b. _____
   c. Karen doesn't travel to New York very often.   c. _____

4. Paul moved from Los Angeles to San Jose last month.
   a. Paul lives in Los Angeles.   a. _____
   b. Paul lives in San Jose.   b. _____
   c. Paul wants to move to San Francisco.   c. _____

5. Tony is taking a math class from Mr. Cortez this semester.
   a. Tony is sitting in his math class right now.   a. _____
   b. Mr. Cortez is teaching math at this moment.   b. _____
   c. The semester ended a few days ago.   c. _____

6. The bus always stops at this corner.
   a. The bus is stopping right now.   a. _____
   b. The bus stopped at this corner yesterday.   b. _____
   c. The bus stops at this corner every day.   c. _____

7. Mai is wrapping a birthday present to send to her father.
   a. The package is in the mail now.   a. _____
   b. Mai took the present to the post office yesterday.   b. _____
   c. Mai is getting the package ready to mail right now.   c. _____

REVIEW OF VERB TENSES

➠ **Direction**: Write your own sentences in the verb tenses that you have studied.

| Verb <u>Be</u> - Simple Present Tense - NO ACTION |

affirmative:

1. _____

_____

negative:

2. _____

_____

yes-no question:

3. _____

_____

| Habitual (Simple) Present Tense - ACTION VERBS |

affirmative:

1. _____

_____

negative:

2. _____

_____

yes-no question:

3. _____

_____

| Present Progressive Tense |

affirmative:

1. _____

_____

REVIEW OF VERB TENSES

Present Progressive Tense (continued)

negative:

2. _____

_____

yes-no question:

3. _____

_____

Verb <u>Be</u> - Simple Past Tense - NO ACTION

affirmative:

1. _____

_____

negative:

2. _____

_____

yes-no question:

3. _____

_____

Simple Past Tense - ACTION VERBS

affirmative:

1. _____

_____

negative:

2. _____

_____

yes-no question:

3. _____

_____

Part 3
The Past Progressive Tense

THE PAST PROGRESSIVE TENSE

➡ In Part 2 of this chapter, you studied the Simple Past Tense of action verbs. In this part, you will study another kind of past tense, the Past Progressive Tense.

> ▶ **Learning Point**
>
> We form the Past Progressive Tense with the past forms of the verb <u>Be</u> (was, were) and the <u>-ing</u> <u>form</u> of a verb (present participle). <u>Be</u> is a helping (auxiliary) verb.
> Example: I <u>was sleeping</u> at 10:30 last night.

➡ **Forms of the Past Progressive Tense**

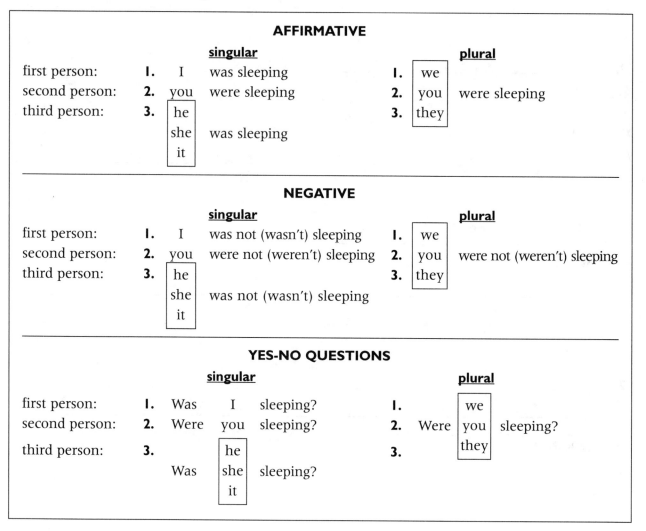

AFFIRMATIVE

			singular			plural
first person:	1.	I	was sleeping	1.	we	were sleeping
second person:	2.	you	were sleeping	2.	you	
third person:	3.	he she it	was sleeping	3.	they	

NEGATIVE

			singular			plural
first person:	1.	I	was not (wasn't) sleeping	1.	we	were not (weren't) sleeping
second person:	2.	you	were not (weren't) sleeping	2.	you	
third person:	3.	he she it	was not (wasn't) sleeping	3.	they	

YES-NO QUESTIONS

			singular			plural
first person:	1.	Was	I	sleeping?	1.		we	sleeping?
second person:	2.	Were	you	sleeping?	2.	Were	you	
third person:	3.	Was	he she it	sleeping?	3.		they	

THE MEANING OF THE PAST PROGRESSIVE TENSE - ACTIONS IN PROGRESS IN THE PAST

> ### Learning Point
>
> We often use the Past Progressive Tense to talk about a past action that was in progress (happening) at a particular point in time, for example: *at 5:00 yesterday afternoon, at 8:00 yesterday morning, at 10:00 last night*.

Exercise 1 Use the Past Progressive Tense to answer the questions below. Then practice asking and answering the questions with a partner.

1. What were you doing at 4:00 this morning?

   _____

2. What were you doing at 7:00 last night?

   _____

3. What were you doing at 2:30 yesterday afternoon?

   _____

4. What were you doing an hour ago?

   _____

5. What were you doing at 8:00 last Saturday night?

   _____

6. What were you doing at 11:00 last Sunday morning?

   _____

7. What were you doing at midnight last Friday night?

   _____

8. What were you thinking about a few minutes ago?

   _____

THE PAST PROGRESSIVE TENSE

➡ **Exercise 2** Counseling services are available at all community colleges to help students with their educational and career goals. Counselors assist students with academic as well as social and personal matters. Mark Hill is a counselor at Foothill College, and his schedule is always very busy. Look at Mr. Hill's schedule from yesterday. Then answer the questions below. Use the Past Progressive Tense in your answers.

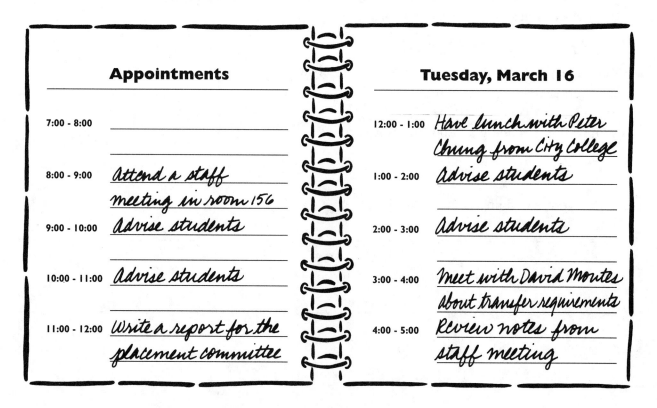

Appointments

Time	
7:00 - 8:00	
8:00 - 9:00	Attend a staff meeting in room 156
9:00 - 10:00	Advise students
10:00 - 11:00	Advise students
11:00 - 12:00	Write a report for the placement committee

Tuesday, March 16

Time	
12:00 - 1:00	Have lunch with Peter Chung from City College
1:00 - 2:00	Advise students
2:00 - 3:00	Advise students
3:00 - 4:00	Meet with David Montes about transfer requirements
4:00 - 5:00	Review notes from staff meeting

1. What was Mr. Hill doing at 8:15 yesterday morning?

_____

2. What was he doing at 9:30?

_____

3. What was he doing at 11:15?

_____

4. What was he doing at 12:30?

_____

5. What was he doing at 3:15?

_____

USING <u>WHEN</u> AND <u>WHILE</u> WITH TWO PAST ACTIONS

> ▶ **Learning Point**
>
> We often use the Past Progressive Tense and the Simple Past Tense in the same sentence to show two past actions.
>
> • The action in the Past Progressive Tense started first and is a **longer** action.
>
> • The action in the Simple Past Tense happened second and is a **shorter** action.

➠ We usually use <u>**while**</u> with the Past Progressive Tense and <u>**when**</u> with the Simple Past Tense.

1. While Sam <u>was painting</u> the house, he <u>fell</u> off the ladder.
          long action   **short action**
          ↑   ↑
    past progressive   **simple past**

2. While we <u>were driving</u> home from work last night, we <u>had</u> a flat tire.
          long action   **short action**
          ↑   ↑
    past progressive   **simple past**

3. I <u>was hurrying</u> to class yesterday when I <u>tripped</u> on the stairs.
       long action   **short action**
         ↑   ↑
    past progressive   **simple past**

4. The waiter <u>was serving</u> dinner when he <u>dropped</u> the plate.
         long action   **short action**
         ↑   ↑
    past progressive   **simple past**

TWO PAST ACTIONS

➡ **Exercise 3** Complete the sentences below. Use <u>while</u> and the Past Progressive Tense with the longer action. Use <u>when</u> and the Simple Past Tense with the shorter action.

1. I __was giving__ a presentation __when__ I __started__ to cough.
   (give)   (start)

2. _____ the teacher _____ the new lesson, the lights _____ out.
                            (explain)   (go)

3. _____ I _____ notes, my pencil _____.
                        (take)   (break)

4. _____ the teacher _____ on me, I _____ attention.
                                    (call)   (not/pay)

5. The fire alarm _____ off _____ we _____ a test.
                    (go)   (take)

6. We _____ our midterms _____ the counselor _____ in.
        (take)   (walk)

7. I _____ asleep _____ I_____ for my history exam last night.
        (fall)   (study)

8. I _____ at the campus bookstore _____ I _____ my wallet.
        (shop)   (lose)

➡ **Exercise 4** Complete the dialog below. Use <u>while</u> and the Past Progressive Tense with the longer action. Use <u>when</u> and the Simple Past Tense with the shorter action.

A Thirtieth Birthday Party

A: Last night we had a surprise birthday party for my sister's thirtieth birthday.

B: Was your sister surprised?

A: Yes! The party was a great success. There were about 20 people there._____

Mary_____ through the front door, everyone_____
        (walk)   (hide)

in the family room. _____ she _____ her hat and coat,
                                        (hang up)

we all _____out of the family room and yelled, "Surprise! Happy Birthday!"
        (run)

_____ she _____ her presents, we _____ in a huge
                    (open)   (carry)

sheet cake with 30 candles! She was really surprised, and we all had a great time.

TWO PAST ACTIONS

▶ **Exercise 5** Complete the sentences below with the Past Progressive Tense or the Simple Past Tense of the verbs in parentheses. Compare your answers with a classmate.

---

1.   Last Friday I **(drive)** _____ to work when I **(run)** _____

out of gas. I pulled over to the side of the freeway and got out of the car. While I **(walk)**

_____ along the freeway, a kind motorist **(offer)** _____

me a ride to the gas station. With his help, I got my gas, and I made it to work on time.

---

2.   Yesterday morning I went to the bank to deposit my paycheck. I **(wait)** _____

in line when I **(meet)** _____ an old friend of mine. We were classmates

in grammar school many years ago. While we **(talk)** _____, her husband

(join) _____ us. What a surprise! He turned out to be my dentist!

---

3.   Last Saturday I had dinner at my sister's house. She and her husband just had a new

baby. When I **(get)** _____ there, my sister **(feed)** _____

the baby, and her husband **(put)** _____ TV dinners into

the microwave. It was fun to see the baby, but dinner wasn't very good!

---

4.   Last night I **(fall)** _____ asleep when I **(hear)** _____

a noise outside my bedroom window. I jumped out of bed and got a flashlight out of the

drawer. While I **(walk)** _____ toward the window, I

(hear) _____ the noise again. My heart **(pound)** _____

when I **(get)** _____ to the window. When I **(pull)** _____

back the curtain, a man **(stand)** _____ outside my window.

USING <u>WHILE</u> AND <u>WHEN</u>

▸ You have learned that we often use <u>while</u> and <u>when</u> in sentences with two past actions.

▶ **Learning Point**

We can use | *while* | or | *when* | first or second in a sentence without a change in meaning.

Note: We use a comma after <u>while</u> and <u>when</u> when we put them at the beginning of a sentence.

1. You can put *while* first or second in a sentence.

| While | I was cooking dinner, I burned my hand.
↑
comma

I burned my hand | while | I was cooking dinner.

2. You can put *when* first or second in a sentence.

| When | I burned my hand, I was cooking dinner.
↑
comma

I was cooking dinner | when | I burned my hand.

WRITING SENTENCES WITH <u>WHILE</u> AND <u>WHEN</u>

▶ **Exercise 6** In the exercise below, the writer is describing a party that she gave for her friends and classmates at the end of last semester. She had one disaster after another!

Use the words in parentheses to write one sentence with two past actions. You can use either <u>while</u> or <u>when</u> to combine the sentences. Use the Simple Past Tense and the Past Progressive Tense in each sentence.

The Party

I. (I / write the guest list for the party)
(my pen / run out of ink)

<u>While I was writing the guest list for the party, my pen ran out of ink.</u>

2. (the handle of my mug / break)
(I / drink a cup of coffee)

_____

_____

3. (I / clean up the mess on the table)
(I / knock over the coffee pot)

_____

_____

4. (I / unpack dishes for the party)
(I / lose one of my contact lenses)

_____

_____

5. (I / cut my finger)
(I / prepare the food for the party)

_____

_____

6. (we / greet our guests)
(the lights / go out)

_____

_____

7. (we / dance by candlelight an hour later)
(the electricity / return)

_____

_____

8. (I / find my contact lens in the bottom of the box)
(I / pack away the party dishes the next day)

_____

_____

REFERENCE CHART - THE PAST PROGRESSIVE TENSE

PAST PROGRESSIVE TENSE - AFFIRMATIVE

		singular			**plural**
first person:	**1.**	I was sleeping	**1.**	we	were sleeping
second person:	**2.**	you were sleeping	**2.**	you	were sleeping
third person:	**3.**	he / she / it was sleeping	**3.**	they	

PAST PROGRESSIVE TENSE - NEGATIVE

		singular			**plural**
first person:	**1.**	I was not (wasn't) sleeping	**1.**	we	were not (weren't) sleeping
second person:	**2.**	you were not (weren't) sleeping	**2.**	you	were not (weren't) sleeping
third person:	**3.**	he / she / it was not (wasn't) sleeping	**3.**	they	

PAST PROGRESSIVE TENSE - YES-NO QUESTIONS

		singular			**plural**
first person:	**1.**	Was I sleeping?	**1.**	we	
second person:	**2.**	Were you sleeping?	**2.**	Were you	sleeping?
third person:	**3.**	Was he / she / it sleeping?		they	

☑ CHECK YOUR UNDERSTANDING

A. Answer the questions below.

1. How do we form the Past Progressive Tense?

_____

_____

2. When do we use the Past Progressive Tense and the Simple Past Tense in the same sentence?

_____

3. Which tense do we use to show the longer action that started first?

_____

4. Which tense do we use to show the shorter action that happened second?

_____

5. Which tense do we usually use with <u>while</u>?

_____

6. Which tense do we usually use with <u>when</u>?

_____

7. When do we use a comma in a sentence with <u>while</u> or <u>when</u>?

_____

B. Write your own sentence with two past actions.

1. Use [while] with the Past Progressive Tense in each sentence.

  a. <u>While I was playing basketball yesterday afternoon, I broke my glasses.</u>

  b. _____

_____

  c. _____

_____

2. Use [when] with the Simple Past Tense in each sentence.

  a. <u>I was thinking about my girlfriend when the teacher called on me.</u>

  b. _____

_____

  c. _____

_____

REVIEW OF VERB TENSES –

Habitual Present, Present Progressive, Simple Past and Past Progressive

➡ **Direction**: Think carefully about the meaning of the sentences below. Then write *true, false,* or *I don't know* on the line after each sentence.

I. David Baxter lives on Sacramento Street in San Francisco.

   a. He lived there five years ago.   **a.** <u>I don't know.</u>

   b. He's living there now.   **b.** <u>true</u>

   c. While David was living in San Francisco, he got married.   **c.** <u>I don't know.</u>

2. Helena was cooking dinner when the earthquake happened.

   a. Helena started to cook before the earthquake happened.   **a.** _____

   b. Dinner was ready before the earthquake happened.   **b.** _____

   c. The family was eating dinner when the earthquake happened.   **c.** _____

3. When Truong got home from work, his children were doing their homework.

   a. The children started their homework before Truong got home.   **a.** _____

   b. The children started their homework after Truong got home.   **b.** _____

   c. The children usually finish their homework before Truong gets home from work.   **c.** _____

4. Joe worked for Intel for five years.

   a. He is working at Intel now.   **a.** _____

   b. He worked at Intel two years ago.   **b.** _____

   c. He is not working at Intel now.   **c.** _____

5. While I was doing my homework in the library last night, my friend Paul walked in.

   a. I finished my homework before Paul got to the library.   **a.** _____

   b. I got to the library before Paul did.   **b.** _____

   c. Paul was studying when I left the library.   **c.** _____

6. My brother and sister-in-law are saving money for a down payment on a larger house.

   a. They have enough money to buy a house.   **a.** _____

   b. They are living in a small house now.   **b.** _____

   c. They started to save money a year ago.   **c.** _____

Writing Assignment

➠ Your writing assignment in this chapter is to write a reason and example paragraph about the best or worst job that you ever had. It can be a job that you had outside the home for pay, a volunteer job, or a job at home. Why was it your best or worst job? What are your reasons? (If you need to review the reason and example paragraph, refer to Chapter 4.)

► **What to do** ◄

1. To help you get ready to write your paragraph, go back to page 212 and re-read Etsuko's paragraph about her worst job.

2. Then choose <u>one</u> of the topic sentences below to write about.

_____ **Topic 1:** The worst job I ever had was _____

_____ **Topic 2:** The best job I ever had was _____

3. Write the first draft and the final draft of your paragraph on separate sheets of paper.

4. Follow the writing steps below.

STEP 1 Before you begin to write, take a few minutes to think about your topic. Then make a *cluster* of your ideas.

STEP 2 Write an *outline* to help you to plan your paragraph.

STEP 3 Follow your outline to write a *first draft (practice paragraph)*.

STEP 4 *Revise and edit* your practice paragraph.

STEP 5 Write your *final draft (final paragraph)*.

Chapter 9
Sentence Structure: Complex Sentences with Time Clauses

To the Student:

One way to make your writing more interesting is to use different kinds of sentences when you write. If you use only one kind of sentence, your writing may become boring to the reader. In previous chapters, you used simple sentences and compound sentences in your exercises and writing assignments. In this chapter, you will study a third kind of sentence - the **complex** sentence.

Part I

Independent and Dependent Clauses

INTRODUCTION

▸ First read the paragraph about **Student Drop-outs** to yourself. Then circle the subjects and verbs in each sentence. Compare your answers with a partner or in a small group.

Student Drop-outs

drop out: quit, leave (two-word verb)

[1]Students drop out* of school for many reasons. [2]First of all, many students drop out of school because they have problems with their work schedules. [3]In some cases, their day-shift schedule suddenly changes to the night shift, so they are unable to attend their night classes. [4]In other cases, students drop out of school because they have to work a lot of overtime. [5]As a result, it is difficult for them to get to class on time or to keep up with* their class work. [6]Second, students often drop out of school for financial reasons. [7]Many students need full-time jobs to pay their living expenses such as rent and utilities*, car insurance, tuition, and books. [8]Some married students even find it necessary to get a second job to support their families. [9]Then they usually find it impossible to meet all of their obligations*, so they drop out of school. [10]Finally, students frequently drop out of school because of family responsibilities. [11]Reliable* childcare is often a problem for mothers with small children. [12]Also, students sometimes have to miss class because of unexpected emergencies such as sick or injured children or elderly parents. [13]In short, most students drop out of school because of circumstances* beyond their control*.

keep up with: maintain

utilities: gas, electricity, water, etc.

obligations: responsibilities, duties, commitments

reliable: dependable, responsible, trustworthy

circumstances: conditions, factors, occurrences

beyond their control: something they cannot help or manage

INDEPENDENT CLAUSES AND DEPENDENT CLAUSES

> ### ▶ Learning Point
>
> A <u>clause</u> is a group of words that has <u>both</u> a **subject** and a **verb**.
>
> There are two kinds of clauses in English: **independent clauses** and **dependent clauses**.

⭢ What Is an Independent Clause?

> An independent clause is a complete thought. The meaning is clear. There are no questions in your mind. An independent clause is a sentence (S - V - C).

                                   s   v   c

1. <u>independent clause:</u> Most students want to stay in school.   (The meaning is clear.)

                                   s   v   c

2. <u>independent clause:</u> Many students have family responsibilities. (The meaning is clear.)

                              s   v   c

3. <u>independent clause:</u> Students often look for jobs on campus.   (The meaning is clear.)

                                 s   v   c

4. <u>independent clause:</u> Financial aid is sometimes available.   (The meaning is clear.)

⭢ What Is a Dependent Clause?

> A dependent clause is *not* a complete idea. A dependent clause often has a S - V - C, but it is not a sentence because the meaning is not clear. There is a question in your mind. You need more information.

                              s   v   c

1. <u>dependent clause:</u> When students miss too many classes ⟶ **What happens???**

                           s   v   c

2. <u>dependent clause:</u> If a student has serious financial problems ⟶ **What happens???**

                            s   v   c

3. <u>dependent clause:</u> Because students have to work a lot of overtime ⟶ **What happens???**

                           s   v   c

4. <u>dependent clause:</u> If parents can't find dependable child care ⟶ **What happens???**

INDEPENDENT CLAUSES AND DEPENDENT CLAUSES

⟫ **Exercise I** Identify each clause as <u>independent</u> or <u>dependent</u>. Remember that an independent clause is a sentence. It is a complete thought. Punctuate each independent clause with a capital letter and a period. Work with a classmate or in a small group.

	independent clause (complete idea)	dependent clause (not a complete idea)
W **I.** work-study jobs help students to pay for their tuition and books.	X	
2. if a student's shift at work changes		X
3. some students have to get a second job		
4. after a student gets a second job		
5. because students have many family obligations		
6. some students have to care for elderly parents or relatives		
7. when an unexpected emergency happens		
8. before a student decides to drop out of school		
9. teachers and counselors encourage students to stay in school		
10. most students do not want to drop out of school		

⟫ **Exercise 2** Follow the same directions as in Exercise 1.

	independent clause (complete idea)	dependent clause (not a complete idea)
I. because they have problems at work		
2. after their work schedule changes		
3. it is hard to find enough time to study		
4. if students get behind in their class work		
5. living expenses such as rent and utilities are expensive		
6. if one of the children gets sick		
7. when there is a death in the family		
8. mothers with small children often have trouble with babysitters		
9. because they don't have reliable transportation		
10. students find it difficult to concentrate on their school work		

Part 2
Time Clauses

WHAT ARE TIME CLAUSES?

> ### ► Learning Point
>
> Time clauses are dependent clauses that begin with words such as *when, while, before, after, as soon as.*
>
> We cannot use a time clause alone in a sentence. A time clause needs a <u>main clause</u> to complete the meaning of the sentence. We call a sentence with a time clause and a main clause a **complex sentence**.

⇒ Read the complex sentences below.

TIME CLAUSE (dependent clause)	MAIN CLAUSE (independent clause)
1. After I get off work,	I always go home first to get ready for class.
2. Before I go to class,	I often stop at McDonald's for a quick dinner.
3. When I get to school,	I usually go to the library to review my notes.
4. While I was driving to class last night,	I had a flat tire.
5. As soon as I changed the tire,	I rushed to class.
6. When I finally got to class,	the teacher was showing a film about China.
7. After we watched the film,	we had an interesting discussion about the film.
8. As soon as we finished our discussion,	the teacher asked us to write a paragraph.
9. When class was over,	my friends and I stopped for coffee.
10. Before I go home,	I always like to relax for a while with my friends.

TIME CLAUSES

⫸ **Exercise I** Read the letter below. Then write the complex sentences that contain time clauses on the lines under the paragraph. There are 5 sentences with time clauses.

May 24, 200_

Dear Fran,

   ¹We're on Day 4 of our China trip, and we're having a wonderful time. ²We arrived in the Chinese capital of Beijing three days ago. ³As soon as we checked into our hotel, we met our local tour guide, Sung Chun. ⁴The next day, Mr. Chun showed us the highlights of Beijing. ⁵First, he took us to Tiananmen Square, and then we visited the Pavilions of the Imperial Palace within the Forbidden City. ⁶At one time, the Forbidden City was accessible only to the Emperors of China, but now it is open to the public. ⁷Before we went back to our hotel, we ended our day in Beijing with a traditional Peking Duck dinner at an elegant restaurant. ⁸When we left Beijing yesterday morning, we traveled north to Badaling to see the Great Wall of China. ⁹The Emperors of China began the wall in the fifth century B.C. as a defense against the Mongols. ¹⁰The wall extends across mountains and valleys for almost 4,000 miles and is a magnificent structure. ¹¹In fact, the Great Wall is the only man-made object visible from outer space! ¹²After we left the Great Wall, we traveled to the Ming Tombs to view the final resting place of many of China's Emperors. ¹³I'm enclosing a picture of our group. ¹⁴While we were walking on the Great Wall, our tour guide took this picture. ¹⁵I'll write again soon.

Love,
Carol

sentence _____ _____
_____

sentence _____ _____
_____

sentence _____ _____
_____

sentence _____ _____
_____

sentence _____ _____
_____

THE ORDER OF TIME CLAUSES IN A SENTENCE

> ### Learning Point
>
> A time clause can come first or second in a sentence without a change in meaning.
>
> When the time clause comes first in a sentence, we put a comma after the time clause.

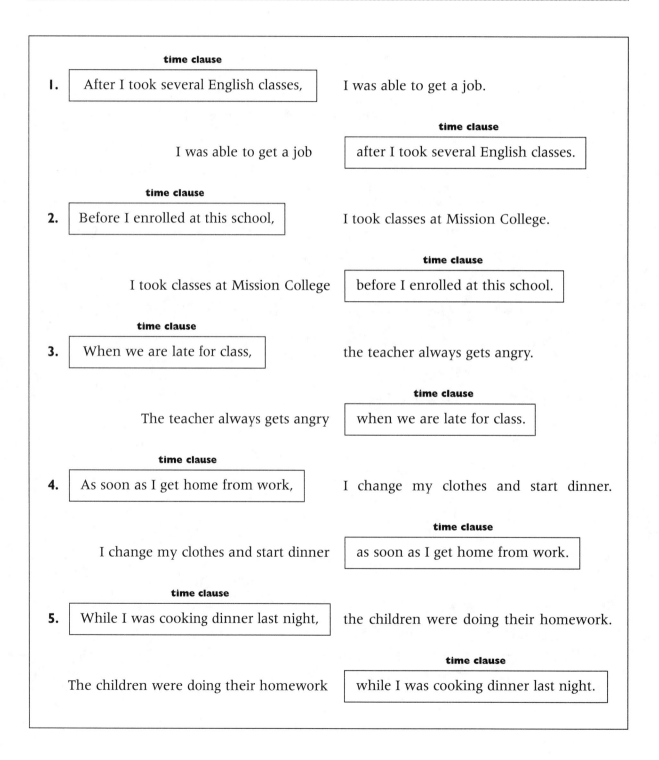

time clause

1. | After I took several English classes, | I was able to get a job.

time clause

I was able to get a job | after I took several English classes. |

time clause

2. | Before I enrolled at this school, | I took classes at Mission College.

time clause

I took classes at Mission College | before I enrolled at this school. |

time clause

3. | When we are late for class, | the teacher always gets angry.

time clause

The teacher always gets angry | when we are late for class. |

time clause

4. | As soon as I get home from work, | I change my clothes and start dinner.

time clause

I change my clothes and start dinner | as soon as I get home from work. |

time clause

5. | While I was cooking dinner last night, | the children were doing their homework.

time clause

The children were doing their homework | while I was cooking dinner last night. |

TIME CLAUSES

▐▌➡ **Exercise 2** Match the clauses in column 1 and column 2 below.

A Success Story

column 1	column 2
1. After I found a job	**a.** before I bought the car
2. I bought a car	**b.** I got a promotion and a raise at work
3. I had to get a driver's license	**c.** as soon as I saved enough money
4. When I had my own transportation	**d.** I was able to open a savings account at the Bank of America
5. I took classes in computer programming	**e.** I enrolled in an evening English class
6. As soon as I completed my certificate in data processing	**f.** after I finished my ESL classes

▐▌➡ **Exercise 3** Use the clauses in columns 1 and 2 above to write complex sentences. Remember to use a comma if the time clause comes first in the sentence.

1. __d__   After I found a job, I was able to open a savings account at the Bank
of America.

2. _____ _____

_____

3. _____ _____

_____

4. _____ _____

_____

5. _____ _____

_____

6. _____ _____

_____

SENTENCE COMBINING

▶ **Exercise 4** David Santos did very well in his English class last semester. In the exercise below, David is describing what he did to get an A in his English class. Combine the simple sentences into one sentence with a time clause. Use a comma if the time clause comes first in the sentence.

A Successful Student

1. (while)   I took careful notes.
                      The teacher was lecturing.

                      I took careful notes while the teacher was lecturing.

2. (after)   The teacher explained a new lesson.
                      I studied all the learning points carefully.

                      _____

                      _____

3. (before)   I started to do an exercise.
                      I read the directions carefully.

                      _____

                      _____

4. (when)   I asked the teacher or a classmate for help.
                      I did not understand something.

                      _____

                      _____

5. (as soon as)   I corrected my mistakes.
                      The teacher returned my papers.

                      _____

                      _____

6. (after)   The teacher wrote an assignment on the board.
                      I copied the assignment into my notebook.

                      _____

                      _____

7. (before)   I started to write a reason and example paragraph.
                      I made a cluster and an outline.

                      _____

                      _____

8. (before)   I watched TV.
                      I finished my homework.

                      _____

                      _____

Note: In a sentence with <u>when</u>, if both clauses are in the Simple Past Tense, the action in the <u>when</u> clause happened first.

SENTENCE COMBINING

▶ **Exercise 5** Chien Pham is a refugee from Vietnam. He often talks about his experiences and the difficulties he had before he was able to come to the U. S. In the exercise below, use *after*, *before*, *when*, or *as soon as* to combine Chien's sentences into one sentence with a time clause.

1. The Communists took over my country.
My parents decided to send me away.

When the Communists took over my country, my parents decided to send me away.

2. I left my country.
I said goodbye to my friends and relatives.

_____

_____

3. I escaped from my country.
I spent 22 months in a refugee camp in Thailand.

_____

_____

4. I felt sad and homesick.
I thought of my country and my family.

_____

_____

5. I was in the camp almost two years.
I received permission to come to the United States.

_____

_____

6. I was very happy.
My plane landed in San Francisco, California.

_____

_____

7. My American sponsor waved to me.
I entered the terminal at the airport.

_____

_____

8. He took me to his home in San Jose.
We picked up my baggage.

_____

_____

9. I said a prayer of thanks for my family and my sponsor.
I went to sleep that night in my new home.

_____

_____

TIME CLAUSES

➠ **Exercise 6** Add a main clause to complete each sentence. Write true statements about your life.

1. After I get up in the morning, _____

_____

2. Before I left the house yesterday morning, _____

_____

3. When the weather is nice, _____

_____

4. After I got home last night, _____

_____

5. While I was eating dinner last night, _____

_____

6. As soon as I have enough money, _____

➠ **Exercise 7** Add a time clause to complete each sentence below.

1. I am always happy when _____

_____

2. I was very tired after _____

_____

3. I made several new friends after _____

_____

4. I like to listen to music when _____

_____

5. I always finish my homework before _____

_____

6. The doorbell rang while _____

_____

Part 3
Avoiding Sentence Fragments

SENTENCE FRAGMENTS

➠ A *sentence fragment* is <u>not</u> a sentence. A sentence fragment is only a <u>part</u> of a sentence.

> ► **Learning Point**
>
> 1. When we use a time clause without a main clause, it is a sentence fragment. It is not a sentence because it is not a complete thought.
>
> 2. We must connect a time clause to a main clause to complete the meaning of a sentence.

➠ Study the examples below.

TIME CLAUSE (dependent clause)	MAIN CLAUSE (independent clause)
1. sentence <u>fragment</u>: When I start a new job.	**? ? ?**
When I start a new job,	I am always nervous.
2. sentence <u>fragment</u>: As soon as I get to know my co-workers.	**? ? ?**
As soon as I get to know my co-workers,	I start to feel more comfortable.
3. sentence <u>fragment</u>: After I am there a few weeks.	**? ? ?**
After I am there a few weeks,	I usually enjoy my job.

CORRECTING SENTENCE FRAGMENTS

➠ **Exercise 1** Teo is an ESL student from Ethiopia. He works very hard to improve his English, and he usually gets good grades in all his classes. Teo's hardest class is English composition. In the paragraph below, Teo has made a very common error. He put periods after time clauses. He forgot that a time clause is not a complete sentence. Find five sentence fragments in Teo's paragraph. Write the numbers of the fragments on the lines under the paragraph. Then do Exercise 2 on page 243.

An Act of Kindness

Marxist: *Communist*

seize: *take by force*

disguise: *hide your true identity*

migrate: *move*

illegal entry: *go into a country without permission or documents*

sponsor: *help, support, take responsibility for someone*

[1]When the Marxist* government took over my country in 1976, it was a terrible time for my country and for my family. [2]As soon as the Communists seized* power. [3]They arrested and killed thousands of people. [4]They executed my uncle and imprisoned my father. [5]My life was also in danger, so my family sent me to the Sudan. [6]I disguised* myself in dirty clothes and walked 200 miles to the Sudanese border. [7]When I reached Khartoum. [8]I found work in a hotel. [9]I cleaned bathrooms all day and slept on the roof at night. [10]After I was able to save a little money. [11]I migrated* to Egypt. [12]As soon as I got to Egypt, the Egyptian police threw me in jail for illegal entry*. [13]They agreed to free me. [14]When I promised to leave Egypt and return to the Sudan. [15]I met a young American on the riverboat on Lake Nasser on the way back to the Sudan. [16]We became friends, and he offered to help me. [17]After my American friend returned to the United States. [18]He asked his parents to sponsor* me. [19]His parents sent a letter to the United Nations, and I arrived at the John F. Kennedy Airport in New York five months later. [20]I was hungry and tired after 72 hours of continuous travel, and I had only 75 cents in my pocket.

sentence fragments: ___2___ _____ _____ _____ _____

CORRECTING SENTENCE FRAGMENTS

➡ **Exercise 2** Correct the five sentence fragments that you found in Teo's paragraph, *An Act of Kindness*, on page 242. Connect each sentence fragment in the paragraph to a main clause to form a complex sentence.

1. Connect sentences 2 and 3.

_____

_____

_____

2. Connect sentences 7 and 8.

_____

_____

_____

3. Connect sentences 10 and 11.

_____

_____

_____

4. Connect sentences 13 and 14.

_____

_____

_____

5. Connect sentences 17 and 18.

_____

_____

_____

Part 4
Simple, Compound, and Complex Sentences

SENTENCE REVIEW

> ▶ **Learning Point**
>
> You have studied three kinds of sentences:
>
> 1   Simple sentences   → one independent clause
>
> 2. Compound sentences   → two or more independent clauses
>
> 3. Complex sentences   → one independent clause and one or more dependent clauses

Simple Sentence

Independent Clause
1. We ate dinner at 6:00 last night.
2. We had chicken, rice, and a salad.
3. We had fresh strawberries for dessert.

Compound Sentence

Independent Clause		Independent Clause
1. Both my husband and I work,	so	we share the household jobs.
2. I usually cook dinner,	and	my husband washes the dishes.
3. I take our son to school in the morning,	and	my husband picks him up after school.

Complex Sentence

Independent Clause (main clause)	Dependent Clause (time clause)
1. I usually start dinner	as soon as I get home from work.
2. My son does his homework	before he watches TV.
3. My husband usually reads the paper	after he finishes the dishes.

SIMPLE, COMPOUND, AND COMPLEX SENTENCES

▶ **Exercise 1** Identify the sentences below. Write *simple, compound,* or *complex* on the line after each sentence.

Monday Morning Blues

1. Monday is the worst day of the week for me.   *simple*

2. When the alarm goes off at 5:30 on Monday morning, it is very hard for me to get out of bed. _____

3. I lie in bed awhile, and I think about the long, hard work week ahead. _____

4. When I finally get up, I immediately jump into the shower to wake up. _____

5. After I take a shower, my next job is to wake up my three children. _____

6. My children hate Monday mornings too, so I have to call them several times. _____

7. Finally, one by one the children drag themselves to the breakfast table. _____

8. While the children are eating breakfast, I make the school lunches. _____

9. As soon as breakfast is over, we immediately begin the search for lost books and homework. _____

10. By this time, it is almost seven o'clock, and it is time to leave. _____

11. Everyone jumps into the car, and we finally drive off. _____

12. At last, the ordeal of Monday morning is over! _____

SIMPLE, COMPOUND, AND COMPLEX SENTENCES

➠ **Exercise 2** Read the paragraph below. Identify the sentences in the paragraph as *simple* (**S**), *compound* (**C**), or *complex* (**CX**). Write *S*, *C*, or *CX* in the parentheses.

A Terrifying* Experience

terrifying: *frightening*

[1]I had a terrifying experience while I was riding my bike to school last Friday. (CX) [2]I was only two blocks from school when I saw a policeman. (   ) [3]He was shouting at a man to stop. (   ) [4]I turned around, and the man was only a few feet away from me. (   ) [5]When he ran by me, he pushed me off my bicycle. (   ) [6]I fell down, and he rode off on my bike. (   ) [7]At that moment, the policeman shouted, "Stop!", but the man did not stop. (   ) [8]Then the policeman fired a warning

all of a sudden: *suddenly, all at once, at that moment*

shot into the air, but the man still did not stop. (   ) [9]All of a sudden*, a car sped* around the corner and hit the man. (   ) [10]He fell off the

sped: *past tense of speed; to go very fast*

bike, and there was blood all around him on the street. (   ) [11]By this time, I was terrified, and I fainted. (   ) [12]When I came to*, the policeman was bending over me. (   ) [13]When I asked him about the

come to: *wake up, regain consciousness*

man, he shook his head. (   ) [14]The man was dead. (   ) [15]I will never forget this terrible experience. (   )

Student Paragraph

✓ CHECK YOUR UNDERSTANDING

A. Answer the questions below.

1. What is a clause? _____

_____

2. What is an independent clause? _____

_____

3. What is a dependent clause? _____

_____

4. Is an independent clause a sentence? _____ yes _____ no

5. Is a dependent clause a sentence? _____ yes _____ no

6. What are time clauses? _____

_____

7. Time clauses begin with words such as:

_____   _____   _____   _____   _____

8. When do we use a comma in a sentence with a time clause? _____

_____

B. Answer the questions below.

1. What is a sentence fragment? _____

_____

2. How do we correct a sentence fragment? _____

_____

3. What are the three kinds of sentences that you have studied?

_____   _____   _____

4. Write a simple sentence. _____

_____

5. Write a compound sentence. _____

_____

6. Write a complex sentence. _____

_____

✓ **CHECK YOUR UNDERSTANDING** (continued)

C. Practice writing complex sentences with time clauses. Give true answers to the questions below.

1. What do you usually do <u>as soon as</u> you get to work?

_____

_____

2. What did you do <u>as soon as</u> you got home last night?

_____

_____

3. What do you usually do <u>when</u> you're upset about something?

_____

_____

4. What do you do <u>when</u> you have a bad cold?

_____

_____

5. What did you do <u>after</u> you had dinner last night?

_____

_____

6. What do you usually do <u>after</u> you finish your homework?

_____

_____

7. What do you do <u>before</u> you take a test?

_____

_____

8. What do you do <u>before</u> you buy a car?

_____

_____

Writing Assignment

⇒ Your writing assignment in this chapter is to write a personal letter to a friend or family member about a funny (humorous) experience that you had recently.

► What to do ◄

1. First read the sample letter below. In the letter, Marta is writing to a friend about a humorous experience that she had recently.

2. Remember that a personal letter includes: (1) the date you are writing, (2) a greeting, and (3) a closing.

3. On a separate sheet of paper, write your own letter to a friend or family member. Describe a humorous experience that you had recently. Use the correct form for a personal letter.

---

greeting   **date**

May 20, 200_

Dear Shirley,

   Thank you for your birthday card and gift. It was nice of you to remember me! I had a great birthday. As you know, it was my fortieth birthday, and everyone teased me about getting old. When I got to work on the morning of my birthday, I found my cubicle decorated with black crepe paper and black balloons. There were several presents on my desk, and they were all wrapped in black paper with black bows. When I opened my gifts, I found a pair of reading glasses, a bottle of vitamins, a box of adult diapers, and a pin that said, "Senior Citizen". Later in the morning, my boss called us into his office for a meeting. When everyone got there, one of my co-workers carried in a huge black cake with 40 black candles. When I blew out the candles, I saw the writing on the cake. It said, "Over the hill"! Everyone was laughing except me! I'll never forget this birthday!

   Thank you again for remembering me. Write soon.

Love,

Marta

closing

Chapter 10
The Narrative Paragraph

To The Student:

In this book you are learning to write different kinds of paragraphs. In Chapter 4, you studied the **Reason and Example** paragraph. You used reasons and examples to support the topic sentence. In Chapter 7, you wrote **Descriptive** paragraphs, and you used description to support the topic sentence. In this chapter, you will study the **Narrative** paragraph. When you write a Narrative paragraph, you support the topic sentence with a story.

Part I
Prewriting

GETTING READY TO WRITE

➠ In this chapter, your writing assignment will be to write a narrative paragraph. In a narrative paragraph, you support your topic sentence with a story about a personal experience. The story might be about a terrible accident you saw on the way to work, about a happy occasion such as a wedding or a special party, about an exciting trip, or about a frightening experience. The word *narrate* means to tell a story.

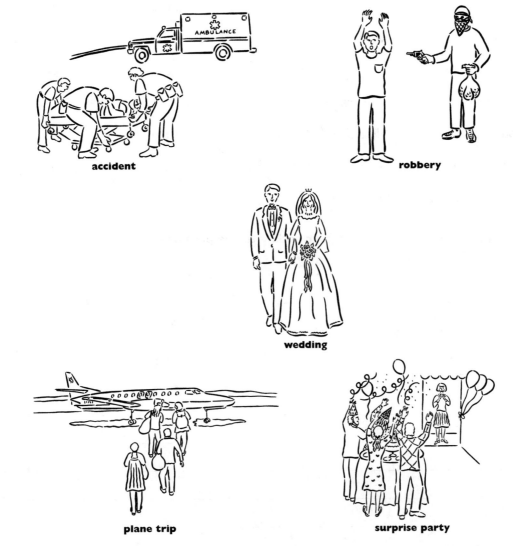

accident

robbery

wedding

plane trip

surprise party

➠ In this chapter, you will write about several personal experiences. To help you to get ready for your writing assignments, follow the prewriting instructions on the next page.

PREWRITING

Activity I

▶ What to do ◀

1. Read the narrative paragraph below about an embarrassing experience. The paragraph does not have an ending. Write an ending to the story on the lines under the paragraph.

2. Now form a group with three or four classmates.

3. How did you and your classmates end the story? Read your ending to the other students in your group.

My Most Embarrassing Experience

[1]My most embarrassing experience happened soon after I graduated from the university. [2]I was a new teacher at a high school in Mexico City. [3]One morning, my alarm clock did not ring because I forgot to wind it the night before. [4]I did not wake up until seven o'clock, and school began at seven-thirty. [5]I quickly washed, shaved, got dressed, jumped into my car, and drove to school. [6]When I arrived, the students were already in class. [7]I walked into the classroom and quickly started the lesson. [8]After two or three minutes, all the students began to laugh, and I could not understand why! [9]Suddenly, I looked down, and I understood.

How do you think the story ended? Write your ending to the paragraph here.

_____

_____

_____

_____

_____

_____

_____

_____

_____

_____

_____

_____

_____

PREWRITING

Activity 2

► **What to do** ◄

1. In Activity 1, you wrote your own ending to a story about an embarrassing experience. Then you shared your ending with the other students in your group.

2. Now read the paragraph below about a painful experience. The paragraph does not have an ending. Write an ending to the story on the lines under the paragraph.

3. Then read your ending to the other students in your group.

A Terrible Misunderstanding

[1]The most painful experience in my life was the misunderstanding that I had with my first girlfriend. [2]Her name was Kien. [3]I fell in love with her when I was in high school in Ho Chi Minh City. [4]After I finished high school, I joined the army. [5]I was stationed in Dalat, about 300 kilometers from Ho Chi Minh City. [6]Kien and I wrote to each other often and maintained a close relationship. [7]After a few months, I had a week's leave*. [8]I called Kien in advance and arranged to pick her up when I got to town. [9]However, when I got to her house, she was not there. [10]I was very upset and went to a snack bar a few blocks from her house. [11]Suddenly, I saw Kien. [12]She was sitting at a table across the room with a young man. [13]I was devastated*. [14]I hurriedly called the waiter, paid for my drink, and rushed out of the snack bar. [15]After that time, I refused to answer Kien's letters and threw them all into the fire. [16]A few months later, Kien brought the same young man to my army camp.

How do you think the story ended? Write your ending to the paragraph here.

_____

_____

_____

_____

_____

_____

_____

_____

Vocabulary Notes   *__leave__: time away from military duty*   *__devastated__: very upset*

Part 2
Using a Story to Support the Topic Sentence

THE NARRATIVE PARAGRAPH

▥➡ In this chapter, you will write a narrative paragraph. When you write a narrative paragraph, you support your topic sentence with a story about a personal experience. You tell your readers what happened to you and why it was important to you. Why was your experience embarrassing? Why was it frightening? Why was it funny? Remember, a paragraph is usually about 150 to 200 words long, so do not try to tell your readers your whole life story in one paragraph. You need to write about a personal experience that happened in a short period of time.

In the student paragraph below, Thanh Ho wrote about a funny experience that happened on the day of his first job interview.

A Humorous Experience

[1]My most humorous* experience happened on the day of my first job interview. [2]At the time, however, I did not think that it was funny at all. [3]My interview was at 1:00, and I did not want to be late. [4]I drove into town and was lucky enough to find a parking space in front of the building. [5]I was just starting to back into the space when another car drove into it. [6]I was furious. [7]I opened my window and yelled angrily at the other driver. [8]He ignored* me and walked away. [9]It took me twenty minutes to find another parking place. [10]As soon as I parked the car, I rushed back to the company. [11]I was very upset because by this time I was ten minutes late for my appointment. [12]When I found the personnel manager's office, I knocked at the door and walked into the office. [13]The man behind the desk was the man who stole my parking place! [14]He smiled and asked me to sit down. [15]He knew why I was late.

Thanh Ho

Vocabulary Notes   *__humorous__: funny, amusing   *__ignore__: pay no attention to, disregard

THE NARRATIVE PARAGRAPH

▌➡ Read the model paragraphs below. Then answer the questions on page 256.

Model Paragraph 1   A Frightening Experience

[1]The most frightening experience in my life happened when I was seventeen years old. [2]I still remember it clearly. [3]It happened on a Friday afternoon in the girls' locker room at my high school. [4]On Fridays, everyone was always in a hurry to get out of school, so I thought that I was the only one in the locker room. [5]I decided to take a shower before I went home. [6]I took off my clothes and underwear and walked to the shower. [7]I did not worry because I did not think that anyone was there to see me. [8]I sang and enjoyed the shower very much. [9]After my shower, I walked back to my locker with no clothes on. [10]While I was drying my hair, I felt that someone was looking at me. [11]I turned my head, and I saw the janitor! [12]I screamed, but luckily for me, the janitor was a woman. [13]After this experience, I never stayed alone in the locker room again.

                                                    Student Paragraph

Model Paragraph 2   A Busy Day

[1]I had cold cereal for breakfast yesterday morning, and then I went to work. [2]A few of us went to Taco Rico for lunch. [3]I had a taco and a beef burrito, and my two friends had enchiladas and soft tacos. [4]We got back to work at about 1:00. I spent the whole afternoon at my computer. [5]First, I typed three letters, and then I made new labels for my file folders. [6]I also answered the phone several times. [7]It was a very busy afternoon. [8]After work, I picked up my jacket and pants at the cleaner's. [9]Then I stopped at Safeway and picked up some TV dinners, a loaf of bread, and a couple of frozen pizzas. [10]When I got home, I put one of the pizzas into the oven and turned on the TV. [11]After dinner, I fell asleep on the couch while I was watching an old movie.

                                                    Student Paragraph

QUESTIONS ABOUT THE MODEL PARAGRAPHS

⟹ **Activity 1** Answer the questions below about the model paragraphs on page 255.

1. Why was the writer of paragraph 1 frightened?

_____

_____

_____

2. What did the writer of paragraph 1 learn from her frightening experience?

_____

_____

_____

3. Which story did you enjoy more, paragraph 1, *A Frightening Experience*, or paragraph 2, *A Busy Day*?

_____

_____

_____

4. Would you like to read more stories by the writer of paragraph 2, *A Busy Day*?

_____

_____

_____

5. After you read paragraph 2, did you ask yourself, "Why did this person write this boring story?"

_____

_____

_____

6. Why do you think that paragraph 2 about *A Busy Day* is boring?

_____

_____

_____

Part 3
Paragraph Skills

THE ORGANIZATION OF A NARRATIVE PARAGRAPH

➡ In a narrative paragraph, we support the topic sentence with a story. All of the sentences in the story explain and support the topic sentence. The concluding sentence usually tells why the experience was important to us or what we learned from the experience.

TOPIC SENTENCE

Tells the reader why you are writing about a personal experience

STORY

A series of events that happened in a short period of time. All the events support the topic sentence.

CONCLUDING SENTENCE

Repeats the idea of the topic sentence or tells why the experience was important to you

TOPIC SENTENCE ______________________________

____

STORY

____

CONCLUDING SENTENCE ______________________________

____

CHRONOLOGICAL ORDER (TIME ORDER)

⟹ When we write a narrative paragraph, we write the events in the story in the order that they happened. We call this <u>chronological order</u>. Chronological order means <u>time order</u>. For example, in the narrative paragraph below, Shahida Kumar used time order to organize the events in her story. She wrote the sentences in the story in the order that they happened.

A Big Fire

¹The most frightening time in my life was the day that my next-door neighbor's house burned down. ²It happened on a hot summer day in July. ³My mother and I were cooking in the kitchen when I saw black smoke outside our kitchen window. ⁴Then we heard the loud sirens of the fire trucks. ⁵My mother and I ran out of our house to see what was happening. ⁶Our neighbor's house was on fire! ⁷Several fire fighters were running toward the house with long hoses. ⁸They quickly hooked up the hoses and began to spray the house with powerful streams of water. ⁹Suddenly, a woman began to scream and point toward the top of the house. ¹⁰A little boy was trapped on the roof. ¹¹The fire fighters immediately placed a tall ladder against the house, and one of them climbed up to the roof and rescued the little boy. ¹²The paramedics put the boy into an ambulance and rushed him to the hospital. ¹³I was too frightened to move, so I just stood and watched. ¹⁴While the fire fighters were fighting the fire at my neighbor's house, they also hosed down the houses on either side to protect them from the fire. ¹⁵In about thirty minutes, the fire was out. ¹⁶My house was safe, but my neighbor's house was burned to the ground.

Shahida Kumar

CHRONOLOGICAL ORDER (TIME ORDER)

➡ **Activity I** The events in the story below are not in chronological order. Write a number in front of each sentence to arrange the events in the correct time order. Sentence number 1 is the topic sentence.

The Good Samaritan*

_____ Then, a few weeks ago, an attorney called me. The attorney told me that Mr. Forbes had died and asked me to stop by his office the next day to pick up a letter.

_____ The paramedics quickly got him out of the car and onto a stretcher and immediately started CPR* (cardiopulmonary resuscitation).

_____ I pulled over to the side of the road to see what was wrong.

___1___ Kindness often has surprising results.

_____ I found the pills and put one under his tongue. Then I rushed off to find an emergency phone to dial 911.

_____ The next day, I called the hospital to find out how the man was, and they told me that Mr. Forbes was doing well and out of danger.

_____ Early last year, I was driving home in heavy traffic when I saw a car stalled* at the side of the highway. I could see that the driver was slumped over the steering wheel.

_____ The window on the passenger side was open, so I leaned in and tried to arouse* the driver. The driver managed to tell me that he had heart trouble and asked me to get his heart pills out of the glove compartment.

_____ After that, I raced back to the stricken* man. He was unconscious. I stayed with him until an ambulance and two police cars arrived.

_____ When I got to the attorney's office, I opened the letter from Mr. Forbes and, to my amazement*, I found that he had left me $100,000 in his will!

_____ Several months passed, and I never thought of the incident* again.

_____ While the paramedics were giving him CPR, the police asked me to describe what happened.

Vocabulary Notes   *__good Samaritan:__ *someone who helps another person in trouble*   *__stricken:__ *seriously ill*
*__amazement:__ *surprise*
*__CPR:__ *revive someone who is not breathing and whose heart has stopped*   *__incident:__ *event*
*__stalled:__ *not running, stopped*
*__arouse:__ *wake up, awaken*

CHRONOLOGICAL ORDER (TIME ORDER)

Activity 2 Use the sentences in Activity 1 on page 259 to write a narrative paragraph about **The Good Samaritan**. Be careful to write the sentences in the correct time order. Remember to write the title of the paragraph and to indent the first sentence.

_____

_____

_____

_____

_____

_____

_____

_____

_____

_____

_____

_____

_____

_____

_____

_____

_____

_____

_____

_____

_____

_____

_____

_____

_____

_____

✓ CHECK YOUR UNDERSTANDING

A. Answer the questions below.

  1. What is a narrative paragraph? _____

  _____

  2. What does the word <u>narrate</u> mean? _____

  _____

  3. What are the three parts of a narrative paragraph?

  _____   _____   _____

  4. How do we support the topic sentence of a narrative paragraph? _____

  _____

  5. What is chronological order? _____

  _____

B. Write *true* or *false* on the line after each statement below.

  When you write a narrative paragraph, you should write about:

  1. the story of your life   _____

  2. one important personal experience   _____

  3. an experience that happened in a short period of time _____

  4. several different experiences that happened to you   _____

  5. why your experience was important to you   _____

Part 4
Getting Ready to Write

GETTING READY TO WRITE A NARRATIVE PARAGRAPH

▶ Now you are ready to write your own narrative paragraph. Before you begin, study the steps that a student, Peter Chang, used when he wrote a narrative paragraph about his automobile accident.

STEP 1 PRE-WRITING: BRAINSTORMING

▶ In Chapter 7, you learned that brainstorming can help you to get your ideas down on paper quickly. When you brainstorm, you make a list of every idea that comes into your mind. A good way to get ideas for a narrative paragraph is to ask yourself questions about the experience that you are going to write about. The most basic question words are <u>who</u>, <u>what</u>, <u>where</u>, <u>when</u>, <u>why</u>, and <u>how</u>. Ask yourself: Who was there? What happened? When did it happen? Why did it happen? How did it happen?

Below is the brainstorming list that Peter made to get ideas for his paragraph about his accident. Notice that Peter did not write complete sentences.

BRAINSTORMING LIST

8 months ago	fainted
thankful - not seriously hurt	woke up in hospital
truck rear-ended* me	couldn't remember anything
driving to work	police came
on Bascom Avenue	called the insurance company
big white truck	had bad dreams
tailgating*	couldn't drive
driving too fast	frightened and upset
not my fault	
stopped at a yellow light	

Vocabulary Notes   ***rear-end:*** *hit the car in front of you*   ***tailgate:*** *drive very close to the car in front of you*

STEP 2 WRITE A FIRST DRAFT (PRACTICE PARAGRAPH)

➡ When Peter finished brainstorming and making a list of ideas about his automobile accident, he chose ideas from his brainstorming list to help him to write his first draft (practice paragraph).

After Peter wrote the first draft of his paragraph, he read the paragraph carefully to see if he could improve it.

1. First, he **revised** his paragraph. **Revise** means to add, move, or take out sentences. Revise also means to rewrite any confusing sentences. As Peter read his paragraph, he asked himself, "Did I use plenty of specific details to show why my accident was frightening? Are any of my details off-topic? Did I write the events of the story in chronological order? Does the paragraph have a concluding sentence?"

2. Then Peter **edited** his paragraph. **Edit** means to correct any errors in grammar, spelling, and the use of capital letters and periods.

The paragraph below is Peter's practice paragraph. Look at the changes and corrections that he made. He made all the changes and corrections on his practice paragraph.

the Accident ← *Capitalize the title*

indent →   *eight months ago*

My most frightening experience happened while I was driving to work. The traffic on highway 280

was   *to (infinitive)*

very heavy, so I decided get off the freeway. I took the Bascom Avenue exit south. As I was driving

looked   *a*

down Bascom Avenue, I look in my rearview mirror and saw big white truck behind me. When I got to

the

the intersection of Bascom and Moorpark, light turned yellow. I stepped on the brakes and

not   *Fix time order*

stopped. He slammed on his brakes, but he couldn't stop in time, so he hit me. The driver of the

truck behind me did not expect me to stop. In fact, he hit me so hard that my car ran up the

sidewalk. I was able to turn off the engine of my car, and then I fainted. When I came to, I was in

the emergency room at the hospital. ~~The emergency room was crowded.~~ My head hurt, and at first

I could not remember anything about the accident. Then the police came and asked me to fill out

After that,

an accident report. I called my wife, and she came to the hospital to take me home.

For the next couple of weeks, I was too frightened to drive my car. To this day, I feel

nervous every time I stop at a yellow light.

Peter Chang

STEP 3 - WRITE THE FINAL DRAFT (FINAL PARAGRAPH)

➡ After Peter **revised** and **edited** (changed and corrected) his practice paragraph on page 263, he was ready to write his final paragraph. Read Peter's final paragraph below.

The Accident

My most frightening experience happened eight months ago while I 1 was driving to work. The traffic on highway 280 was very heavy*, so I decided to get off the freeway. I took the Bascom Avenue exit south. As I was driving down Bascom Avenue, I looked in my rearview mirror and saw a big white truck behind me. When I got to the intersection of 5 Bascom and Moorpark, the light turned yellow, and I stopped. The driver of the truck behind me did not expect me to stop. He slammed on his brakes*, but he could not stop in time, so he hit me. In fact, he hit me so hard that my car ran up onto the sidewalk. Fortunately*, there were no pedestrians* on the sidewalk. I was able to turn off the 10 engine of my car, and then I fainted. When I came to, I was in the emergency room at the hospital. My head hurt, and at first I could not remember anything about the accident. Then the police came and asked me to fill out an accident report. After that, I called my wife, and she came to the hospital to take me home. For the next couple of weeks, I 15 was too frightened to drive my car. To this day, I feel nervous every time I stop at a yellow light.

Peter Chang

traffic was very heavy: there were a lot of cars on the road

slammed on his brakes: hit his brakes hard

fortunately: luckily

pedestrians: people who are walking, people on foot

📝 Writing Assignment

▦➡ Your writing assignment in this chapter is to write a narrative paragraph about a personal experience that was important to you.

▶ **What to do** ◀

1. Think of an experience that you want to write about.

2. Choose an adjective from the box below to describe your experience.

happiest	most memorable
saddest	most frightening

3. Write a topic sentence for your paragraph on the lines below.

Note: If you need help writing your topic sentence, use one of the following sentence patterns:

My _____ experience happened on the day that _____.
    (adjective)

My _____ experience happened when _____.
    (adjective)

My _____ experience was the time when _____.
    (adjective)

your topic _____
sentence:

_____

_____

Writing Assignment

STEP 1 - BRAINSTORMING

➡ Now that you have chosen a personal experience from page 265 to write about, take a few minutes to think about your topic. Write your topic sentence here.

your topic   _____
sentence:
                  _____

                  _____

Now make a brainstorming list to help you to get your ideas down on paper quickly. Write every idea that comes into your mind. To help you to get started, ask yourself *who? what? where? when? why?* and *how?* Do not write complete sentences, and do not worry about grammar or spelling in your list.

BRAINSTORMING LIST

_____   _____

_____   _____

_____   _____

_____   _____

_____   _____

_____   _____

_____   _____

_____   _____

_____   _____

_____   _____

_____   _____

_____   _____

_____   _____

_____   _____

Writing Assignment

STEP 2 - WRITE A FIRST DRAFT (PRACTICE PARAGRAPH)

▶ **What to do** ◀

1. Now that you have written the basic facts of your story on your brainstorming list on page 266, you are ready to write the first draft of your paragraph.

2. You need to use clear, specific details to make your readers see and understand your experience. Do not write off-topic details that do not explain and support your topic sentence.

3. Put the events of your story in chronological order (time order).

4. Limit your paragraph to a short period of time. Do not write your whole life story. Write about <u>one</u> specific experience to support your topic sentence.

5. Double space your paragraph, and circle the subject(s) and verb(s) in each sentence. Be sure to give your paragraph a title.

Writing Assignment

FIRST DRAFT (CONTINUED)

_____

_____

_____

_____

_____

_____

_____

_____

_____

_____

_____

_____

_____

_____

_____

STEP 3 - REVISE AND EDIT YOUR PARAGRAPH

► What to do ◄

1. When you are finished writing your practice paragraph, read your paragraph to yourself.

2. Revise your paragraph.

   Are all of your sentences clear and easy to understand? Do you want to add, move, or take out sentences? If you need to make changes, make them on your practice paragraph.

3. Edit your paragraph.

   Are there any mistakes in grammar, spelling, capital letters, or periods? Did you use correct paragraph form? If you need to make corrections, make them on your practice paragraph.

4. When you are finished revising and editing your paragraph, write your name on the Review Sheet on page 269, and give your book to a partner. Your partner will read and review your paragraph.

Partner Review Sheet

Paragraph written by _____

Paragraph reviewed by _____

➡ *To the Reviewer:* Read your partner's paragraph carefully. Then answer the questions below about your partner's paragraph. Do not write on your partner's paper.

1. Does your partner's paragraph have a title?

_____ yes　　　_____ no

2. Write the topic sentence of your partner's paragraph here.

_____

_____

3. Does the paragraph have a story that explains and supports the topic sentence and a concluding sentence?

_____ yes　　　_____ no

4. Did your partner put the events of his/her story in chronological order?

_____ yes　　　_____ no

5. Which sentence is true about your partner's paragraph?

_____ **a.** All the sentences in my partner's paragraph support the topic sentence.

_____ **b.** My partner's paragraph is not clear because some of the sentences are off-topic.

6. Do all of the sentences in the paragraph begin with a capital letter and end with a period?

_____ yes　　　_____ no

7. Did your partner circle the subject(s) and verb(s) in each sentence?

_____ yes　　　_____ no

➡ *To the Reviewer:* When you are finished reviewing your partner's paragraph, return your partner's book.

Writing Assignment

STEP 5 - WRITE YOUR FINAL DRAFT (FINAL PARAGRAPH)

When your partner returns your book, make any necessary changes or corrections on your practice paragraph. Now you are ready to write the final draft of your paragraph.

▶ **What to do** ◀

1. Write your final paragraph in ink on a separate sheet of paper. Write as neatly as possible, and use correct paragraph form.

2. Double space your paragraph, and write on only one side of the paper.

3. When you finish your paragraph, underline or highlight the topic sentence and the concluding sentence.

4. Circle the subject(s) and verb(s) in each sentence.

 Additional Writing Topics

Reason and Example Paragraphs

Topic 1: My Funniest Experience

Topic 2: My Worst Experience

Topic 3: My Most Embarrassing Experience

Chapter 11
Writing About the Future

Part 1: The Future with <u>Will</u>

Part 2: The Future with <u>Be Going to</u>

Part 3: Future Time in Time Clauses

Writing Assignment

To the Student:

You have learned that verbs tell us the time that an action in a sentence happened. In previous chapters you used different verb tenses to write about present time and past time. In this chapter, you will study two ways to write about future time. You will study future with <u>will</u> and future with <u>be going to.</u>

Part I
The Future with <u>Will</u>

THE SIMPLE FUTURE TENSE

➠ In this chapter you will use <u>will</u> and <u>be going to</u> to express future time. You will begin with the Simple Future Tense with <u>will</u>.

> ### Learning Point
>
> We use <u>will</u> to talk about events that will happen in the future or events that will probably happen in the future.

➠ Study the examples below.

FUTURE TIME WORDS
tomorrow
tomorrow night
next <u>week</u>
soon
in two hours

At Home

1. My son <u>will be</u> twenty-one on his next birthday.

2. We <u>will</u> probably <u>have</u> a big party to celebrate this special occasion.

3. We <u>will invite</u> all our friends and relatives to join in our celebration.

At Work

1. My boss <u>will retire</u> next year.

2. He <u>will</u> probably <u>move</u> to a place with a warmer climate such as Florida or Arizona.

3. All the employees in our group <u>will miss</u> him.

At School

1. Next semester our school <u>will buy</u> twenty new computers and <u>install</u> them in the school library.

2. Students <u>will have</u> access to the Internet.

3. They <u>will be</u> able to send E-mail to students at colleges and universities all over the world.

Leisure Time

1. My family and I <u>will fly</u> to London next week.

2. My brother <u>will</u> probably <u>drive</u> us to the airport.

3. It <u>will take</u> about nine hours to get to London.

<u>Note</u>: You will study future with <u>be going to</u> in Part 2.

FORMING THE SIMPLE FUTURE TENSE (WILL)

> ▶ **Learning Point**
>
> I. We use the helping verb <u>will</u> + the <u>root form</u> of the main verb to form the Simple Future Tense.
>
> 2. To form contractions in the Simple Future Tense, we combine the subject pronoun and the helping verb <u>will</u>. (I will→ I'll   he will → he'll   they will → they'll)

⟶ Forms of the Simple Future Tense

<u>singular</u>

I.	I will (I'll)	
2.	you will (you'll)	work
3.	he will (he'll) she will (she'll) it will (it'll)	

<u>plural</u>

I.	we will (we'll)	
2.	you will (you'll)	work
3.	they will (they'll)	

⟶ Word Order of Affirmative Sentences

SUBJECT	HELPING VERB	MAIN VERB (ROOT FORM)	COMPLEMENT
I. I	will	see	you in class tomorrow.
2. You	will	enjoy	the new Internet class next semester.
3. He	will	graduate	in June.
4. She	will	give	a speech at the graduation ceremony.
5. It	will	be	a busy semester.
6. We	will	work	hard to pass all our classes.
7. You	will	have	final exams in the last week of May.
8. They	will	transfer	to the university next September.

<u>Note:</u>   It is not common to use <u>shall</u> in American English. However, you will sometimes hear <u>shall</u> in questions with first person pronouns (I, we) to make a suggestion.

<u>Example:</u> Are you cold? Shall I close the windows?

THE SIMPLE FUTURE TENSE

➡ My roommate Sally buys a lottery ticket every week. She believes that one day she will win the lottery. Last night she had a wonderful dream. In her dream she was holding the winning ticket. The numbers on the ticket were 63216. When she woke up, she rushed to the store to buy a ticket. She marked the ticket with the numbers from her dream. She is sure that she will win $1 million in next Saturday's drawing!

➡ **Exercise 1** Use your imagination! What do you think Sally will do with her million dollars if she wins the lottery next Saturday? Write future sentences with the verbs in parentheses. Practice using contractions in your sentences.

(take)   **1.** <u>She'll take a trip around the world.</u>

(buy)   **2.** _____

(quit)   **3.** _____

(go)   **4.** _____

(travel)   **5.** _____

(move)   **6.** _____

(sleep)   **7.** _____

(give)   **8.** _____

(get)   **9.** _____

(visit)   **10.** _____

(donate)   **11.** _____

*(pay off) **12.** _____

Vocabulary Note ***pay off:*** *(two-word verb) pay all of a debt*

MAKING PREDICTIONS ABOUT THE FUTURE WITH <u>WILL</u>

▶ **Exercise 2** A <u>prediction</u> is what we think will happen in the future. Think about your classmates. What do you think they will do in the future? Use <u>will</u> to make predictions about some of your classmates.

PREDICTIONS ABOUT SOME OF MY CLASSMATES

Classmate 1: *Peter will move to Hollywood and become a famous movie star.*

Classmate 2: _____

_____

Classmate 3: _____

_____

Classmate 4: _____

_____

Classmate 5: _____

_____

▶ **Exercise 3** Now think about <u>your</u> future. What do you think you will do in the future? Use <u>will</u> to make predictions about your own future.

PREDICTIONS ABOUT MY FUTURE

Prediction 1: _____

_____

Prediction 2: _____

_____

Prediction 3: _____

_____

Prediction 4: _____

_____

Prediction 5: _____

_____

FORMING NEGATIVE SENTENCES WITH <u>WILL</u>

> ### Learning Point
>
> 1. To form negative sentences in the Simple Future Tense, we use the helping verb <u>**will**</u> + <u>**not**</u> and the <u>**root form**</u> of the main verb.
>
> 2. We combine <u>will</u> and <u>not</u> to form the negative contraction <u>**won't**</u>.
>   Notice the change in spelling (will not ⟶ won't).

<u>Example:</u> 1. affirmative: We will have our final exam next Thursday.

   negative: We <u>will not</u> (won't) have our final exam next Thursday.
                     ↑   ↑
                    hv   **main verb**

2. affirmative: The exam will be very difficult.

   negative: The exam <u>will not</u> (won't) be very difficult.
                         ↑   ↑
                        hv   **main verb**

Simple Future Tense - Negative Form

	<u>singular</u>			<u>plural</u>	
1.	I		**1.**	we	
2.	you	will not (won't) work	**2.**	you	will not (won't) work
3.	he		**3.**	they	
	she				
	it				

Word Order of Negative Sentences

SUBJECT	HELPING VERB + NOT	MAIN VERB (ROOT FORM)	COMPLEMENT
1. I		be	ready for a few more minutes.
2. You		have	a test next week.
3. He		take	a history class next semester.
4. She	will not (won't)	attend	the meeting next Friday.
5. It		be	hot tomorrow.
6. We		forget	to call you tonight.
7. You		have	any trouble with the next homework assignment.
8. They		return	to school next year.

NEGATIVE SENTENCES

▶ **Exercise 4** When students start a new quarter or semester, they usually have a lot of good intentions. They don't want to repeat their mistakes and bad habits from the previous semester. Use the verbs in the chart below to complete the list of one student's good intentions. Use each verb only once. The sentences will all be negative.

copy	fall	do	* turn in
go	forget	be	* stay up
talk	miss	✔ leave	wait

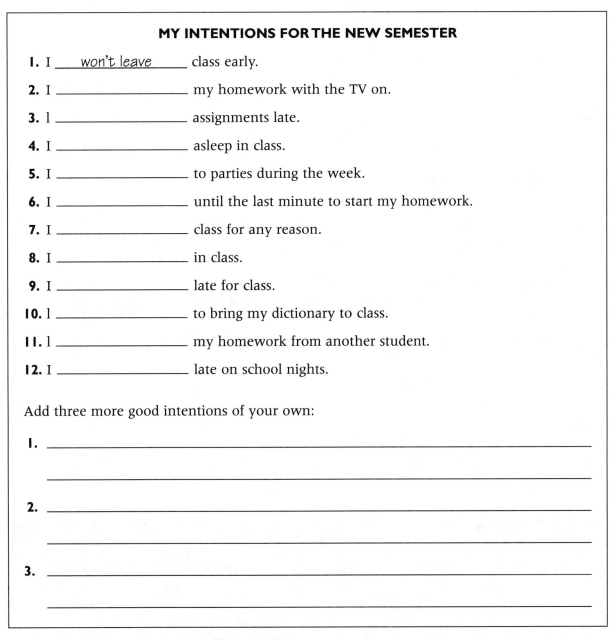

MY INTENTIONS FOR THE NEW SEMESTER

1. I ____won't leave____ class early.

2. I _____ my homework with the TV on.

3. I _____ assignments late.

4. I _____ asleep in class.

5. I _____ to parties during the week.

6. I _____ until the last minute to start my homework.

7. I _____ class for any reason.

8. I _____ in class.

9. I _____ late for class.

10. I _____ to bring my dictionary to class.

11. I _____ my homework from another student.

12. I _____ late on school nights.

Add three more good intentions of your own:

1. _____

_____

2. _____

_____

3. _____

_____

Vocabulary Notes * **turn in**: *(two-word verb) give, hand in*
* **stay up**: *(two-word verb) not go to bed*

AFFIRMATIVE AND NEGATIVE SENTENCES

Exercise 5 Use the Simple Future Tense with <u>will</u> and the verbs in parentheses to complete the conversations below. Then practice the conversations with a partner.

I. *A Company Picnic:* It is the end of the summer, and Nancy and her co-workers want to have a picnic at a park near their office.

Nancy: Let's have the picnic at Jefferson Park at lunch time next Friday. I <u>'ll call</u> **(1. call)** the Parks and Recreation Department and reserve an area for our group.

Peter: Good idea. I _____ **(2. provide)** the hamburgers and hot dogs, and Dave _____ **(3. help)** me to barbecue them.

Carmen: I _____ **(4. bring)** potato salad, and I_____ **(5. bring)** lettuce and tomatoes from my garden for the sandwiches.

Nancy: I _____ **(6. ask)** Wendy to make one of her famous triple chocolate cakes for dessert. They're delicious.

Carmen: Can Ted bring his CD player and cassettes?

Peter: No. Ted _____ **(7. not / be)** able to come to the picnic. He has an important meeting with some customers that day.

2. *A Worried Student:* Thanh is having a lot of trouble in his history class, and he is worried about his grades. He is talking to his friend Paul about his problems.

Paul: Did you have your midterm last night?

Thanh: Yes, I did. It was hard.

Paul: How did you do?

Thanh: I don't know. We _____ **(1. not / get)** our tests back until next week. The teacher _____ **(2. correct)** them over the weekend.

Paul: That's too bad. You _____ **(3. worry)** about your grade all weekend.

Thanh: You're right. In fact, I _____ **(4. worry)** about this class for the rest of the semester. If I pass this course, I _____ **(5. not / take)** another history class!

Note: In conversation, we can use contractions with both nouns and pronouns (Mary'll come, she'll come). In writing, we do not use contractions with nouns (~~Mary~~'ll come).

USING <u>PROBABLY</u> IN SENTENCES WITH <u>WILL</u>

> ▶ **Learning Point**
>
> 1. When we talk about the future, we are not always sure what will happen. For this reason, it is very common to use the word **probably** in sentences with <u>will</u>.
>
> 2. You must be careful where you put the word <u>probably</u> in affirmative and negative sentences.

▸ Affirmative Sentences

Put <u>probably</u> between the helping verb <u>will</u> and the main verb.

a. It's getting cloudy. It will ⟨hv⟩ | probably | rain ⟨mv⟩ tomorrow.

b. We'll ⟨hv⟩ | probably | have ⟨mv⟩ a quiz in our math class on Monday. We just finished Chapter 8.

c. I need to buy a birthday present for my cousin. I'll ⟨hv⟩ | probably | give ⟨mv⟩ him a gift certificate.

▸ Negative Sentences with <u>Won't</u>

Put <u>probably</u> before the negative contraction <u>won't</u>.

a. I | probably | won't be in class tomorrow. My cold is getting worse.

b. The plane was delayed in Chicago. It | probably | won't arrive for another two hours.

c. The big football game is nearly sold out, so we | probably | won't be able to get tickets.

▸ Negative Sentences with <u>Will Not</u>

In formal sentences, put <u>probably</u> between the helping verb <u>will</u> and <u>not</u>.

a. The President will ⟨hv⟩ | probably | not ⟨not⟩ attend the trade conference in Canada next week.

b. The doctor is at the hospital. He will ⟨hv⟩ | probably | not ⟨not⟩ be able to see you until tomorrow.

c. Jerry's job interview at IBM did not go very well. He will ⟨hv⟩ | probably | not ⟨not⟩ get the job.

USING **PROBABLY** IN SENTENCES WITH **WILL**

▶ **Exercise 6** Use probably and the words in parentheses to make a prediction about each situation below. Some of your predictions will be affirmative, and some will be negative. Work with a partner.

Situation 1   Our landlord just raised our rent again, and we're having trouble meeting our expenses.

(look for)   We'll probably look for a cheaper apartment.

Situation 2   Susan and Jeff met each other at a friend's party about eight months ago. Now they spend all their time together.

(get married)   _____

Situation 3   My friends and I ate at a new Italian restaurant last night. The food was okay, but the restaurant was very noisy, and the service was slow.

(go back)   _____

Situation 4   My mother is very angry at my new puppy. He cries all night and keeps her awake. Yesterday, he chewed the legs of her dining room table.

(give away)   _____

Situation 5   Mike had a job interview yesterday. He got there late and didn't bring a resume.

(get the job)   _____

Situation 6   My department at work is very busy, and we have a big deadline at the end of next week.

(work overtime)   _____

Situation 7   James wants to go camping in Wyoming on his vacation this year, but his wife and children want to go to Disney World in Florida.

(spend their vacation)   _____

Situation 8   Peter and Kim need to get a new car, but Peter just got laid off.

(be able to buy)   _____

ASKING YES-NO QUESTIONS WITH <u>WILL</u>

> ### ▶ Learning Point
>
> To form Yes-No Questions in the Simple Future Tense, we put the helping verb <u>will</u> in front of the subject. We always use the <u>root form</u> of the main verb in questions.

Example: **1.** **A:** Will you be home tomorrow night?

B: Yes, I will. I'll be home all evening.

2. **A:** Will you lend me $10.00?

B: No, I won't. You still owe me $10.00 from last week.

➡ Simple Future Tense – Yes-No Questions

	singular			plural	
1.			**1.**		
2. Will	I / you / he / she / it	work?	**2.** Will	we / you / they	work?
3.			**3.**		

➡ Word Order of Yes-No Questions

	HELPING VERB	SUBJECT	MAIN VERB (ROOT FORM)	COMPLEMENT	SHORT ANSWERS FOR CONVERSATION
1.	Will	Ruth	leave	for college soon?	Yes, she will.
2.	Will	she	live	in an apartment?	No, she won't.
3.	Will	she	take	her computer and her printer?	Yes, she will.
4.	Will	her parents	help	her to move her things?	Yes, they will.
5.	Will	Ruth	feel	sad to leave home?	No, she won't.

YES-NO QUESTIONS

➤ **Exercise 7** Although no one knows for sure what will happen in the future, everyone has some ideas about what the future will be like. In the paragraph below, Dr. Valerie Whiteson talks about her predictions for the future. Read Dr. Whiteson's paragraph.

The World of the Future

cycle of life: be born, mature, grow old, and die

physical characteristics: what someone looks like, for example, hair color, color of eyes, etc.

conceived in test tubes: test-tube baby, a baby born as the result of artificial insemination

transplanted organs: organs (such as heart or liver) moved from one person to another

¹What will the world be like in the future? ²In the future, people will go through the same cycle of life* and have the same problems as people do today. ³They will be born. ⁴They will go to schools and a university. ⁵They will fall in love. ⁶They will find a job. ⁷They will have children. ⁸They will grow old and die. ⁹However, the way of doing these things will be different. ¹⁰Parents will choose their babies' sex and physical characteristics*, and babies will probably be conceived in test tubes*. ¹¹They will attend school in electronic classrooms and will see their teachers only on TV. ¹²They will fall in love through computer dating. ¹³They will work at home through a computer hook-up to their jobs. ¹⁴They will grow old with transplanted organs* and die when they are 150 years old. ¹⁵Will the world be better? ¹⁶There will be less disease, but social problems will probably increase and war will continue.

➤ **Exercise 8** Use the words in parentheses to write yes-no questions about the paragraph. Use the Simple Future Tense with <u>will</u>. Answer each question with a short answer. When you are finished, take turns asking and answering the questions with a partner. (Note that questions 3–10 continue on the next page.)

1. (people / go through the same cycle of life in the future)

   Q: <u>Will people go through the same cycle of life in the future?</u>

   A: <u>Yes, they will.</u>

2. (people's problems / be very different in the future)

   Q: _____

   A: _____

YES-NO QUESTIONS

▐▶ **Exercise 8** (continued)

3. (people / be born, grow up, have families, grow old, and die)

    Q: _____

    A: _____

4. (the way of doing these things / be the same in the future)

    Q: _____

    A: _____

5. (parents / be able to choose the sex and physical characteristics of their children)

    Q: _____

    A: _____

6. (students / have close personal relationships with their teachers)

    Q: _____

    A: _____

7. (people / meet and fall in love through the computer)

    Q: _____

    A: _____

8. (people / work at home and telecommute* through a computer)

    Q: _____

    A: _____

9. (people / live longer in the future)

    Q: _____

    A: _____

10. (the world of the future / have fewer social problems, violence, and war)

    Q: _____

    A: _____

Vocabulary Note * **telecommute:** *work at home and communicate with the job through a computer*

Part 2
The Future with <u>Be Going to</u>

TALKING ABOUT THE FUTURE WITH <u>BE GOING TO</u>

➡ You have learned that we use the Simple Future Tense (<u>*will*</u> + *root form*) to talk about the future. We can also use <u>***be going to***</u> to talk about future time.

> ▶ **Learning Point**
>
> We can express future time with:
>
>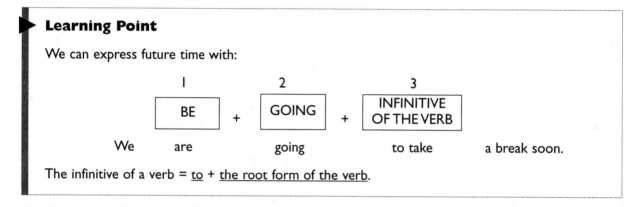
>
> | | 1 | | 2 | | 3 | |
> |------|---|---|---|---|---|---|
> | | **BE** | + | **GOING** | + | **INFINITIVE OF THE VERB** | |
> | We | are | | going | | to take | a break soon. |
>
> The infinitive of a verb = <u>to</u> + <u>the root form of the verb</u>.

➡ **Future with <u>Be Going To</u> - Affirmative Form**

	singular			plural	
1.	I am (I'm)		1.	we are (we're)	
2.	you are (you're)	going to eat	2.	you are (you're)	going to eat
3.	he is (he's)		3.	they are (they're)	
	she is (she's)				
	it is (it's)				

➡ **Word Order of Affirmative Sentences**

SUBJECT	VERB BE	+ GOING +	INFINITIVE OF THE VERB	COMPLEMENT
1. I	am	going	to play	tennis next week.
2 You	are	going	to get	an A in this class.
3. He	is	going	to be	out of town next week.
4. She	is	going	to clean	house tomorrow.
5. It	is	going	to be	a nice day tomorrow.
6. We	are	going	to eat	out tomorrow night.
7. You	are	going	to have	a lot of homework tonight.
8. They	are	going	to give	a party next Saturday.

Note: <u>Will</u> and <u>be going to</u> usually have the same meaning. You will study one difference between <u>will</u> and <u>be going to</u> on page 290.

FUTURE WITH <u>BE GOING TO</u>

➡️ **Exercise 1** Use Future with <u>be going to</u> and the verb in parentheses to complete each sentence.

1. My niece is very excited. She <u> is going to spend </u> **(spend)** her junior year in college as a foreign exchange student in Italy.

2. I travel a lot on business. In fact, I _____ **(be)** out of town all next week.

3. My husband was not happy with his last job, so he found a new job at a local software company. He _____ **(start)** his new job at Datalink next week.

4. My neighbors just bought a new house in the Silver Creek area. They _____ _____ **(move)** in a few weeks.

5. I can't go shopping with you on Saturday because I have a lot of things to do. I _____ **(wash)** my car, pay bills, and write some letters.

6. Everyone in my family is very happy. My son and daughter-in-law _____ **(have)** their first baby in a few months.

➡️ **Exercise 2** Each sentence below contains an error in the use of future with <u>be going to</u>. Circle the error in each sentence. Then write the sentence correctly. Compare your answers with a classmate.

1. Mohammed ⟨are going⟩ to return to his country next month.

   <u>Mohammed is going to return to his country next month.</u>

2. We are go to take a cruise through the Panama Canal on our next vacation.

   _____

3. Some of my classmates going to transfer to another school next year.

   _____

4. The class will going to have a party at the end of the semester.

   _____

5. We are going see a play in San Francisco and spend the night at the St. Francis Hotel.

   _____

6. I am go to have a job interview tomorrow morning.

   _____

<u>Note</u>:   Remember that we can omit repeated words in sentences with <u>and</u>. See sentence 5, Exercise 1 and sentence 5, Exercise 2. (Refer to Chapter 6, pages 152–153.)

FORMING NEGATIVE SENTENCES IN THE FUTURE WITH <u>BE GOING TO</u>

> ## ▶ Learning Point
>
> 1. To form negative sentences in the future with <u>be going to</u>, we put **not** after the verb <u>Be</u>.
>
>   <u>Example:</u>   affirmative: He is going to play golf next weekend.
>
>   negative: He is **not** going to play golf next weekend.
>
> 2. Remember that there are two ways to form negative contractions with <u>Be</u> + <u>not</u>:
>
>   <u>Example:</u>   He <u>is not</u> going to play. = He<u>'s not</u> going to play. = He <u>isn't</u> going to play.

▥ Future with <u>Be Going To</u> - Negative Form

	singular			plural	
1.	I am **not**		1.	we are **not**	
2.	you are **not**	going to eat	2.	you are **not**	going to eat
3.	he is **not**		3.	they are **not**	
	she is **not**				
	it is **not**				

▥ Word Order of Negative Sentences

SUBJECT	VERB BE	+ NOT +	GOING +	INFINITIVE OF THE VERB	COMPLEMENT
1. I	am	not	going	to take	a math class next semester.
2. You	are	not	going	to like	that book.
3. He	is	not	going	to move	before April of next year.
4. She	is	not	going	to accept	Mr. Wilson's offer of a job.
5. It	is	not	going	to be	a nice day tomorrow.
6. We	are	not	going	to leave	on our trip until next month.
7. You	are	not	going	to have	enough time to finish the job.
8. They	are	not	going	to come	to dinner next Sunday.

AFFIRMATIVE AND NEGATIVE SENTENCES

▸ **Exercise 3** It's nearly time for spring break, and everyone is looking forward to the time off. Both the teachers and the students are discussing their vacation plans. Use the Future with <u>be going to</u> to complete the dialogs below. Some of the sentences will be affirmative, and some will be negative.

The Cafeteria

Marta: I can't wait for spring break! My roommates and I ___<u>are going to rent</u>___ a house at
                                                                                                (1. rent)

Lake Tahoe. We _____ skiing for the whole week.
                                (2. go)

Steve: That sounds like fun. I _____ the week on the beach in San Diego.
                                              (3. spend)

I _____ in the sun all day, and I _____ all night.
          (4. lie)   **(5. party)**

Hung: Well, I _____ town, but I _____ a good time.
                    (6. not/leave)   **(7. have)**

I _____ before 9:00. I _____ my bed, and
        (8. not/get up)   **(9. not/make)**

I _____ the dishes. I _____ the phone. I
        (10. not/do)   **(11. not/answer)**

_____ about my classes. I _____ a book or write a
    (12. not/think)   **(13. not/open)**

paragraph. I _____ a great week!
                      (14. have)

▸ **Exercise 4** The teachers' conversations in the faculty lounge are very similar to the conversations in the cafeteria.

The Faculty Lounge

Mrs. Moll: Spring break will begin next week, and I really need the time off. My husband

and I _____ a cruise to Mexico. It's our first cruise, so
              (1. take)
we're really looking forward to it.

Mr. Sola: My idea of a good break is to stay home and forget about school.

I _____ any lessons, and I _____
        (2. not/plan)   **(3. not/correct)**

any papers. I _____ the phone or make any calls, and
              (4. not/answer)

I _____ any meetings.
        (5. not/attend)

ASKING QUESTIONS IN THE FUTURE WITH <u>BE GOING TO</u>

> ### Learning Point
>
> To form Yes-No Questions in the Future with <u>be going to</u>, we put the helping verb <u>Be</u> (*am, is, are*) in front of the subject.

Example: 1. **A:** Are you going to do something special for your sister's fortieth birthday?

            B: Yes, we are. My brother and I are going to give her a big surprise party.

        2. **A:** Is it going to be a nice day tomorrow?

            B: No, it isn't. It's going to be cool and cloudy.

➠ Future with <u>Be Going To</u> - Yes-No Questions

singular

1.	Am	I
2.	Are	you
3.	Is	he
	Is	she
	Is	it

going to eat?

plural

1.	Are	we
2.	Are	you
3.	Are	they

going to eat?

➠ Word Order of Yes-No Questions

VERB BE	SUBJECT	GOING	INFINITIVE	COMPLEMENT	SHORT ANSWERS FOR CONVERSATION
1. Are	Kim and Ed	going	to have	an anniversary party?	Yes, they are.
2. Is	the party	going	to be	at their home?	No, it isn't.
3. Is	it	going	to be	at a hotel?	Yes, it is.
4. Is	the hotel	going	to prepare	a large buffet dinner ?	Yes, it is
5. Are	Kim and Ed	going	to have	a live dance band?	Yes, they are.

ASKING QUESTIONS WITH <u>BE GOING TO</u>

▶ **Exercise 5** Write the missing yes-no questions in the conversations below. Use <u>be going to</u> and the words in parentheses to form each question. Practice the conversations with a partner.

| Two Co-workers |
---

1. <u>Vinh:</u>   (you / take your car to the mechanic tomorrow)

    Are you going to take your car to the mechanic tomorrow? _____

   <u>Carl:</u>   Yes, I am. I think that there's a problem with the brakes.

2. <u>Vinh:</u>   (it / be expensive)

   _____

   <u>Carl:</u>   I hope not! I just spent $800.00 on it a couple of months ago.

| Husband and Wife on the Phone |
---

1. <u>Mark:</u>   (your boss / have a staff meeting this afternoon)

   _____

   <u>Julie:</u>   Yes, he is. It's going to start at 4:00.

2. <u>Mark:</u>   (the meeting / last very long)

   _____

   <u>Julie:</u>   It probably is. We have a lot to discuss to get ready for the conference next week.

3. <u>Mark:</u>   (you / be home for dinner)

   _____

   <u>Julie:</u>   Yes, I am, but I'm probably going to be late.

| Two Friends |
---

1. <u>Emily:</u>   (your sister and her boyfriend / get married soon)

   _____

   <u>Kendal:</u> Yes, they are. In fact, they are looking for a place to have their reception right now.

2. <u>Emily:</u>   (they / have a big wedding)

   _____

   <u>Kendal:</u> No, they're only going to invite family and a few close friends.

SPECIAL POINT – FUTURE PLANNED ACTIONS WITH <u>BE GOING TO</u>

➠ You have learned that <u>will</u> and <u>be going to</u> usually have the same meaning. Read the pairs of sentences below. Sentences **a** and **b** have the same meaning.

Example: 1. a. The teacher <u>will</u> return our exams next week. ⎱
              b. The teacher <u>is going to</u> return our exams next week. ⎰ **same meaning**

          2. a. It <u>will</u> probably rain tomorrow. ⎱
             b. It <u>is</u> probably <u>going to</u> rain tomorrow. ⎰ **same meaning**

➠ Sometimes, however, <u>will</u> and <u>be going to</u> do not have the same meaning.

> ▶ **Learning Point**
>
> When we talk about a future planned action, we use <u>be going to</u>. We do not use <u>will</u>. A future planned action is an action that:
>
> 1. You have thought about in advance.
>
> 2. You have decided to do.
>
> 3. You have made plans to do.

➠ Study the examples below. We use <u>be going to</u> in these sentences because the speaker has given the action thought and planning. We do not use <u>will</u> in this kind of sentence.

1. Tom: <u>I'm going to visit</u> my parents in June. I bought my plane ticket last week.

   (Tom uses *be going to* because he made definite plans to visit his parents.)

2. Sue: <u>I'm going to have</u> a party tomorrow night. I called my friends last week. I bought the food and cleaned the house yesterday.

   (Sue uses *be going to* because she made definite plans to have a party.)

3. Joe: <u>I'm going to paint</u> my house next weekend. I bought a ladder and eight gallons of light brown paint last night.

   (Joe uses *be going to* because he made definite plans to paint his house.)

4. Bob: <u>I'm going to propose</u> to Maria at dinner tonight. I bought a beautiful diamond engagement ring today.

   (Bob uses *be going to* because he made definite plans to ask his girlfriend to marry him.)

SPECIAL POINT - FUTURE PLANNED ACTIONS WITH <u>BE GOING TO</u>

➠ **Exercise 6** Use the words in parentheses to write sentences with <u>be going to</u>. We do not use <u>will</u> in these sentences because the sentences all talk about a future planned action.

I. I just picked up some maps at the Automobile Association.

   (take a trip) *I'm going to take a trip up the Pacific coast from California to Oregon.*

2. My friend took out a home equity loan last week.

   (remodel his house) _____

3. My husband and I are taking a German class at City College this semester.

   (spend our next vacation in Germany) _____

4. My sister picked out a pattern and bought five yards of material.

   (make her daughter a dress) _____

5. I packed a lunch of sandwiches, potato salad, chips, fruit, and cookies, and my daughter filled a thermos with lemonade.

   (have a picnic at the beach) _____

6. Kim picked up a schedule of classes at City College and made an appointment with a counselor.

   (register for the next semester) _____

➠ **Exercise 7** Read the situations below. Then use <u>be going to</u> to answer the questions.

I. Sue wasn't sure where to go on her vacation. Then she read about the beautiful beaches on St. Martin Island in the Caribbean, and she decided to go there.

   Where is Sue going to spend her vacation?

   _____

2. Maria's class is going to have a potluck. Maria decided to make her favorite dessert for the potluck. Her favorite dessert is chocolate cake.

   What is Maria going to take to the potluck?

   _____

3. My nephew Ben is very happy because he was accepted at the University of Texas Law School. He plans to complete law school and then join his father's law firm.

   What profession is Ben going to practice?

   _____

4. Karl began to plan for his retirement about ten years ago, and he now has enough money to retire at age 62. Karl is 61 now, and his birthday is in February.

   When is Karl going to retire?

   _____

✓ CHECK YOUR UNDERSTANDING

A. Answer the questions below.

1. Write five future time words:

_____ _____ _____ _____ _____

2. What form of the verb do we always use with the helping verb <u>will</u>?

_____

3. What is a prediction?

_____

4. What is the negative contraction for <u>will not</u>?

_____

5. Why is it common to use the word <u>probably</u> when we talk about the future?

_____

_____

6. How do we form yes-no questions with <u>will</u>?

_____

7. We can use <u>will</u> + the root form of the verb to talk about the future.

We can also use _____ + _____ + _____ to talk about the future.

8. How do we form yes-no questions with <u>be going to</u>?

_____

9. What is a future planned action?

_____

10. Do we use <u>will</u> or <u>be going to</u> when we talk about a future planned action?

_____

B. Write about <u>your</u> future plans.

1. What are you going to do on the weekend?

_____

2. Where are you going to go on your next vacation?

_____

3. What is your class going to do at the end of the semester?

_____

4. Are you going to attend class here next semester?

_____

Part 3
Future Time in Time Clauses

USING TIME CLAUSES TO EXPRESS FUTURE TIME

➠ In Chapter 9, you studied time clauses. You learned that a time clause is a clause that begins with a word such as *when, while, before, after, as soon as.* You learned that a time clause cannot stand alone in a sentence. A time clause must have a main clause to complete the meaning of the sentence.

When + subject + verb = time clause   **main clause**

1. When my nephew learns enough English, | he'll enroll in a computer science course.

After + subject + verb = time clause   **main clause**

2. After he completes his course, | he's going to look for a job at an Internet company.

▶ **Learning Point**

When we use a time clause in a future tense sentence, we usually use the <u>Simple Present Tense</u> in the time clause and <u>will</u> or <u>be going to</u> in the main clause.

We do not use <u>will</u> or <u>be going to</u> in the time clause.

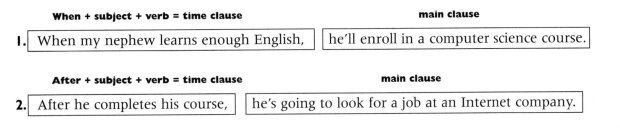

TIME CLAUSE	MAIN CLAUSE
<u>Simple Present Tense</u>	<u>Future (*will or be going to*)</u>
1. **As soon as** I <u>save</u> enough money,	I'<u>m going to take</u> a trip to Lake Louise, Canada.
2. **When** Antonio <u>has</u> some time off,	he'<u>ll go</u> to Mexico to visit his grandmother.
3. **After** Ana <u>graduates</u> next June,	she'<u>ll</u> probably <u>spend</u> a few months in Europe.
4. **Before** I <u>leave</u> on my vacation,	I'<u>m going to get</u> some traveler's checks at the bank.

➠ Remember that a time clause can come first or second in a sentence without a change in meaning. When a time clause comes first in a sentence, we put a comma after the time clause.

time clause

After I get off work tomorrow, | I'm going to meet some friends for dinner.

time clause

I'm going to meet some friends for dinner | after I get off work tomorrow.

USING TIME CLAUSES TO EXPRESS FUTURE TIME

➡ **Exercise 1** Complete each sentence with the correct form of the verb in parentheses. Use the Simple Present Tense in the time clause and the Future Tense in the main clause. In sentences 1 - 4, the time clause comes first in the sentence. In sentences 5 - 8, the time clause comes second.

1. When I **(see)** ___see___ John tomorrow, I **(invite)** ___am going to invite___ him to the party.

2. As soon as the rain **(stop)** _____, the children **(go)** _____ outside to play.

3. After I **(leave)** _____ the doctor's office, I **(stop)** _____ at the drugstore and pick up my prescription.

4. Before I **(do)** _____ another thing, I **(sit)** _____ down and relax for a few minutes.

5. I **(transfer)** _____ to the university as soon as I **(get)** _____ my AA Degree.

6. Ana **(finish)** _____ her homework before she **(watch)** _____ TV.

7. The class **(begin)** _____ as soon as the teacher **(get)** _____ here.

8. I **(visit)** _____ the art museum when I **(travel)** _____ to Chicago next month.

➡ **Exercise 2** In the dialog below, two classmates are talking about what they are going to do after they graduate. Complete the dialog with the correct form of the verbs in parentheses. Use only the Simple Present Tense in the time clause and the Future Tense with either <u>will</u> or <u>be going to</u> in the main clause.

Tran: I _____ probably _____ a few weeks off before I _____
                                    (1. take)   **(2. look)**

      for a full-time job. As soon as I _____ enough money, I _____ a
                                  (3. have)   **(4. rent)**

      three-bedroom house with a yard for the children. I want to buy a house, but I won't have

      enough money for a down payment for a long time.

Joe: When I _____ my classes, I _____ to a small town.
                 (5. finish)   **(6. move)**

      My wife and I want to open a small business such as a yogurt shop or a video store. We

      _____ the business opportunities in the area very
               (7. investigate)

      carefully before we _____ to buy. After we _____ our
                        (8. decide)   **(9. find)**

      business, we _____ very hard to make it a success.
            (10. work)

USING TIME CLAUSES TO EXPRESS FUTURE TIME

➡ **Exercise 3** Choose the correct form of the to complete each sentence in the paragraph. Compare your answers with a classmate.

A Different Life

When I **(1.)** _____finish_____ my classes at the Vocational Center,
(**will finish / finish / finishes**)

I **(2.)** _____ my own auto repair shop. My life **(3.)** _____
(**open / is opening / am going to open**)   (**will be / am going to be / is**)

very different when I **(4.)** _____ responsible for a business. For one thing,
(**will be / am going to be / am**)

I will need to work long hours, seven days a week to get the business established. After I

(5.) _____ the repairs on the cars, I **(6.)** _____
(**finish / am going to finish / will finish**)   (**am having / have / will have**)

to clean the shop, check out my tools and equipment, order parts, and update my accounts. For

another thing, I will need to learn how to satisfy my customers to get their return business in the

future. I **(7.)** _____ to be fair and accurate when I **(8.)** _____
(**will need / need / needs**)   (**will give / give / are giving**)

a customer an estimate for a job. I will also have to schedule my jobs carefully and be sure to

complete them on time. Finally, when I **(9.)** _____ the owner of a business,
(**am going to be / am / to be**)

I **(10.)** _____ responsible for the well-being of my employees. Before I
(**will be / am / are**)

(11.) _____ anyone, I **(12.)** _____ the labor laws
(**hire / am going to hire / will hire**)   (**study / am studying / will study**)

and learn about social security, health insurance, and workers' compensation. It is my dream to own

my own business. It is also a big responsibility.

☑ CHECK YOUR UNDERSTANDING

A. Answer the questions below.

1. What is a time clause?

_____

_____

2. We often use a time clause in a future tense sentence.

   a. When we use a time clause in a future tense sentence, what tense do we usually use in the time clause?

   _____

   b. What tense do we usually use in the main clause?

   _____

3. When a time clause comes first in a sentence, we put a _____ after the time clause.

B. Add a time clause to complete each future sentence below. Write <u>true</u> sentences about yourself.

1. I'm going to look for a better job after _____

2. I'm going to shop carefully before _____

3. I'll call you as soon as _____

4. My life will be easier after _____

5. I'll be happier when _____

C. Add a main clause in future tense to complete each sentence. Write <u>true</u> sentences.

1. As soon as I get home tonight, _____

2. Before I go to bed tonight, _____

3. When I have some spare time, _____

4. After I get the information, _____

5. When my class is over at the end of the semester, _____

Writing Assignment

⟹ Your writing assignment in this chapter is to write a paragraph about the future.

▶ What to do ◀

1. Choose <u>one</u> of the topic sentences below to write about.

_____ **Topic 1:** My life will be very different ten years from now.

When you think about the future, what predictions can you make about yourself? What do you think your life will be like ten years from now? How will it be different? Write three predictions about the way your life will be different in the future.

_____ **Topic 2:** The world of the future will be better in many ways.

Are you optimistic about the future? Do advances in medicine, the use of computers, the Internet, space exploration, etc., make you think that the future will be a better place? If so, why? Give three reasons to support your topic sentence.

_____ **Topic 3:** The world of the future will be worse in many ways.

Perhaps you are pessimistic about the future. When you think about things such as over-population, damage to the environment, man's ability to make war, etc., do you think that the future will be a worse place to live? If so, why? Give three reasons to support your topic sentence.

2. Write the first draft and the final draft of your paragraph on separate sheets of paper.

3. Follow the writing steps below.

STEP 1 Before you begin to write, take a few minutes to think about your topic. Make a *brainstorming list* of your ideas.

STEP 2 Choose three ideas from your brainstorming list, and write a *first draft (practice paragraph)*. Use the following transition words in your paragraph:

> *For one thing,*
> *For another thing,*
> *Last of all,*

STEP 3 *Revise and edit* your practice paragraph.

STEP 4 Write your *final draft (final paragraph)*.

Chapter 12
The Example Paragraph

To the Student:

In previous chapters, you studied several different kinds of paragraphs. In this chapter, you will learn to write another kind of paragraph, the **Example** paragraph. In an Example paragraph, you use examples to explain and support the topic sentence. Examples help your readers to see for themselves that what you are saying is true.

Part I
Prewriting

GETTING READY TO WRITE

In this chapter, you will learn how to write an example paragraph. In an example paragraph, we use examples to explain statements that we make. Examples help our readers to see for themselves that our statements are true.

Suppose that you want a friend to go to San Francisco with you for a week's vacation. An easy way to convince your friend that San Francisco is a great place to visit is to give your friend several examples of San Francisco's tourist attractions.

San Francisco has many famous tourist attractions.

(example)	the Golden Gate Bridge
(example)	Fisherman's Wharf
(example)	Chinatown
(example)	Golden Gate Park
(example)	Alcatraz

In the same way, you might want a friend to go with you to try a new restaurant in your neighborhood. It would be easy to convince your friend to have dinner there if you gave some examples of the dishes on the restaurant's menu.

Giorgio's Italian Diner has wonderful food.

(example)	spaghetti and ravioli
(example)	meatball sandwiches
(example)	minestrone soup
(example)	lasagna
(example)	all kinds of pizza

In this chapter, you will use examples to support your topic sentences. To help you to prepare for your writing assignments, follow the prewriting instructions on the next page.

PREWRITING

Activity 1

▶ What to do ◀

1. Work with a partner.

2. Read each statement below. How many examples can you and your partner think of to show that each statement is true?

3. Write your examples on the lines below each statement.

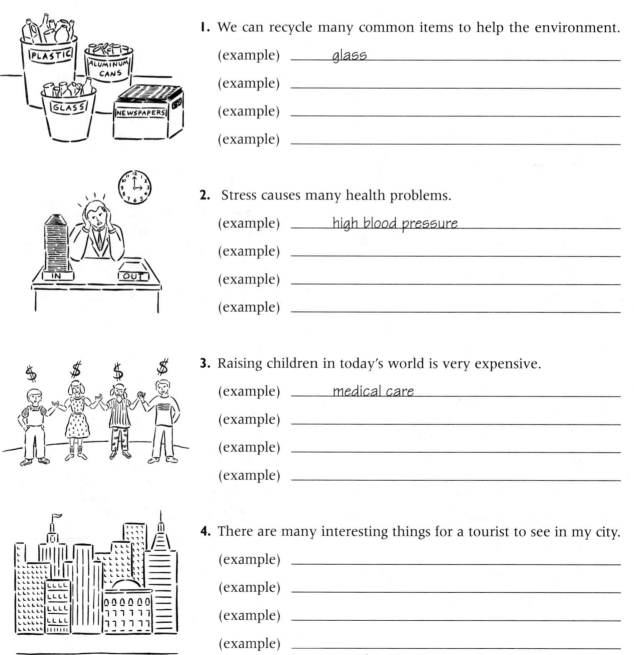

1. We can recycle many common items to help the environment.

(example) _____glass_____

(example) _____

(example) _____

(example) _____

2. Stress causes many health problems.

(example) _____high blood pressure_____

(example) _____

(example) _____

(example) _____

3. Raising children in today's world is very expensive.

(example) _____medical care_____

(example) _____

(example) _____

(example) _____

4. There are many interesting things for a tourist to see in my city.

(example) _____

(example) _____

(example) _____

(example) _____

(name of the city where you live)

Part 2
Using Examples to Support the Topic Sentence

THE EXAMPLE PARAGRAPH

➡ In this chapter, you will write an example paragraph. The most important thing to remember about writing an example paragraph is to use plenty of detailed and specific examples to support your topic sentence. One or two short examples will not convince your readers that what you are saying is true.

➡ Read the student paragraph below. Nha Loi began her paragraph with the topic sentence, **My best friend Susan is a very generous person.** Nha then gave three detailed and specific examples of Susan's generosity. When you are finished reading the paragraph, answer the questions on page 302.

MODEL PARAGRAPH

My Best Friend

generous: *willing to give or share time, money, gifts, etc. with other people*

Alzheimer's Disease: *a brain disease that causes loss of memory and personality changes*

concerned: *worried*

donate: *give, contribute*

homeless shelter: *a place that provides temporary housing for people without homes*

¹ My best friend Susan is a very generous* person. ²For example, Susan spends every Saturday afternoon at a local retirement home. ³While other young people her age spend Saturday at the mall or at the movies, Susan donates her time to help elderly people with Alzheimer's Disease*. ⁴She takes them for walks, helps them with art projects, and sometimes takes her guitar and leads them in singing and dancing. ⁵For another thing, Susan is also concerned* about homeless people. ⁶At Christmastime or New Year's, she donates* money and warm clothes to one of the homeless shelters* in our city. ⁷Finally, Susan volunteers every Thursday night in an English class for new immigrants. ⁸She works with small groups of students to give them a chance to practice conversation with a native speaker of English. ⁹Susan is a truly generous person, and I am proud to be her friend.

Nha Loi

THE EXAMPLE PARAGRAPH - MODEL PARAGRAPH

⟶ **Activity I** Answer the questions below about Nha Loi's paragraph, My Best Friend, on page 301.

1. What is the topic sentence of the paragraph?

_____

_____

2. Where does Susan spend every Saturday afternoon?

_____

_____

3. Who does Susan help on Saturday afternoons?

_____

_____

4. What does she do to help the people with Alzheimer's Disease?

_____

_____

5. Who else is Susan concerned about?

_____

_____

6. What does Susan donate to the homeless at Christmastime and New Year's?

_____

_____

7. Where does Susan volunteer every Thursday night?

_____

_____

8. What does Susan do in the English class?

_____

_____

9. What is the concluding sentence of the paragraph?

_____

_____

Part 3
Paragraph Skills

USING TRANSITION WORDS IN AN EXAMPLE PARAGRAPH

➠ You have learned that it is important to use transition words when you write a paragraph. Transition words help the reader to follow the ideas in your paragraph. Transition words are like road signs or traffic signals that tell you which way to go.

There are many different kinds of transition words in English. In this chapter, you will study some common transition words that we use in example paragraphs.

transition words to introduce examples

For example,	For one thing,	Also,
For instance,	For another thing,	Finally,
First of all,	In addition,	Last of all,

➠ We usually put transition words at the beginning of a sentence. We put a comma after the transition word. (Example: For one thing, he works fifty to sixty hours a week.)

↑
comma

➠ **Activity I** In the paragraph below, Joe Ramirez used three examples to support his topic sentence, ***My next-door neighbor Mike is a workaholic.*** Read the paragraph. Then circle the transition words that Joe used to introduce each example.

A Workaholic

[1]My next-door neighbor Mike is a workaholic. [2]For one thing, he works fifty to sixty hours a week and usually brings work home from the office. [3]He leaves home before 6:00 every morning and does not get home until 6:00 or 6:30 at night. [4]When he gets home, he eats a quick dinner with the family and then turns on the computer for another two or three hours of work. [5]In addition, Mike is always "connected" to the office. [6]He has a pager and a cell phone, and his boss can call him at any time in case of an emergency at work. [7]Last month, his boss called him into work three Saturdays out of four. [8]Finally, Mike has very little time for his family because of work. [9]He often has to miss a school activity or other family event because he cannot leave work. [10]His wife is unhappy with him, his children are unhappy with him, and he often feels guilty and upset. [11]I feel sorry for my young neighbor. [12]He needs to learn how to balance work and home, or he will cause himself and his family many problems in the future.

Joe Ramirez

TRANSITION WORDS

➡ **Activity 2** Read the paragraph below. Then fill the blanks with transition words to introduce the examples that support the topic sentence. Refer to the box on page 303. Be sure to use a comma after each transition word.

My New Roommate

¹My new roommate Paula is the most inconsiderate person I know. ²_____ she never does her share of the housework. ³Whenever it is time to clean, Paula always has something else to do. ⁴She gets a phone call or has a date or needs to study for an exam. ⁵On the few occasions when she cleans, she leaves the vacuum cleaner in the middle of the living room floor and the dust rags and furniture polish on the coffee table for me to put away. ⁶_____ my roommate does not like to do her laundry. ⁷As a result, she lets her dirty sheets and towels pile up in the corner of her room, and when she runs out of clean clothes, she borrows my clothes without asking. ⁸_____ Paula leaves the bathroom in a big mess every day. 1When she takes a shower, she leaves wet towels all over the bathroom floor. ⁹She never puts the cap on the toothpaste and always leaves her toothbrush on the edge of the sink. ¹⁰By the time she is finished, her hair and make-up look great. ¹¹In the bathroom, however, there is hair in the sink, hairspray on the mirror, and lipstick-stained tissues all over the counter. ¹²I need a new roommate!

➡ **Activity 3** Answer the questions below about the paragraph. Use complete sentences.

Housework

1. What often happens when it is time to clean the apartment?

_____

2. What does Paula do with the vacuum cleaner when she finishes vacuuming?

_____

Laundry

3. What can you see in the corner of Paula's bedroom?

_____

4. What does she do when she runs out of clean clothes?

_____

Bathroom

5. Where does Paula put her towels after she takes a shower?

_____

6. Does Paula leave the bathroom neat and clean every day?

_____

TRANSITION WORDS

➡ **Activity 4** Read the paragraph below. Then fill the blanks with transition words to introduce the examples that support the topic sentence. Refer to the box on page 303. Be sure to use a comma after each transition word.

Pay Attention!

¹My sister Eileen is very absent-minded. ²_____ last week she had a job interview with my boss. ³When I got to work that day, Eileen was already in my boss's office. ⁴Three of my co-workers were standing by the door of the office and smiling. ⁵Of course, I was curious, so I walked over to the door and looked in. ⁶I couldn't believe my eyes. ⁷My sister was sitting with her back to the door, and she had three large pink rollers on the back of her head! ⁸_____ _____ a couple of nights ago, she was shopping at Sears and almost got arrested for shoplifting. ⁹She tried on several sweaters and decided to buy a pink one. ¹⁰She gathered up the pink sweater, her purse and her other bags and left the dressing room. ¹¹She stopped to look at some jeans on a sale rack and also noticed some purses at 50% off. ¹²By this time, the store was closing, so she headed for the front door. ¹³Suddenly, an alarm went off, and a security officer stopped her. ¹⁴She forgot to pay for the sweater! ¹⁵After this latest incident, Eileen decided to get help from a therapist to improve her memory!

➡ **Activity 5** Answer the questions below about the paragraph. Use complete sentences.

Job Interview

1. When did Eileen have a job interview?

_____

2. Why were the writer's co-workers smiling?

_____

3. What did Eileen forget to do when she was getting ready to go for her interview?

_____

Shopping

4. Where was Eileen shopping a couple of nights ago?

_____

5. After she decided to buy the pink sweater, did Eileen go directly to the cashier's?

_____

6. What did Eileen forget to do before she tried to leave the store?

_____

☑ CHECK YOUR UNDERSTANDING

A. Answer the questions below.

1. In this chapter, you used _____ to support the topic sentence.

2. Good, clear examples help the reader to see that _____

_____

3. What is the most important thing to remember about writing an example paragraph?

_____

_____

4. Why do we use transition words in a paragraph?

_____

5. Write six transition words that we often use in example paragraphs.

_____ _____ _____

_____ _____ _____

6. When a transition word comes at the beginning of a sentence, we put a _____

after the transition word.

B. Match each statement in column A with the correct example in column B.

column A - Statement	column B - Example
1. Peter Lee is a very honest man.	**a.** Whenever he sees an injured bird or a lost dog or kitten, he brings it home and feeds it.
2. My neighbor's son is a soft-hearted little boy.	**b.** She has photo albums in every room of the house and loves to look at pictures and remember happy times from long ago.
3. My brother is often irresponsible.	**c.** When he was at the hardware store last week, he found a wallet with $200.00. He immediately turned it in to the manager of the store.
4. Sarah's boyfriend is very jealous.	**d.** Last week he forgot to lock his bicycle when he went to the store, and someone stole it.
5. My grandmother is very sentimental.	**e.** He doesn't like her to go out with her friends, and he gets angry whenever she talks to another man.
6. My niece Kathy is very shy.	**f.** Whenever a boy talks to her, she turns red and can't find a word to say.

Part 4
Getting Ready to Write

GETTING READY TO WRITE AN EXAMPLE PARAGRAPH

➠ Your writing assignment in this chapter will be to write an example paragraph about one quality of a family member, a close friend, a neighbor, or someone else that you know well. Qualities are words such as *generous, inconsiderate, honest, or absent-minded*.

➠ Before you begin, study the steps that Patricia Solano used when she wrote an example paragraph about her brother. When Patricia thought about her brother, she immediately thought about how well-organized he is. Therefore, she chose as her topic sentence, *My brother Tony is a very organized person.*

STEP 1 - PRE-WRITING: LIST OF EXAMPLES

The first thing that Patricia did was to make a list of examples to support her topic sentence. She thought of all the ways that her brother showed himself to be a very organized person. To save time, Patricia did not use complete sentences in her list.

LIST OF EXAMPLES

bedroom	school work
makes his bed	organizes his notebooks
hangs up his clothes	takes careful notes in class
lines up clothes and shoes	reviews homework before class
keeps his desk neat	palm pilot
organizes his books	names, addresses of friends
bathroom	birthdays and appointments
medicine cabinet is neat	list of everything he has to do
keeps tub and shower clean	car
towels neatly folded on rack	keeps litter bag by front seat
exercise	plastic holder for tapes and CDs
equipment in garage	glove compartment is neat
fills in chart each day	special place for his maps

STEP 2 - WRITE A FIRST DRAFT (PRACTICE PARAGRAPH)

➡ After Patricia finished making a list of specific examples to show how organized her brother Tony is, she chose two or three of the best examples and wrote her first draft (practice paragraph).

After Patricia wrote the first draft of her paragraph, she read the paragraph carefully to see if she could improve it.

1. First, she **revised** her paragraph. **Revise** means to add, move, or take out sentences. Revise also means to rewrite any confusing sentences. As Patricia read her paragraph, she asked himself, "Did I use plenty of specific examples to show that Tony is an organized person? Are any of my examples off-topic? Did I use clear transition words? Does my paragraph have a concluding sentence?"

2. Then Patricia **edited** her paragraph. **Edit** means to correct any errors in grammar, spelling, and the use of capital letters and periods.

➡ The paragraph below is Patricia's practice paragraph. Look at the changes and corrections that she made on her practice paragraph.

A Place for Everything

indent⟶ For instance, everything an exact
My brother Tony is a very organized person. Everything in his room has a place. He makes his bed every morning. The top of his desk is never cluttered, and he has special holders for his pens,

pencils, paper clips, and erasers. He keeps his books in a bookcase next to his desk and arranges
            alphabetical
them in order by author. Even his closet is organized. His jackets go on the left, then his shirts,

pants, ties, and belts, and his shoes are lined up on the floor of the closet. For another thing,
        is   a
Tony very organized in his school work. He has separate notebook for each class. He takes precise

notes at each class session and always writes down his homework assignments. Before each
                        previous   to (infinitive)
class, he reviews the material from the class before. He hates surprises and does not want go to

class and find out that there is a quiz or a paper due.
                                        P   P
Finally, Tony never goes anywhere without his palm pilot. This little organizer has the names,
            and e-mail addresses
addresses, and phone numbers of all his friends. The Palm Pilot date book contains everyone's

birthday as well as Tony's appointments, and the "To Do" list reminds him of everything that he

has to do. Because he is so organized, Tony makes good use of his time. He is a good model for me

to follow.

STEP 3 – WRITE THE FINAL DRAFT (FINAL PARAGRAPH)

➠ After Patricia revised and edited (changed and corrected) her practice paragraph on page 308, she was ready to write her final paragraph.

Read Patricia's final paragraph below. Draw a circle around the transition words that Patricia used to introduce the examples in her paragraph.

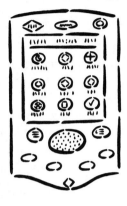

A Place for Everything

My brother Tony is a very organized person. For instance, everything in his room has an exact   **1**

place. The top of his desk is never cluttered, and he has special holders for his pens, pencils, paper

clips, and erasers. He keeps his books in a bookcase next to his desk and arranges them in

alphabetical order by author. Even his closet is organized. His jackets go on the left, then his

shirts, pants, ties, and belts, and his shoes are precisely lined up on the floor of the closet. For   **5**

another thing, Tony is very organized in his schoolwork. He has a separate notebook for each class.

He takes precise notes at each class session and always writes down his homework assignments.

Before each class, he reviews the material from the previous class. He hates surprises and does

not want to go to class and find out that there is a quiz or a paper due. Finally, Tony never goes

anywhere without his Palm Pilot. This little organizer has the names, addresses, phone numbers,   **10**

and e-mail addresses of all his friends. The Palm Pilot date book contains everyone's birthday as

well as Tony's appointments, and the "To Do" list reminds him of everything that he has to do.

Because he is so organized, Tony makes good use of his time. He is a good model for me to follow.

Patricia Solano

✎ Writing Assignment

➡ Your writing assignment in this chapter is to write an example paragraph about one quality of a family member, a close friend, a neighbor, or someone else that you know well.

▶ **What to do** ◀

1. Think of the person that you want to write about.

2. Choose one quality from the box below that applies to that person:

Qualities		
ambitious	generous	reliable
brave	honest	self-centered
cheerful	irresponsible	selfish
considerate	jealous	shy
dishonest	lazy	sloppy
energetic	neat	stubborn
friendly	patient	

3. Write a topic sentence for your paragraph on the lines below. Include the name of the person you want to write about, your relationship to that person, and the specific quality that applies to that person.

To help you write your topic sentence, use one of the following sentence patterns:

My _____sister_____ _____Kim_____ is a very _____patient_____ person.
          (relationship)   **(name)**   **(quality)**

My __brother-in-law__ __Arthur__ is __the most stubborn__ person that I know.
          (relationship)   **(name)**   **(quality)**

your topic _____
sentence: _____

Writing Assignment

STEP 1 - LIST OF EXAMPLES

Now that you have chosen a person to write about and a quality from the box on page 310, take a few minutes to think about your topic. Write your topic sentence here.

your topic
sentence:
_____

_____

Now make a list of specific examples to support your topic sentence. Think of all the ways that the person shows the quality that you have chosen. Write every example that comes into your mind. Do not write complete sentences, and do not worry about grammar or spelling in your list.

LIST OF EXAMPLES

_____	_____
_____	_____
_____	_____
_____	_____
_____	_____
_____	_____
_____	_____
_____	_____
_____	_____
_____	_____
_____	_____
_____	_____
_____	_____
_____	_____

Writing Assignment

STEP 2 - WRITE A FIRST DRAFT (PRACTICE PARAGRAPH)

▶ What to do ◀

1. Now that you have made a list of examples on page 311, you are ready to write the first draft of your paragraph.

2. Pick two or three of the best examples from your list to support your topic sentence. Be sure to pick the examples that will clearly show the reader the quality of the person you are writing about.

3. Use transition words from page 303 to help the reader follow the ideas in your paragraph.

4. Double space your paragraph, and circle the subject(s) and verb(s) in each sentence. Be sure to give your paragraph a title.

Writing Assignment

FIRST DRAFT (CONTINUED)

_____

_____

_____

_____

_____

_____

_____

_____

_____

_____

_____

_____

_____

_____

_____

_____

_____

STEP 3 - REVISE AND EDIT YOUR PARAGRAPH

▶ **What to do** ◀

1. When you are finished writing your practice paragraph, read your paragraph to yourself.

2. Revise your paragraph.

   Are all of your sentences clear and easy to understand? Do you want to add, move, or take out sentences? If you need to make changes, make them on your practice paragraph.

3. Edit your paragraph.

   Are there any mistakes in grammar, spelling, capital letters, or periods? Did you use correct paragraph form? If you need to make corrections, make them on your practice paragraph.

4. When you are finished revising and editing your paragraph, write your name on the Review Sheet on page 314, and give your book to a partner. Your partner will read and review your paragraph.

 **Partner Review Sheet**

Paragraph written by _____

Paragraph reviewed by _____

⟹ *To the Reviewer:* Read your partner's paragraph carefully. Then answer the questions below about your partner's paragraph. Do not write on your partner's paper.

1. Does your partner's paragraph have a title?

_____ yes   _____ no

2. Write the topic sentence of your partner's paragraph here.

_____

_____

3. Does the paragraph have a topic sentence, two or three supporting examples, and a concluding sentence?

_____ yes   _____ no

4. Which sentence is true about your partner's paragraph?

_____ **a.** My partner used detailed and specific examples to support the topic sentence.

_____ **b.** My partner's examples need more detail.

5. Did your partner use transition words in his or her paragraph?

_____ yes   _____ no

6. Do all of the sentences in the paragraph begin with a capital letter and end with a period?

_____ yes   _____ no

7. Did your partner circle the subject(s) and verb(s) in each sentence?

_____ yes   _____ no

⟹ *To the Reviewer:* When you are finished reviewing your partner's paragraph, return your partner's book.

Writing Assignment

STEP 5 - WRITE YOUR FINAL DRAFT (FINAL PARAGRAPH)

When your partner returns your book, make any necessary changes or corrections on your practice paragraph. Now you are ready to write the final draft of your paragraph.

► What to do ◄

1. Write your final paragraph in ink on a separate sheet of paper. Write as neatly as possible, and use correct paragraph form.

2. Double space your paragraph, and write on only one side of the paper.

3. When you finish your paragraph, underline or highlight the topic sentence and the concluding sentence.

4. Circle the subject(s) and verb(s) in each sentence.

Additional Writing Topics

Reason and Example Paragraphs

Topic 1: _____ is a very _____ person.

Think of someone you admire. What do you admire most about that person? What is his/her most outstanding quality?

Topic 2: My friends think that I am a _____ person.

Think about yourself. What do your friends like about you? What is your best quality?

Topic 3: Sometimes I am a very _____ person.

Think about yourself. What is your worst quality? What would you like to change about yourself if you could?

Chapter 13
Modals

To the Student:

In this chapter you will study a small group of helping (auxiliary) verbs called <u>modals</u>. Modals are very common in English and have many different meanings. The modals that you will study in this chapter are:

can	could	should	must	may	might

You will begin with the modals **<u>can</u>** and **<u>could</u>**.

Part I
Can and Could (Ability, Possibility)

THE MODAL CAN TO SHOW ABILITY

> ### Learning Point 1
>
> The modal **can** shows the ability to do something in present time.

1. My daughter is very musical. She can play both the piano and the guitar. **(ability)**

2. Our teacher can speak three languages. She speaks English, Spanish, and Chinese. **(ability)**

> ### Learning Point 2
>
> **1.** The modal **can** is a helping (auxiliary) verb. We always use <u>can</u> with the root form of a verb.
>
> **2.** The negative form of <u>can</u> is **cannot** (one word). The negative contraction of <u>cannot</u> is **can't**.

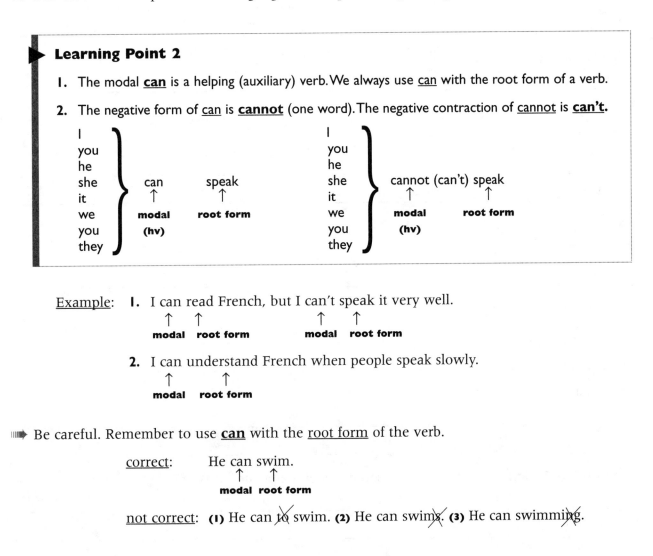

Example: **1.** I can read French, but I can't speak it very well.
                  ↑   ↑   ↑   ↑
               modal root form   **modal root form**

          2. I can understand French when people speak slowly.
                  ↑   ↑
               modal   root form

⟹ Be careful. Remember to use **can** with the <u>root form</u> of the verb.

          <u>correct</u>:   He can swim.
                                ↑   ↑
                             modal root form

          <u>not correct</u>: **(1)** He can ~~to~~ swim. **(2)** He can ~~swims~~. **(3)** He can ~~swimming~~.

<u>Note</u>: You will study the modal <u>can</u> to show possibility on pages 319 - 321.

THE MODAL CAN TO SHOW ABILITY

➧ **Exercise 1** Complete each sentence below. Tell what you <u>can</u> and <u>can't</u> do.

1. I can _____ *drive a car* _____ , but I can't _____ *fly a plane.* _____

2. I can _____ , but I can't _____

3. I can _____ , but I can't _____

4. I can _____ , but I can't _____

5. I can _____ , but I can't _____

6. I can _____ , but I can't _____

➧ **Exercise 2** Write <u>true</u> answers to the questions below. Use complete sentences in your answers. Then take turns asking and answering the questions with a partner.

1. What can you do very well?

   _____

   _____

2. What can't you do very well?

   _____

   _____

3. How many languages can you speak?

   _____

   _____

4. Can you play a musical instrument?

   _____

   _____

5. Can you use a computer?

   _____

   _____

6. What can't a child do?

   _____

   _____

7. In the United States, what can a person do when he or she turns 18?

   _____

   _____

THE MODAL <u>CAN</u> TO SHOW POSSIBILITY

▶ You have learned that the modal <u>can</u> shows <u>ability</u>. The modal <u>can</u> also has another important meaning. We often use <u>can</u> to show <u>possibility</u>.

> ### ▶ Learning Point
>
> The modal <u>can</u> shows that it is possible to do something in present or future time.

<u>Example:</u>

1. I can drive you to school tomorrow because I don't have to go to work.

(***meaning:*** It is possible for me to drive you to school tomorrow.)

2. I can go to the movies with you today, but I can't go with you tomorrow.

(***meaning:*** It is possible for me to go to the movies with you today, but it is not possible for me to go tomorrow.)

3. You can't get a driver's license until you are sixteen.

(***meaning:*** It is not possible for you to get a driver's license until you are sixteen.)

▶ **Exercise 3** Practice writing sentences with <u>can to show possibility</u>.

1. Name 3 things that you can do on the weekend that you can't do during the week.

   a. <u>I can sleep late on the weekend.</u> _____

   b. _____

   c. _____

2. What is your favorite place to visit? Name 3 things that you can do there.

   a. _____

   b. _____

   c. _____

3. Name 3 things that you can do in your hometown.

   a. _____

   b. _____

   c. _____

THE MODAL <u>CAN</u> TO SHOW POSSIBILITY

> **Exercise 4** Read the paragraph below. Then do the exercise on page 321.

Something for Everyone

¹If you want to spend a wonderful day at a beautiful park, visit Golden Gate Park in San Francisco. ²There are many free or inexpensive ways for both adults and children to have fun in the park. ³For example, Stowe Lake is a popular attraction for families. ⁴Here visitors **<u>can</u>** rent paddle boats, rowboats, or small power boats to navigate the lake. ⁵Bicycles are also available for rent at this location. ⁶Nearby, there are numerous grassy areas with picnic tables, barbecue grills, and play areas for children. ⁷Golden Gate Park also offers many activities for sports-lovers. ⁸For instance, golfers **<u>can</u>** play nine holes of golf at a hilly and challenging* golf course near the Pacific Ocean. ⁹For tennis players, there are twenty-one tennis courts with restrooms, lockers, and a snack bar. ¹⁰Visitors to the park **<u>can</u>** rent horses from the Golden Gate Park Stables and explore the park on horseback. ¹¹The stables are open to the public seven days a week and offer guided trail rides through the park. ¹²Finally, visitors **<u>can</u>** enjoy many cultural* activities at Golden Gate Park. ¹³One of the most famous museums in San Francisco, the De Young Museum, is located in Golden Gate Park. ¹⁴Here visitors **<u>can</u>** view* a wonderful collection of paintings, sculptures, and artifacts* from ancient Africa to twenty-first-century America. ¹⁵In the same building, there is an impressive collection of Asian art. ¹⁶Across from the De Young Museum at the Museum of Natural History, visitors **<u>can</u>** learn about different species* of animals in their natural habitat*. ¹⁷At the Steinhart Aquarium, they **<u>can</u>** see hundreds of different kinds of fish and sea life. ¹⁸Finally, at the Morrison Planetarium, they **<u>can</u>** study the movement of the earth, learn about the stars and constellations*, and view exhibits of the planets. ¹⁹Clearly, Golden Gate Park has something for everyone!

Vocabulary Notes

*<u>**challenging:**</u> *difficult*

*<u>**cultural:**</u> *pertaining to the art, music, literature, institutions, etc. of a certain group of people*

*<u>**view:**</u> *see*

*<u>**artifact:**</u> *object made by human work*

*<u>**species:**</u> *kind, variety, type*

*<u>**habitat:**</u> *home, environment*

*<u>**constellations:**</u> *groups of stars that form a picture or pattern*

THE MODAL <u>CAN</u> TO SHOW POSSIBILITY

▶ **Exercise 5** Complete the sentences below. Refer to the paragraph about Golden Gate Park on page 320 if necessary. Use <u>can</u> or <u>can't</u> in your sentences. When you are finished, compare your answers with a partner.

San Francisco's Golden Gate Park

1. If you want to spend a wonderful day at a beautiful park, you *can visit Golden Gate*

   Park in San Francisco.

2. There are many things to do at Stowe Lake. People _____

   _____

3. There are large, grassy areas near Stowe Lake where people _____

   _____

4. Golden Gate Park has many activities for the sports lover. For example, they _____

   _____

   _____

5. If people like horseback riding, they _____

   _____

6. The park has several snack bars and restaurants. When visitors get hungry, they _____

   _____

7. There are many cultural activities in the park. For example, you _____

   _____

   _____

8. If people want to learn about fish and other sea life, they _____

   _____

9. If people want to learn about the stars and planets, they _____

   _____

10. Tourists like to visit Golden Gate Park because they _____

   _____

   _____

THE MODAL <u>COULD</u> TO SHOW PAST ABILITY

▷ The modal <u>could</u> is one of the most difficult modals in English because it is used in many different ways. One of the most common uses of the modal <u>could</u> is to show a past ability to do something. When <u>could</u> is used in this way, <u>could</u> is the past form of <u>can</u>.

> ### ▶ Learning Point 1
>
> The modal **could** often shows the ability to do something in the past.

1. My nephew is very intelligent. He could read before he started kindergarten last year. **(past ability)**

2. When I lived in Mexico several years ago, I could speak Spanish fluently. **(past ability)**

> ### ▶ Learning Point 2
>
> **1.** The modal **could** is a helping (auxiliary) verb. We always use <u>could</u> with the root form of a verb.
>
> **2.** The negative form of <u>could</u> is **could not.** The negative contraction of <u>could not</u> is **couldn't.**

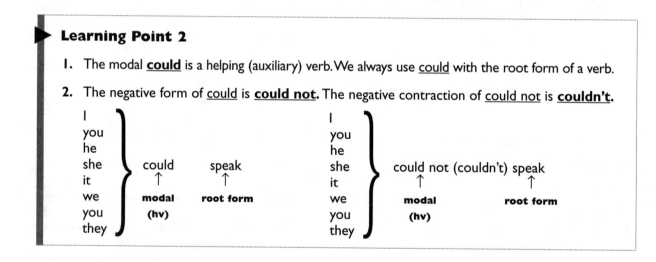

Example: **1.** I could use a computer after I took some classes last semester.
                    ↑   ↑
                 modal root form

2. I couldn't speak English very well last year, but I can now.
           ↑   ↑
        modal   root form

▷ Be careful. Remember to use **could** with the <u>root form</u> of the verb.

<u>correct</u>:   My niece <u>could</u> <u>use</u> a computer when she was only four years old.
                              ↑   ↑
                           modal root form

<u>not correct</u>: My niece could to use
                     could used   } a computer when she was only four years old.
                     could using

THE MODALS <u>CAN</u> AND <u>COULD</u> TO SHOW ABILITY

⟹ **Exercise 6** Use the modals <u>can</u>, <u>can't</u>, <u>could</u>, or <u>couldn't</u> and the verbs in parentheses to complete the paragraphs below. Work with a partner or in a small group.

Paragraph I   **Computer Phobia**

[1]Until a few months ago, I **(use)** ___couldn't use___ a computer. [2]I was afraid of computers, and I **(understand)** _____ how they worked. [3]Then I signed up for an introductory computer class through our adult education program. [4]I felt very nervous the first day of class. [5]In fact, I **(turn on)** _____ the computer without help from one of the other students. [6]However, our teacher was excellent and understood how to help students with "computer phobia". [7]After only two or three classes, I learned how to use the computer. [8]Now I **(send)** _____ e-mail, make charts, and do my personal finances on my "friendly" PC.

Paragraph 2   **Friends to the Rescue**

[1]When I got married last year, I **(boil)** _____ an egg, so I signed up for the course, "Learn to Cook in 5 Easy Lessons". [2]However, when I finished the fifth lesson a few weeks ago, I was disappointed because I still **(cook)** _____. [3]Then I bought several cookbooks and spent many hours in the kitchen, but I still **(prepare)** _____ a decent meal. [4]Finally, I asked five of my best friends for help. [5]They each gave me their easiest recipe. [6]Now I **(cook)** _____ at least five good meals!

Paragraph 3   **Getting in Shape**

[1]A few weeks ago, my doctor told me to get more exercise, so I got my old ten-speed bicycle out of the garage. [2]To my surprise, however, when I got on my bike, I **(ride)** _____ to the corner grocery store. [3]By the time I got to the store, I was sweating and my heart was beating very fast. [4]When I was younger, **(ride)** _____ my bike several miles to and from work, and on weekends I **(ride)** _____ for hours up and down mountain trails. [5]For the next several weeks, I worked hard to get back into shape. [6]I got up early every morning and rode my bike for an hour a day until I **(ride)** _____ for several miles without getting tired. [7]Now, I **(ride)** _____ as well as I could when I was young. Well, almost as well!

✓ CHECK YOUR UNDERSTANDING

A. Answer the following questions in complete sentences.

1. What is a modal?_____

_____

2. What are two meanings of the modal <u>can</u>?

    a. _____

    b. _____

3. What time does the modal <u>can</u> show in a sentence? _____

_____

4. What is a common use of the modal <u>could</u>? _____

_____

5. What form of the verb do we use with the modals <u>can</u> and <u>could</u>? _____

_____

B. *EDITING* - Each sentence below contains a mistake in the use of the modals <u>can</u> and <u>could</u>. Circle the mistake in each sentence. Then write the sentence correctly.

1. My father could ⟨speaks⟩ Japanese when he lived in Tokyo many years ago.

    My father could speak Japanese when he lived in Tokyo many years ago. _____

2. My sister can't to meet us for dinner tonight because she has to work overtime.

_____

_____

3. I can going shopping with you next Friday, but I can't go on Saturday.

_____

_____

4. I could not picked you up yesterday because I had a flat tire.

_____

_____

5. I can to walk to school when the weather is nice.

_____

_____

6. My neighbor could not pays his phone bill, so the phone company disconnected his phone yesterday.

_____

_____

Part 2
<u>Should</u> (Advice)

THE MODAL <u>SHOULD</u> TO GIVE ADVICE

▶ **Learning Point 1**

We use the modal **should** to give advice. The modal <u>should</u> shows present or future time.

1. A: Tom, you look terrible! What's the matter?

   B: I was up late last night, so I didn't get much sleep.

   A: You <u>should go</u> to bed early tonight. **(good advice)**

2. A: I don't know what to do. My son got another speeding ticket today. That's two this month!

   B: You <u>should take</u> away his license until he can learn to be more responsible. **(good advice)**

▶ **Learning Point 2**

1. The modal **should** is a helping (auxiliary) verb. We always use <u>should</u> with the root form of a verb.

2. The negative form of <u>should</u> is **should not**. The negative contraction of <u>should not</u> is **shouldn't**.

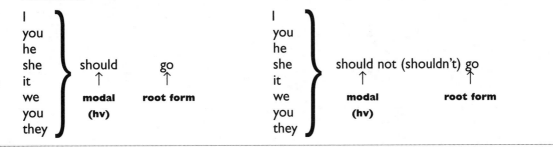

Example: **1.** You <u>should</u> always <u>lock</u> your car.
               ↑   ↑
             modal   **root form**

           2. You <u>shouldn't</u> <u>walk</u> alone at night because the streets can be dangerous.
               ↑   ↑
            modal **root form**

        3. You <u>shouldn't</u> <u>pick</u> up hitchhikers.
               ↑   ↑
          modal root form

THE MODAL <u>SHOULD</u> TO GIVE ADVICE

➡ **Exercise 1** The person in each dialog below has a problem. Use <u>should</u> or <u>shouldn't</u> to give advice in each situation.

1. A: My brother is in poor health. He is at least 30 pounds overweight, and he has high blood pressure. He sits at a desk all day at work, and when he gets home, he sits and watches TV all evening. What should he do to improve his health?

B: _First of all, your brother should go on a diet and lose some weight. He should also avoid salt and fried food. These are bad for people with high blood pressure. Finally, he should stay active and get at least twenty minutes of exercise a day._

2. A: I hate going to work every morning because my job is so boring that I almost fall asleep at my desk. I do the same thing over and over again. I can't complain, however, because I didn't finish high school, and I don't have the necessary skills to get a better job. What should I do?

B: _____

_____

_____

_____

3. A: I miss my parents very much. I don't live near them anymore, so I don't see them very often. I'm so busy at work and school that I don't have time to write to them either. I want to be a better son to them. What should I do?

B: _____

_____

_____

4. A: I live by myself in my own apartment, and I'm having a hard time paying the rent. Maybe I should get a roommate to share expenses with me. Is this a good idea, or am I asking for problems? I really like living alone, but I could use the extra money to help pay the rent and utilities.

B: _____

_____

_____

SPECIAL POINT – USING <u>OUGHT TO</u> AND <u>HAD BETTER</u> TO GIVE ADVICE

➠ You have learned that we use the modal <u>should</u> to give advice in present or future time. The expressions <u>ought to</u> and <u>had better</u> are very similar in meaning to the modal <u>should</u>.

▶ **Learning Point 1**

We can use the expressions **<u>ought to</u>** and **<u>had better</u>** to give advice in present or future time.

---

1. Ted has a bad cough. He $\begin{cases} \text{should} \\ \text{ought to} \\ \text{had better} \end{cases}$ call the doctor tomorrow. **(good advice)**

2. Mary has a terrible headache. She $\begin{cases} \text{should} \\ \text{ought to} \\ \text{had better} \end{cases}$ take some Tylenol. **(good advice)**

3. My aunt has diabetes, so she $\begin{cases} \text{should} \\ \text{ought to} \\ \text{had better} \end{cases}$ watch her diet more carefully. **(good advice)**

▶ **Learning Point 2**

1. **<u>Had better</u>** is stronger than **<u>should</u>** or **<u>ought to</u>.** <u>Had better</u> often means that something bad will happen if you don't follow the advice.

   <u>Example:</u> Susan <u>had better</u> lock her doors at night, or someone might break into her house.

2. The contraction of <u>had better</u> is <u>'d better</u>.

   <u>Example:</u> He<u>'d better</u> study harder, or he'll flunk out of school.

3. The negative form of <u>had better</u> is <u>had better not</u>.

   <u>Example:</u> I<u>'d better</u> not go out tonight. I'm getting a cold.

➠ Study the examples below.

1. I <u>had better</u> take some classes to improve my job skills, or I'll never get a better job.

2. Bob <u>had better</u> get some help. If he continues to take drugs, he'll ruin his life.

3. She<u>'d better</u> not be late for work again, or her boss will fire her. She was late three times last week.

4. I<u>'d better</u> cut down on desserts and eat more fresh fruit instead. I gained five pounds last month.

SHOULD, OUGHT TO, AND HAD BETTER TO GIVE ADVICE

▶ **Exercise 2** We have many good counselors at my school, but a favorite counselor with all the students is Mr. Nguyen. He is always ready to listen to students' problems whether they are academic or personal. Select the correct modal to complete Mr. Nguyen's advice in the conversations below.

1.

Student: My girlfriend wants to get married, but I don't think that we can afford to get married until we finish school. She says that two people can live as cheaply as one. I don't agree, but I don't want to lose my girlfriend. We agreed to follow your advice.

Mr. Nguyen: Your girlfriend needs a class in finances. Two people cannot live as cheaply as one. You **(shouldn't / ought to)** _____ get married until you both finish school and have good jobs. Then you can get married.

2.

Student: I'm very angry with my best friend. She said that I cheated on my midterm because I got an A and she got an F. It's not true. I studied hard for my midterm, and she didn't study at all. I think that she is jealous. We've been friends for a long time, but now I don't think that I can continue to be her friend. What should I do?

Mr. Nguyen: Good friends are hard to find. You **(had better not / ought to)** _____ meet with your friend to discuss the misunderstanding. You should try to save the friendship.

3.

Student: I have a big problem. I can't decide whether to buy a used car or a new car. If I buy a new car, I will have to take out a bank loan at a high interest rate to pay for it. Then I would have to work overtime to make the car payments. I really think that I can work more hours and still keep up my grades.

Mr. Nguyen: Be sensible. You have a C- average. You **(had better / shouldn't)** _____ buy the used car and concentrate more on your grades. You need better grades more than you need a new car. You can buy a new car after you graduate.

4.

Student: When I was young, I didn't have the opportunity to go to college. Now I'm almost 50 years old. My children are grown, and I have the time to return to school. I want to take some literature and history classes. However, I'm afraid that I'm too old. I don't know if I can do the work or keep up with the other students. What do you think?

Mr. Nguyen: You **(ought to / shouldn't)** _____ worry. It's never too late to get an education. You have the motivation, and you're willing to work hard. You'll do fine.

SHOULD, OUGHT TO, AND HAD BETTER TO GIVE ADVICE

➠ Many people write to their local newspaper to ask for advice. Advice columns are one of the most popular features in most newspapers. Pretend that you give advice in a local newspaper. Your name is **Dr. Knowsit.** Your first letter is from a high school student who needs your advice.

> Dear Dr. Knowsit,
>
> I'm a high school student, and I'm having problems with one of my teachers. I don't think that she likes me. First of all, I'm usually only 10 or 15 minutes late for class, so I don't know why she gets so angry. She also yells at me when I don't turn in my homework. I really don't like homework, so I never do it. Also, she won't let me sit in the back of the room with my friends. She makes me sit right in front of her desk. This really embarrasses me. Then she calls on me to answer the hardest questions, especially when I don't know the answers. When I get an "F" on a test, she makes me take it again. Worst of all, she even makes me erase the boards after class! What should I do to make her like me?
>
> Worried in Wisconsin

➠ **Exercise 3** Answer the letter from "Worried in Wisconsin". Use **should, should not, ought to, had better,** and **had better not** to give advice. Write about 8 - 10 sentences so that your reply will fit in the newspaper.

<u>Dear Worried,</u>

✓ CHECK YOUR UNDERSTANDING

A. Answer the following questions in complete sentences.

1. When do we use the modal <u>should</u>?

_____

2. What two expressions are similar in meaning to the modal <u>should</u>?

a. _____

b. _____

3. What time do the modals <u>should</u>, <u>ought to</u>, and <u>had better</u> show in a sentence?

_____

4. Write your own sentences.

a. (should) _____

b. (ought to) _____

c. (had better _____

B. *EDITING* - Each sentence below contains a mistake in the use of the modal <u>should</u>, <u>ought to</u>, or <u>had better</u>. Circle the mistake in each sentence. Then write the sentence correctly.

1. My sister gained a lot of weight over the holidays, so she (should to go) on a diet.

My sister gained a lot of weight over the holidays, so she should go on a diet.

2. Peter ought get a haircut because he has a job interview tomorrow.

_____

3. The gas gauge is on empty, so we better stop for gas.

_____

4. ESL students should tries to speak English as much as possible.

_____

5. Bob has better not forget his wife's birthday tomorrow, or she'll be angry.

_____

6. If you hate your job, you will ought to look for another one.

_____

Part 3
<u>Must</u> (Necessity)

THE MODAL <u>MUST</u> TO SHOW NECESSITY

▶ Learning Point 1

We use the modal <u>**must**</u> to show that it is necessary to do something. <u>Must</u> shows present or future time.

1. You have a high temperature. You must see a doctor right away. **(action is necessary)**

2. My driver's license will expire next week, so I must renew it. **(action is necessary)**

▶ Learning Point 2

1. The modal <u>**must**</u> is a helping (auxiliary) verb. We always use <u>must</u> with the root form of a verb.

2. The negative form of <u>must</u> is <u>**must not.**</u> The negative contraction of <u>must not</u> is <u>**mustn't.**</u>

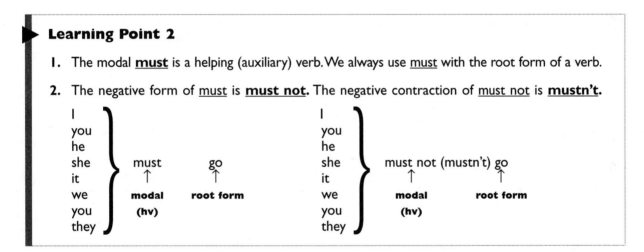

Example:

1. I must make a deposit to my checking account tomorrow, or my account will be overdrawn.
   ↑   ↑
 modal   root form

2. People in the United States must file an income tax return no later than April 15 every year.
               ↑ ↑
           modal root form

3. Maria wants to become a U. S. citizen, so she must take the citizenship test next month.
                  ↑   ↑
              modal   root form

4. I must not forget to pay my rent. It's due tomorrow.
 ↑   ↑
 modal   root form

THE MODAL __MUST__ TO SHOW NECESSITY

➠ **Exercise 1** Use the modal __must__ to show that an action is necessary in the sentences below.

1. The students in my English class _must turn in all their assignments_ in order to pass the course.

2. You_____if you want to get a good job.

3. I _____, or I'll lose my job.

4. You _____ if you want to be a lawyer.

5. Students _____, or the teacher will get angry.

6. Everyone _____ before they can travel to Europe.

7. Drivers _____, or they'll get a ticket.

8. You_____ if you want to keep your car in good condition.

9. People _____ in order to stay healthy.

10. You _____ if you want to live to be 100.

11. You _____ so that you'll have a good credit rating.

12. You _____ if you want to have a secure retirement.

➠ **Exercise 2** Practice writing sentences with __must__.

1. Name two things that you __must do__ to get ready for a vacation.

   a. _____

   _____

   b. _____

   _____

2. Name two things that you __must do__ to get a driver's license.

   a. _____

   _____

   b. _____

   _____

3. Name two things that you __must do__ before an important test.

   a. _____

   _____

   b. _____

   _____

THE DIFFERENCE BETWEEN <u>SHOULD</u> AND <u>MUST</u>

▶ **Exercise 3** David Carter is a student in a driver's education class, and he has an excellent instructor. He teaches his young students the driving laws, and he also gives them advice on how to be good drivers. David has written down the following lists of instructions. Some instructions are necessary actions (things he must do) and some are advisable actions (things he should do). Identify each instruction as something David <u>must</u> do or something he <u>should</u> do. Work with a partner or in a small group.

List 1 - How To Be a Good Driver	**Things he must do**	**Things he should do**
1. Observe the speed limit.	X	
2. Change your oil every 3000 miles.		
3. Have a valid driver's license.		
4. Look over your shoulder before you change lanes.		
5. Have proof of insurance.		
6. Rotate your tires regularly.		
7. Keep the windshield wipers in good working order.		
8. Turn your wheels away from the curb and set the parking brake when you park uphill.		
9. Turn on your headlights when it is cloudy, raining, snowing, or foggy.		
10. Wear a seatbelt.		

List 2 - How To Be a Good Driver	**Things he must do**	**Things he should do**
1. Always set your parking brake.		
2. Yield to the person on your right at a four-way stop.		
3. Have a regular maintenance schedule.		
4. Be sure that your speedometer works properly.		
5. Turn your wheels into the curb and set the parking brake when you park downhill.		
6. Drive no faster than 25 mph near a school when children are present.		
7. Put children under six or less than 60 pounds in car seats.		
8. Slow down at the first sign of rain because this is when the roads are most slippery.		
9. Come to a complete stop at a stop sign.		
10. Lock your car doors when you park your car.		

SPECIAL POINT - USING <u>HAVE TO</u> TO SHOW NECESSITY

▸ You have learned that we use the modal <u>must</u> to show that it is necessary to do something in present or future time. We can also use the expression <u>have to</u> to show that an action is necessary in present or future time.

> ▶ **Learning Point**
>
> <u>**Have to**</u> is very similar in meaning to the modal <u>**must**</u>. <u>**Have to**</u> means that an action is necessary.

1. My Visa bill was due yesterday. I $\left\{\begin{array}{c}\text{must}\\\text{have to}\end{array}\right\}$ pay it right away. **(action is necessary)**

2. Our trip is next month. We $\left\{\begin{array}{c}\text{must}\\\text{have to}\end{array}\right\}$ get our tickets next week. **(action is necessary)**

▸ **Exercise 4** Although <u>must</u> and <u>have to</u> have similar meanings, it is more common to use <u>have to</u> than <u>must</u> in everyday speaking and writing. Answer the questions below. Use <u>have to</u> in your answers. Give true information about your activities in the present or future.

1. What do you <u>have to do</u> after class today? _____

_____

_____

2. What do you <u>have to do</u> tomorrow? _____

_____

_____

3. What do you usually <u>have to do</u> on the weekend? _____

_____

_____

4. What do you <u>have to do</u> when you get a speeding ticket? _____

_____

_____

5. What do you <u>have to do</u> to pass this class? _____

_____

_____

Note: We can also use the expression <u>have got to</u> to show necessity in present or future time. We use <u>have got to</u> only in informal speaking and writing. <u>Have got to</u> does not show past time.
Example: I have to study tomorrow = I have got to study tomorrow.

USING **MUST NOT** AND **DO NOT HAVE TO**

Be careful. **Must not** and **do not have to** have different meanings.

> ### ▶ Learning Point 1
> **Must not** means that an action is <u>not permitted</u>. You must not do this.

<u>Example:</u>

1. People <u>must not drink</u> and <u>drive</u>. It is against the law to drink and drive. **(They must not do this.)**

2. Students <u>must not cheat</u> when they take a test. It is dishonest. **(They must not do this.)**

3. I <u>mustn't be</u> late for work again, or I'll lose my job. **(I must not do this.)**

4. Children <u>mustn't play</u> with matches. They might hurt themselves or start a fire. **(They must not do this.)**

5. You <u>mustn't use</u> electric appliances near the water. You might get electrocuted. **(You must not do this.)**

> ### ▶ Learning Point 2
> **Do not have to** means that it is <u>not necessary</u> to do something.

<u>Example:</u>

1. We <u>do not have to go</u> to work tomorrow because it's a holiday. **(The action is not necessary.)**

2. My daughter found her glasses, so she <u>does not have to get</u> new ones. **(The action is not necessary.)**

3. I <u>don't have to do</u> any homework tonight. I finished it at the library. **(The action is not necessary.)**

4. My first class isn't until 9:00, so I <u>don't have to leave</u> home until 8:00. **(The action is not necessary.)**

5. Luis <u>doesn't have to take</u> the quiz tomorrow. He got an A on the last test. **(The action is not necessary.)**

USING <u>MUST NOT</u> AND <u>DO NOT HAVE TO</u>

▶ **Exercise 5** Complete the negative sentences below with <u>must not</u> or <u>do not have to</u>.

1. We _____*must not*_____ make noise or speak too loudly in the library because other people are trying to study. The library should be quiet at all times.

   a. (must not)   **b.** do not have to   **c.** does not have to

2. During the week, I have to get up at 4:30 a.m. every day. I look forward to Saturday and Sunday because I _____ get up early.

   a. must not   **b.** do not have to   **c.** does not have to

3. I made an appointment to see the doctor tomorrow, but I'm feeling much better now, so I _____ see the doctor after all.

   a. must not   **b.** do not have to   **c.** does not have to

4. Our city has strict "No Smoking" laws. People _____ smoke in public places.

   a. must not   **b.** do not have to   **c.** does not have to

▶ **Exercise 6** Follow the same directions as in Exercise 5.

1. Yesterday I locked myself out of my car, and I had to call a locksmith. I _____ forget to put a spare key in my wallet in the future.

   a. must not   **b.** do not have to   **c.** does not have to

2. Everyone understands the chapter on time clauses, so the teacher _____ review it.

   a. must not   **b.** do not have to   **c.** does not have to

3. I usually pick my daughter up after school, but sometimes she has to walk home. I always remind her of two important rules. "You _____ talk to strangers, and you _____ walk by yourself. You must always walk with a friend."

   a. must not   **b.** do not have to   **c.** does not have to

4. It's my mother's birthday. We're taking her out so she _____ cook.

   a. must not   **b.** do not have to   **c.** does not have to

USING <u>MUST</u>, <u>HAVE TO</u>, <u>MUST NOT</u>, AND <u>DO NOT HAVE TO</u>

⟫ **Exercise 7** Write the correct letter in the blank according to the meaning of the sentence.

Final Exam Requirements

1. Most students _____*a*_____ complete a final examination for every college course that they take.

   a. must / have to   b. must not   c. do not have to

2. At Evergreen Valley College, all intermediate and advanced writing students _____ take a board-graded final exam.

   a. must / have to   **b.** must not   **c.** do not have to

3. However, lower-level classes _____ take a board-graded final exam.

   a. must / have to   **b.** must not   **c.** do not have to

4. Every student _____ purchase a special examination booklet at the bookstore.

   a. must / has to   **b.** must not   **c.** does not have to

5. Students _____ bring a dictionary to the exam, but it is a good idea.

   a. must / have to   **b.** must not   **c.** do not have to

6. Students _____ talk during the exam or give help to another student.

   a. must / have to   **b.** must not   **c.** do not have to

7. Students _____ write their final exam in ink and double space.

   a. must / have to   **b.** must not   **c.** do not have to

8. In addition, students _____ finish their exam during a required time limit.

   a. must / have to   **b.** must not   **c.** do not have to

9. If students finish the exam early, they _____ leave the classroom until the exam is over.

   a. must / have to   **b.** must not   **c.** do not have to

10. In order to pass the final exam, students _____ receive a grade of C- or better.

   a. must / have to   **b.** must not   **c.** do not have to

11. Any student who fails to show up for the final exam _____ take the entire course again.

   a. must / has to   **b.** must not   **c.** does not have to

✓ CHECK YOUR UNDERSTANDING

A. Answer the following questions in complete sentences.

1. When do we use the modal <u>must</u>?_____

_____

2. What time does the modal <u>must</u> show in a sentence?_____

_____

3. What form of the verb do we use with the modal <u>must</u>? _____

_____

4. What is the difference in meaning between <u>should</u> and <u>must</u>?_____

_____

5. What expression is similar in meaning to the modal <u>must</u>?

_____

6. Do <u>must not</u> and <u>do not have to</u> have the same meaning? _____ yes _____ no

    a. <u>Must not</u> means _____

    b. <u>Do not have to</u> means _____

B. Think carefully about the meaning of the sentences below. One sentence is true, and one sentence is false. Write *T* or *F* on the line after each sentence.

1. Ann should take more classes because she wants to graduate next June.

    a. Ann already has enough units to graduate next June. _____

    b. Ann needs more classes if she plans to graduate next June. _____

2. Pete doesn't have to lose any more weight. He's already too thin.

    a. Pete needs to go on a diet. _____

    b. Pete lost too much weight when he went on a diet. _____

3. Cal's Restaurant doesn't take checks or credit cards, so you'd better get some cash from the bank.

    a. If you don't have cash to pay the bill, don't eat at Cal's Restaurant. _____

    b. If you eat at Cal's Restaurant, you can pay by check. _____

4. It's illegal to sell alcoholic beverages to anyone under the age of 21. It's also illegal to sell cigarettes to anyone under 18.

    a. People 21 and over are not able to purchase beer or wine. _____

    b. If you sell cigarettes to a minor, you are breaking the law. _____

Part 4

<u>Must</u> (Logical Conclusion)

THE MODAL <u>MUST</u> TO SHOW LOGICAL CONCLUSION

▪▶ In Part 3 you learned that the modal <u>must</u> shows that an action is necessary. The modal <u>must</u> also has another important meaning.

> ▶ **Learning Point**
>
> We often use the modal <u>**must**</u> to make a logical conclusion about a situation in present time. A logical conclusion is your best guess about a situation.

▪▶ Study the examples below.

1. Situation: Bob doesn't look well. He is coughing and sneezing and blowing his nose.

(What do you think is probably wrong with Bob? What is your best guess or conclusion?)

Logical conclusion: He <u>must have</u> a cold.

2. Situation: It's 10:00, and it's past the children's bedtime. They usually go to bed at 8:00. They're yawning and starting to get irritable.

(What do you think is probably wrong with the children? What is your best guess?)

Logical conclusion: They <u>must be</u> tired and sleepy.

3. Situation: The guests look bored, and several people are leaving the party early.

(Why do you think people are leaving? What is your best guess?)

Logical conclusion: It <u>must be</u> a boring party. No one is having a good time.

4. Situation: The new restaurant on Almaden Avenue often advertises in the local newspaper, and its prices appear to be reasonable. They even offer 2-for-1 dinner coupons. However, whenever I drive by, the parking lot is always empty.

(Why do you think the parking lot is always empty? What is your best guess?)

Logical conclusion: The food <u>mustn't be</u> very good at the new restaurant.

THE MODAL <u>MUST</u> TO SHOW LOGICAL CONCLUSION

➡ **Exercise 1** Make logical conclusions with <u>must</u> or <u>must not</u> to complete the dialogs below.

1. A: Tran looks sick. He's holding his head, and he just took some aspirin. What do you think is wrong with him?

   B: *He must have a headache.*
                  (have a headache / be bored / not like the class)

2. A: Lupe is a very conscientious student. She studies hard and gets good grades. She's never late or absent, but she's not in class today. Why do you think she isn't here?

   B: _____
                  (be at the movies / be sick / be out with her boyfriend)

3. A: Bill is going to have a serious accident one of these days. He just got his third speeding ticket in eight months. What's his problem?

   B: _____
        (like to pay high insurance premiums / be a careless driver / have a red sports car)

4. A: The man in the next apartment is a very nice man, but he keeps his stereo and TV on so loud that it disturbs the neighbors. In fact, when he watches TV at night, I can't sleep because the volume is so loud. Why does he keep his stereo and TV so loud?

   B: _____
             (be deaf / like loud music / hate the neighbors)

5. A: Mike invited Sue to the new Chinese restaurant on Second Street, but she told him that she had to stay home and do her homework. A few minutes ago, Richard called her, and now she's fixing her hair, putting on her make-up, and getting ready to go out. Why did she change her mind?

   B: _____
       (not like Chinese food / like Richard better than Mike / not want to do her homework)

6. A: Los Angeles is about 450 miles from San Francisco, and it takes about 8 hours to drive there. My brother and sister-in-law left San Francisco at 6:00 this morning, and it's 4:00 now. Where do you think they are?

   B: _____
       (be on the way to Los Angeles / be in San Francisco / be in Los Angeles)

THE MODAL <u>MUST</u> TO SHOW LOGICAL CONCLUSION

▶ **Exercise 2** Use the information in each situation to write a logical conclusion with <u>must</u> or <u>must not</u>. The subject is given. Compare your answers with a classmate.

<u>Situation 1</u>   Ted's car is stalled at the intersection of Bascom and Camden, and he can't start the engine. The lights won't go on, and the radio and the windshield wipers don't work either.

logical
conclusion: *The battery must be dead.*

<u>Situation 2</u>   It's 11:50, and the students are standing up and putting their books and papers into their backpacks and briefcases. The teacher is erasing the board.

logical
conclusion: *Class*

<u>Situation 3</u>   The Stanford Theater shows classic, old-time movies from the 1930's, 1940's, and 1950's. The theater is always crowded, especially on the weekend, and people sometimes have to wait in line to get a ticket.

logical
conclusion: *Old movies*

<u>Situation 4</u>   On Monday and Tuesday nights, my friend Susan orders pizza from the Pizza Express or picks up Chinese food from The Golden Dragon on her way home from work. On Wednesday and Thursday nights, she always has dinner at her mother's house. On Friday nights, her boyfriend cooks dinner, and on Saturday and Sunday, they eat out.

logical
conclusion: *Susan*

<u>Situation 5</u>   Brian takes the bus to and from school every day. Right now, he's standing at the bus stop in front of the library and glancing at his watch every few minutes.

logical
conclusion: *The bus*

<u>Situation 6</u>   All the lights are on at my neighbor's house, and there's an ambulance in their driveway.

logical
conclusion: *Someone*

Part 5
May and Might (Uncertainty)

THE MODALS MAY AND MIGHT

> ### Learning Point 1
>
> We use the modals **may** and **might** when we are not sure if something will happen.
> May and might have the same meaning.
>
> May and might show present or future time.

1. A: What are you going to do tonight?

    B: I'm not sure. I $\left\{ \begin{array}{l} \text{may} \\ \text{might} \end{array} \right\}$ go to the movies with a friend, or I $\left\{ \begin{array}{l} \text{may} \\ \text{might} \end{array} \right\}$ go shopping.

2. A: I really don't like my job. It's boring.

    B: Are you going to quit?

    A: I don't know. I $\left\{ \begin{array}{l} \text{may} \\ \text{might} \end{array} \right\}$ look for a new job during the summer. I'm not sure.

> ### Learning Point 2
>
> 1. The modals **may** and **might** are helping (auxiliary) verbs. We always use may and might with the root form of a verb.
>
> 2. The negative form of may is **may not.** The negative form of might is **might not.**
>
> $\left. \begin{array}{l} \text{I} \\ \text{you} \\ \text{he} \\ \text{she} \\ \text{it} \\ \text{we} \\ \text{you} \\ \text{they} \end{array} \right\}$ $\begin{array}{cc} \text{may} & \text{go} \\ \text{might} & \text{go} \\ \uparrow & \uparrow \\ \textbf{modal} & \textbf{root form} \\ \textbf{(hv)} & \end{array}$ $\left. \begin{array}{l} \text{I} \\ \text{you} \\ \text{he} \\ \text{she} \\ \text{it} \\ \text{we} \\ \text{you} \\ \text{they} \end{array} \right\}$ $\begin{array}{ccc} \text{may} & \text{not} & \text{go} \\ \text{might} & \text{not} & \text{go} \\ \uparrow & & \uparrow \\ \textbf{modal} & & \textbf{root form} \\ \textbf{(hv)} & & \end{array}$

1. I don't want to go to the beach tomorrow because it $\left\{ \begin{array}{l} \text{may} \\ \text{might} \end{array} \right\}$ rain.

                                                                                   ↑   ↑
        modal   **root form**

2. I $\left\{ \begin{array}{l} \text{may not} \\ \text{might not} \end{array} \right\}$ come to class tomorrow. I think I'm coming down with the flu.

           ↑   ↑
   modal   **root form**

THE MODALS <u>MAY</u> AND <u>MIGHT</u>

▶ **Exercise I** We use the modals <u>may</u> and <u>might</u> when we are not sure if something will happen. <u>May</u> and <u>might</u> have the same meaning. You can use either <u>may</u> or <u>might</u> to complete each dialog below.

1. **A:** I'm having trouble with our writing assignment in our English 92 class. I can't think of a good topic. What are you going to write about?

   B: *I don't know. I'm having trouble too. I might write about a childhood experience, or I might write about my plans for the future.*

2. **A:** What are you going to do tonight?

   B: I can't make up my mind. _____

3. **A:** There's a three-day weekend at the end of the month. Are you going to do anything special?

   B: I don't know yet. _____ , or

4. **A:** I'm looking forward to Kim's birthday party on Saturday, but I don't know what to give her for her birthday. What are you going to get her?

   B: I can't decide. _____ , or

5. **A:** I found a great apartment just a few blocks from school, but the landlord wants the first and last month's rent and a cleaning deposit. I'm about $300.00 short.

   B: What are you going to do?

   A: I'm not sure. _____

6. **A:** We just moved into a new house with a beautiful back yard, and we are going to the nursery tomorrow to buy some flowers and plants.

   B: What kind of plants are you going to buy?

   A: We're trying to decide. _____ , or

7. **A:** Where are you planning to go on your vacation?

   B: I'm not sure. I want to go somewhere warm with beautiful beaches. _____

REFERENCE CHART - MODALS

Review the meaning of the modals you have studied in this chapter.

MODALS REFERENCE CHART

	modal	meaning	example
1.	can	ability	I can speak English and Spanish.
2.	can	possibility	I got my car back from the mechanic, so I can drive you home after class.
3.	could	past ability	My daughter could read when she was four years old.
4.	should ought to had better	good advice	You don't look well. You $\begin{Bmatrix} \text{should} \\ \text{ought to} \\ \text{had better} \end{Bmatrix}$ call the doctor.
5.	must have to	necessity	Everyone $\begin{Bmatrix} \text{must} \\ \text{has to} \end{Bmatrix}$ obey the law.
6.	must not	not permitted	People must not drink and drive.
7.	do not have to	not necessary	Tomorrow is a holiday, so we don't have to go to work.
8.	must	logical conclusion	There's an ambulance in my neighbor's driveway. Someone must be ill.
9.	may might	uncertainty	I'm not sure what classes to take next semester. I $\begin{Bmatrix} \text{may} \\ \text{might} \end{Bmatrix}$ take biology, or I $\begin{Bmatrix} \text{may} \\ \text{might} \end{Bmatrix}$ take a math class.

✔ CHECK YOUR UNDERSTANDING

A. Complete the dialogs with the correct expression from the box. Use each expression only one time.

don't have to	should go	couldn't get
can multiply and divide	mustn't call	had better be
mustn't be	could count	✔ can't find

I. A: I bought these pants at Macy's last week, but they don't fit right. I want to return them, but I __can't find__ the receipt.

    B: You _____ worry about the receipt. If the original tags are on the pants, Macy's will take them back and give you a store credit.

2. A: My little sister is very good at math. She _____ to 100 when she was two years old.

    B: That's amazing. Is she still good at math?

    A: Yes, she's only eight years old, and she _____ fractions.

3. A: I was really disappointed because I _____ into Professor Tran's history class last semester. His classes are very popular, and they always close early.

    B: That's too bad. He is a very good teacher. You should try again this semester.

4. A: Paul _____ more serious about his job, or he's going to get fired.

    B: Why do you say that?

    A: His boss yelled at him today. He told him that he _____ late for work anymore, and he _____ in sick so often. He called in sick four times last month.

5. A: This restaurant looks crowded. Should we put our name on the waiting list?

    B: Well, there's an hour's wait.

    A: That's too long to wait for a table. We _____ somewhere else for dinner.

✓ CHECK YOUR UNDERSTANDING

B. The following products came from a local drugstore. Read the label on each product. Then complete the sentences below with can, should, or must not.

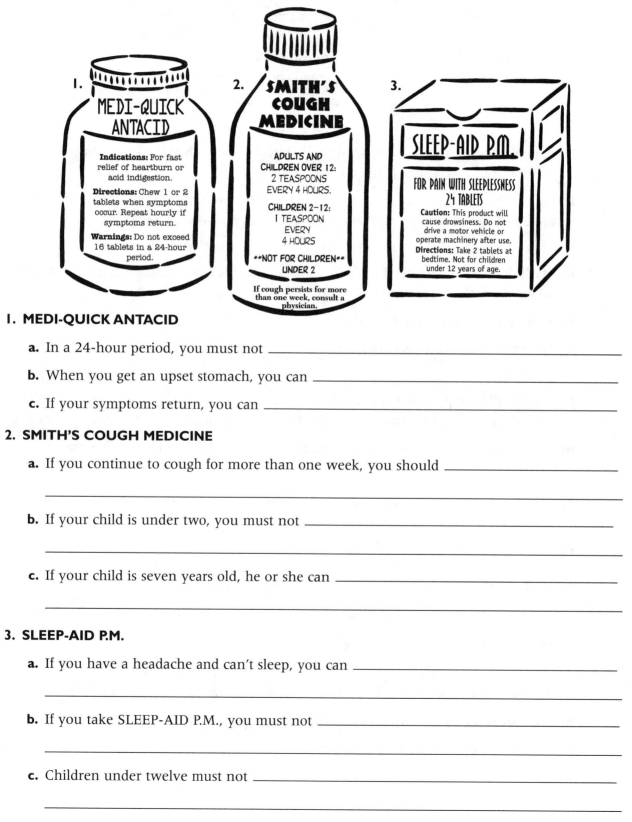

1. MEDI-QUICK ANTACID

Indications: For fast relief of heartburn or acid indigestion.

Directions: Chew 1 or 2 tablets when symptoms occur. Repeat hourly if symptoms return.

Warnings: Do not exceed 16 tablets in a 24-hour period.

2. SMITH'S COUGH MEDICINE

ADULTS AND CHILDREN OVER 12: 2 TEASPOONS EVERY 4 HOURS.

CHILDREN 2–12: 1 TEASPOON EVERY 4 HOURS

NOT FOR CHILDREN UNDER 2

If cough persists for more than one week, consult a physician.

3. SLEEP-AID P.M.

FOR PAIN WITH SLEEPLESSNESS 24 TABLETS

Caution: This product will cause drowsiness. Do not drive a motor vehicle or operate machinery after use.

Directions: Take 2 tablets at bedtime. Not for children under 12 years of age.

1. MEDI-QUICK ANTACID

a. In a 24-hour period, you must not _____

b. When you get an upset stomach, you can _____

c. If your symptoms return, you can _____

2. SMITH'S COUGH MEDICINE

a. If you continue to cough for more than one week, you should _____

_____

b. If your child is under two, you must not _____

_____

c. If your child is seven years old, he or she can _____

_____

3. SLEEP-AID P.M.

a. If you have a headache and can't sleep, you can _____

_____

b. If you take SLEEP-AID P.M., you must not _____

_____

c. Children under twelve must not _____

_____

Writing Assignment

➡ Your writing assignment is to write a paragraph about one of the topics below.

▶ What to do ◀

1. Choose **one** of the topic sentences below to write about.

   _____ **Topic 1:** Parents can help their children to become successful adults in several ways.

   All parents want their children to grow up to be successful, independent, responsible adults. However, raising children is not an easy job. Parents must teach and guide their children to prepare them for adulthood. What are the most important things that parents can teach their children? How can parents help their children to succeed in life?

   _____ **Topic 2:** There are several important things that people should do to have a long, healthy life.

   Good health is one of the most important things in life, but many people do not take care of themselves. What advice would you give to these people? What are the three most important things that people should do to have a long, healthy life?

2. Write the first draft and the final draft of your paragraph on separate sheets of paper.

3. Follow the writing steps below.

STEP 1   Before you begin to write, take a few minutes to think about your topic. Then make a *list* of your ideas.

STEP 2   Choose three ideas from your list, and write a *first draft (practice paragraph)*.

STEP 3   *Revise and edit* your practice paragraph.

STEP 4   Write your *final draft (final paragraph)*.

Chapter 14
Gerunds and Infinitives

To the Student:

In this chapter you will study special forms of verbs called **gerunds** and **infinitives.** We can use gerunds and infinitives in many of the same ways that we use nouns in sentences. Before you begin to use gerunds and infinitives in your writing, you will review some of the ways that we use nouns in sentences.

Part I
Review of Nouns

NOUN REVIEW

➠ Read the paragraph about Disneyland below. Then do the noun review exercise on page 350.

If you are planning a vacation to Southern California, Disneyland is the place to go. Disneyland 1

is one of the most popular amusement parks in the world and offers visitors of all ages many

wonderful things to do and see. When my family and I were in Disneyland last summer, we arrived

at the park about 9:30 and began our day in Adventureland. We boarded a small boat and took a

cruise along a jungle river where we saw monkeys, elephants, lions, and tigers. Adventureland looks 5

exactly like a jungle in Africa. After that, we visited Frontierland. In Frontierland, we saw an old-

fashioned western town from the 1800s with wooden buildings, horses and wagons, cowboys, and

gold mines. By this time, everyone was hungry, so we stopped at a snack bar for lunch. After lunch,

the children wanted to go to Fantasyland, where we met many well-loved characters such as

Mickey Mouse, Cinderella, and Donald Duck. We ended our day in Tomorrowland. In Tomorrowland, 10

we learned about space travel and life in the future. At the end of the day, we all agreed that

Disneyland was not only fun but an unforgettable experience for the whole family.

NOUN REVIEW

▐▶ You have learned that a noun is a word that names a person, place, thing, idea, or quality.

Most nouns you can see or touch.			Some nouns you cannot see or touch.	
persons	places	things	ideas	qualities
visitor	restaurant	boat	happiness	honesty
tourist	park	elephant	fun	courage
children	town	hamburger	future	kindness
Donald Duck	United States	tickets	time	thoughtfulness
Walt Disney	Disneyland	ride	experience	generosity

▐▶ **Exercise 1** The sentences below are about the Disneyland paragraph on page 349. Circle the nouns in each sentence.

1. A (visit) to (Disneyland) is not only (fun,) but it is also a wonderful (experience). **(4 nouns)**

2. Disneyland changes people of all ages into children. **(4)**

3. Adventureland looks like a jungle in Africa. **(3)**

4. Visitors to Adventureland can take a cruise through the jungle where they see monkeys, elephants, lions, and tigers. **(8)**

5. Visitors to Frontierland can go back in time to when the United States was a young, new country. **(5)**

6. In Fantasyland, visitors meet well-loved characters such as Mickey Mouse, Cinderella, and Donald Duck. **(6)**

7. Fantasyland also has many popular rides. **(2)**

8. Visitors can tour a castle, sail on a pirate ship, or take a ride on a train around the park. **(6)**

9. Tomorrowland teaches people about life in the future. **(4)**

10. Visitors to Tomorrowland can take a ride through space. **(4)**

11. Disneyland is not just another amusement park. **(2)**

12. It is unlike any other place in the world and offers visitors an unforgettable experience. **(4)**

NOUN REVIEW

➠ A noun is a word that names a person, place, thing, idea, or quality. We use nouns in different ways in sentences. Three of the ways that we use nouns in sentences are:

1. Nouns as <u>subjects</u> of verbs: My <u>family</u> just won a trip to Disneyland in a newspaper contest.

2. Nouns as <u>objects</u> of verbs: The newspaper called my <u>family</u> with the good news last week.

3. Nouns as <u>objects of prepositions</u>:   The paper is making all the necessary arrangements for my <u>family</u>.

➠ **Exercise 2** One noun in each sentence below is underlined. Write the underlined noun on the line. Then tell how the noun is used in the sentence: subject of verb (<u>s of v</u>), object of verb (<u>o of v</u>), or object of preposition (<u>o of p</u>).

1. My <u>family</u> won a free trip to Disneyland.   *family - s of v*

2. We have a lot to do before we leave on our <u>trip</u> next week. _____

3. First, everyone wants new <u>clothes</u>.   _____

4. My <u>sister</u> and I need new bathing suits, and my brother needs new jeans.   _____

5. My mother wants some cotton <u>slacks</u> and comfortable shoes.   _____

6. My <u>father</u> says that he doesn't need anything.   _____

7. However, we are giving my father a new <u>camera</u> as a surprise. _____

8. Before we leave, we need to ask one of our neighbors to feed our cat and keep an eye on the <u>house</u>.   _____

9. We also have to call the newspaper to stop delivery of the <u>paper</u>. _____

10. We're leaving early on Tuesday, so we need to pack by Monday <u>night</u>.   _____

11. The newspaper will send a <u>limousine</u> to pick us up at 6:30 a.m. _____

12. Our <u>flight</u> to Los Angeles leaves at 8:00 from the San Jose airport. _____

13. Someone from the <u>hotel</u> will meet us when we arrive at the airport.   _____

14. We're staying at the Disneyland Hotel close to the <u>park</u>.   _____

15. My <u>family</u> expects to have a wonderful three days!   _____

Part 2
Introduction to Gerunds

GERUNDS

➤ In previous chapters, you used the <u>-ing form</u> of the verb in the Present Progressive Tense to show an action that is happening now.

Example: **1.** We are reading about Disneyland now. **(action - Present Progressive Tense)**
                                ↑   ↑
                            hv verb (action)

            2. We are planning a trip to Disneyland. **(action - Present Progressive Tense)**
                                ↑   ↑
                            hv verb (action)

> ▶ **Learning Point**
>
> We can also use the <u>-ing form</u> of the verb as a noun. When we use the <u>-ing form</u> as a noun, we call it a **gerund.** A gerund does not show action.

Example: **1.** Reading is an enjoyable pastime. **(no action)**
                    ↑
            gerund (subject noun)

            2. Planning a trip can be a lot of fun. **(no action)**
                    ↑
            gerund (subject noun)

➤ **Exercise 1** Compare the use of the <u>-ing form</u> in the following sentences. In some of the sentences, the <u>-ing form</u> is a verb. In some of the sentences, the <u>-ing form</u> is a gerund.

1. We are <u>flying</u> to Los Angeles at 6:30 tomorrow morning.   _____*flying - verb*_____

2. <u>Flying</u> to Los Angeles takes about 45 minutes.   _____*flying - gerund*_____

3. <u>Driving</u> to Los Angeles takes about seven hours.   _____

4. Everyone is <u>getting</u> ready for our trip to Disneyland.   _____

5. My sister is <u>taking</u> three suitcases and a backpack.   _____

6. <u>Going</u> to Disneyland is one of our favorite vacations.   _____

7. We are also <u>going</u> to the Universal Studios in Hollywood.   _____

8. <u>Visiting</u> the studios and the movie sets will be very interesting.   _____
    We might even get to see some famous movie stars!

GERUNDS

On the previous page, you learned that a gerund is the <u>-ing form</u> of a verb used as a noun.

> ### ▶ Learning Point
>
> We use gerunds in the same way that we use nouns in sentences. Gerunds can be used as subjects of verbs, objects of verbs, and objects of prepositions.

1. Gerunds as <u>subjects</u> of verbs:

   <u>Traveling</u> is my sister's favorite pastime.
   gerund

2. Gerunds as <u>objects</u> of verbs:

   She enjoys <u>traveling</u> more than any other activity.
   gerund

3. Gerunds as <u>objects of prepositions</u>:

   She dreams about <u>traveling</u> around the world someday.
   gerund

Exercise 2 Read each sentence below. Then tell how the underlined gerund is used in the sentence: subject of verb **(s of v)**, object of verb **(o of v)**, or object of preposition **(o of p)**.

1. Visitors of all ages enjoy <u>spending</u> a day at Disneyland.   *spending - o of v*

2. <u>Planning</u> the day is important because there are so many things to see and do.

3. Children are always excited about <u>going</u> on the many different kinds of rides in the park.

4. <u>Looking</u> in the shops along Main Street is another favorite thing for tourists to do at Disneyland.

5. No one leaves the park without <u>buying</u> a souvenir such as a Mickey Mouse hat, a Donald Duck T-shirt, or a video tape of a favorite Disney movie.

6. There are many good snack bars and restaurants in the park, so <u>eating</u> is another favorite pastime,

7. In the evening, everyone enjoys <u>watching</u> the spectacular fireworks over Sleeping Beauty's castle at the entrance to Fantasyland.

8. The world will always remember Walt Disney for <u>giving</u> us characters such as Mickey Mouse and magical places like Disneyland.

Part 3
Verbs Followed by Gerunds

GERUNDS USED AS OBJECTS OF VERBS

➠ You have learned that we can use gerunds (-ing form) as subjects of verbs, as objects of verbs, and as objects of prepositions. In the exercises that follow, you will practice using gerunds as objects of verbs.

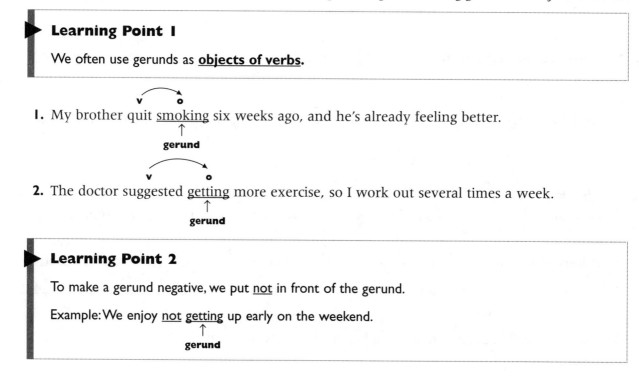

> ▶ **Learning Point I**
>
> We often use gerunds as **objects of verbs.**

    I. My brother quit <u>smoking</u> six weeks ago, and he's already feeling better.
               gerund

    2. The doctor suggested <u>getting</u> more exercise, so I work out several times a week.
              gerund

> ▶ **Learning Point 2**
>
> To make a gerund negative, we put <u>not</u> in front of the gerund.
>
> Example: We enjoy <u>not getting</u> up early on the weekend.
>   **gerund**

➠ **Exercise I** Use a gerund after each verb. Some sentences are affirmative, and some are negative.

  I. I appreciated **(receive)** <u>receiving</u> your postcard from Disneyland.

  2. Our travel agent recommended **(not/go)** _____ to Southern California in August.

  3. During the summer, I always enjoy **(visit)** _____ my parents in Canada.

  4. We considered **(drive)** _____ to Los Angeles, but we decided to fly instead.

  5. I'm a procrastinator. I always postpone **(make)** _____ my travel plans until the last minute.

  6. I dislike **(fly)** _____ on a holiday because the airports are always very crowded.

  7. My sister regrets **(not / take)** _____ more pictures when she went to Europe last year.

  8. I had to work overtime last night, so I couldn't finish **(pack)** _____ for my trip until this morning.

VERBS FOLLOWED BY GERUNDS (VERB + GERUND)

➡ We often use gerunds (-ing form) after certain verbs. Study the verbs in the list below. We can use gerunds after these verbs.

VERBS FOLLOWED BY GERUNDS			
admit	deny	finish	quit
appreciate	discuss	mind	recommend
avoid	dislike	postpone	resist
consider	enjoy	practice	

➡ **Exercise 2** Complete the dialogs below with verbs followed by gerunds. Take turns asking and answering the questions with a partner.

1. A: What should ESL students do to improve their English?

   B: They should ____practice speaking____ outside of class as often as they can.
                  (practice / speak)

2. A: You look nervous. What's the matter?

   B: I have to give a speech in my speech class today, and I always _____
                                                (dislike / speak)
     in front of an audience.

   A: I know. It's difficult to speak in front of a group, but I'm sure you'll do well.

3. A: I don't have my book. I must have left it at home. Would you _____
     yours with me?   **(mind / share)**

   B: Sure. I'd be glad to.

4. A: When did your class _____ the chapter on modals?
                           (finish / study)

   B: We finished it last week. Now I know the difference between the modals <u>should</u> and <u>must</u>!

5. A: Did you and Minh decide to study together for the final exam?

   B: No, we didn't. We _____ together, but we decided against it.
                        (discuss / study)
     We have different work schedules, and we couldn't find a time that was good for both of us.

6. A: Did Jack _____ on the test?
               (admit / cheat)

   B: No, he didn't, but everyone knows that he did.

VERBS FOLLOWED BY GERUNDS (VERB + GERUND)

➥ **Exercise 3** Choose an expression from the list to complete the sentences below. Use a gerund in each sentence.

join a health club	add salt to his food	eat high fiber foods	smoke
✔ walk three miles	make an appointment	receive your card	buy a chocolate cake

I. My neighbor <u>enjoys</u> <u> walking three miles </u> every morning. This form of exercise is fun, easy, and convenient. I'm going to try it.

2. My friend Mary feels great since she joined a health club. I'<u>m considering</u> _____

_____ too.

3. My brother smokes at least two packs of cigarettes a day. He <u>should quit</u> _____, or he will ruin his health.

4. My father-in-law has high blood pressure, so he <u>avoids</u> _____.

5. People need fiber in their diets. Doctors and nutritionists <u>recommend</u> _____

_____ such as cereal and grains.

6. I know that I should lose weight, but whenever I go into a bakery, I can't <u>resist</u> _____

_____ or a banana cream pie.

7. I <u>appreciated</u> _____ and flowers when I was in the hospital.

8. Chris is afraid of the dentist. As a result, she <u>postponed</u> _____

until she got a bad toothache.

➥ **Exercise 4** Answer the questions below. Use a gerund after the underlined verb in your answers. Then practice asking and answering the questions with a partner.

I. What do you <u>enjoy</u> doing on the weekend?

_____

_____

2. What don't you <u>enjoy</u> doing on the weekend?

_____

_____

3. What do you often <u>postpone</u> doing?

_____

_____

4. What time do you usually <u>finish</u> doing your homework during the week?

_____

SPECIAL POINT - GO + GERUND (-ING)

> ▶ **Learning Point**
>
> In conversation, we often use a gerund after the verb go to talk about sports and other recreational activities.

EXPRESSIONS WITH GO + ING

go bowling	go fishing	go ice skating	go sightseeing
go camping	go golfing	go sailing	go skiing

➠ Be careful. Do not use **to** in front of the gerund.

correct: **1.** I usually go shopping for groceries on Saturday morning.
not correct: I usually go ~~to~~ shopping for groceries on Saturday morning.

correct: **2.** My brother went fishing last weekend, but he didn't catch any fish.
not correct: My brother went ~~to~~ fishing last weekend, but he didn't catch any fish.

➠ **Exercise 5** Answer the questions below. Use **go + ing** in your answers.

1. My sister spends every Saturday and Sunday at the mall. She always comes home with bags full of clothes, shoes, and jewelry. What does she do every weekend?

    She goes shopping every weekend.

2. My brother has a new 15-foot sailboat. He and his friends went to the lake last weekend. What did they do at the lake last weekend?

_____

3. My uncle enjoys his favorite sport all year long. He spends every Saturday and Sunday swinging a club at a little white ball. What does he do every weekend?

_____

4. Last summer my neighbors spent a week in the mountains. They slept in tents and cooked their food over a campfire. What did they do last summer?

_____

5. What is <u>your</u> favorite recreational activity? What do <u>you</u> usually do in your free time?

_____

_____

✓ CHECK YOUR UNDERSTANDING

A. Answer the questions below.

1. What is a noun?

_____

2. Write 5 examples of nouns on the lines below.

_____ _____ _____ _____ _____

3. Name 3 ways that we use nouns in sentences.

   a. _____

   b. _____

   c. _____

4. What is a gerund?

_____

5. Name 3 ways that we use gerunds in sentences.

   a. _____

   b. _____

   c. _____

6. Write 5 verbs that can be followed by a gerund.

_____ _____ _____ _____ _____

B. Use the pairs of verbs below to write sentences with verbs followed by gerunds. Use any tense (present, past, or future). Circle the verb and the gerund in each sentence.

1. finish + write I'll finish writing my composition next weekend. _____

_____

2. practice + speak _____

_____

3. enjoy + watch _____

_____

4. dislike + eat _____

_____

5. postpone + take _____

_____

Part 4
Verbs Followed by Infinitives

VERBS + INFINITIVES

▶ In previous pages, you studied verbs followed by gerunds. Now you will study verbs followed by **infinitives**.

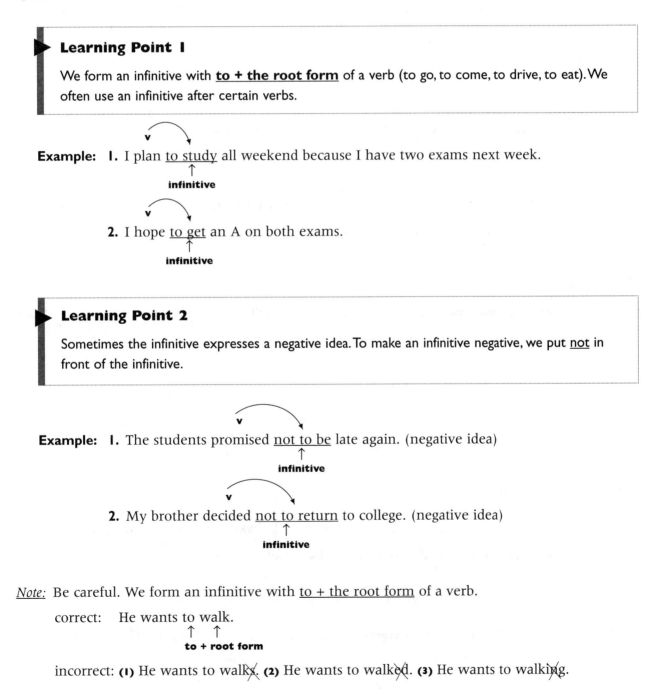

> ▶ **Learning Point 1**
>
> We form an infinitive with **to + the root form** of a verb (to go, to come, to drive, to eat). We often use an infinitive after certain verbs.

Example: **1.** I plan <u>to study</u> all weekend because I have two exams next week.
infinitive

2. I hope <u>to get</u> an A on both exams.
infinitive

> ▶ **Learning Point 2**
>
> Sometimes the infinitive expresses a negative idea. To make an infinitive negative, we put <u>not</u> in front of the infinitive.

Example: **1.** The students promised <u>not to be</u> late again. (negative idea)
infinitive

2. My brother decided <u>not to return</u> to college. (negative idea)
infinitive

<u>Note:</u> Be careful. We form an infinitive with <u>to + the root form</u> of a verb.

correct: He wants to walk.
to + root form

incorrect: **(1)** He wants to walks. **(2)** He wants to walked. **(3)** He wants to walking.

VERBS FOLLOWED BY INFINITIVES (VERB + INFINITIVE)

➡ Be careful. Some verbs can only be followed by gerunds (-ing form of the verb), and some verbs can only be followed by infinitives (to + root form). The verbs in the list below are followed by **infinitives.** We cannot use a gerund after these verbs.

VERBS FOLLOWED BY INFINITIVES			
verb + infinitive	**verb + infinitive**	**verb + infinitive**	**verb + infinitive**
agree to _____	hope to _____	plan to _____	want to _____
decide to _____	learn to _____	promise to _____	can't afford to _____
expect to _____	need to _____	seem to _____	can't wait to _____
forget to _____	offer to _____	try to _____	

➡ **Exercise I** Complete the dialogs below with an infinitive (to + root form) after the verb. Then take turns asking and answering the questions with a partner.

I. A: Do you have a computer?

   B: No, I don't. I want **(get)** ___to get___ one, but I need **(save)** _____ another

   $200.00. When I have the money, I plan **(buy)** _____ a PC.

2. A: What are you learning in this class?

   B: I'm learning **(understand)** _____ English grammar, and I'm also learning

   (write) _____ well-organized paragraphs.

3. A: Is your teacher in a good mood today?

   B: Yes, she seems **(be)** _____ in a good mood. She was in a bad mood yesterday,

   so she gave us a lot of homework.

4. A: What grade do you expect **(get)** _____ in this class?

   B: I expect **(get)** _____ an A because I always study the Learning Points, and I

   do all my homework. Besides, the teacher likes me!

5. A: I left a message for you yesterday, but you didn't return my phone call.

   B: I'm sorry. I sometimes forget **(return)** _____ phone calls when I'm very busy.

VERBS FOLLOWED BY INFINITIVES (VERB + INFINITIVE)

➡ **Exercise I** (continued)

6. A: Are you still driving that old car?

    B: Yes, I am. I need a new car, but I can't afford **(buy)** _____ one right now.

7. A: Did you have homework over the weekend?

    B: No, we didn't. Our teacher agreed **(not / give)** _____ us any homework because all the students did well on their last test.

8. A: Can you have coffee with me after work?

    B: I'd like to, but I can't today. When I get off work, I need **(stop)** _____ at the grocery store on my way home. My refrigerator is empty.

9. A: Doesn't your brother ever go to a movie or a dance?

    B: No, he doesn't. He's trying **(save)** _____ all his money so he can move into his own apartment. He can't wait **(have)** _____ his own place.

10. A: What are you going to do after you graduate? Are you going to get a job right away?

    B: No, I'm not. I decided **(take)** _____ some time off before I look for a job. I need some time to relax before I go to work.

11. A: When are you going to return the $5.00 that I lent you last week?

    B: Oh, I'm sorry! I forgot all about it. I promise **(bring)** _____ the money tomorrow. In fact, I'll take you to lunch, too.

12. A: Where are you going? Why are you leaving class early?

    B: I'm going to buy some lottery tickets. I buy ten tickets every Tuesday.

    A: Do you really expect **(win)** _____ anything? It's a waste of money.

    B: No, it isn't. I hope **(win)** _____ a million dollars one of these days!

VERBS FOLLOWED BY INFINITIVES (VERB + SOMEONE + INFINITIVE)

➠ Sometimes we put "someone" between the verb and the infinitive.

Example: **verb + (someone) + infinitive**
1. The doctor <u>advised</u> <u>my sister</u> <u>to get</u> more rest. She works too hard.

   verb + (someone) + infinitive
2. He <u>encouraged</u> <u>her</u> <u>to take</u> a long, restful vacation.

VERB + (SOMEONE) + INFINITIVE

allow (someone) to ____	instruct (someone) to ____	tell (someone) to ____
ask (someone) to ____	permit (someone) to ____	trust (someone) to ____
forbid (someone) to ____	remind (someone) to ____	want (someone) to ____
help (someone) to ____	require (someone) to ____	warn (someone) to ____

➠ **Exercise 2**   Complete the sentences below with a verb and an infinitive.

Airline Safety

              verb   **+**   **(someone)**   **+**   **infinitive**
1. **(require / attend)** All airlines <u> require </u> their flight attendants <u> to attend </u> training programs to learn safety measures and procedures.

2. **(allow / board)** The airlines _____ handicapped people and people with small children _____ the plane first.

3. **(tell / fasten)** The flight attendants _____ the passengers _____ their seat belts on take-off and landing.

4. **(forbid / smoke)** The law _____ passengers _____ on planes.

5. **(instruct / locate)** The flight attendants always _____ the passengers _____ the emergency exits.

6. **(warn / fasten)** When there is a lot of turbulence, the attendants _____ everyone _____ their seat belts.

7. **(help / remain)** The crew _____ everyone _____ calm in an emergency.

8. **(remind / stay)** The flight attendants _____ the passengers _____ in their seats until the plane comes to a complete stop.

9. **(trust / get)** Passengers _____ the captain and crew _____ them to their destination safely.

<u>Note:</u>   Sometimes we do not use <u>to</u> after the verb <u>help</u>. Both forms are correct.
       <u>Example</u>: He helped me **to cook** dinner. = He helped me **cook** dinner.

☑ CHECK YOUR UNDERSTANDING

A. *EDITING* - Each sentence below contains a mistake in the use of infinitives. Circle the mistake in each sentence. Then write the sentence correctly.

1. Lana expects ⟨gets⟩ a good grade on her composition.

   Lana expects to get a good grade on her composition.

2. I promised not forgetting my homework again.

   _____

3. I need to returning my books to the library after class today.

   _____

4. When my car broke down yesterday, my friend offered drove me home.

   _____

5. My parents want me get all A's this semester.

   _____

6. My car is in terrible condition, but I can't afford buying a new one.

   _____

B. Use the pairs of verbs below to write sentences with <u>verb + infinitive</u> or <u>verb + someone + infinitive</u>. Use any tense (present, past, future).

1. decide + look _I decided to look for another job when my company cut our_

   health benefits.

2. offer + help _____

   _____

3. try + save _____

   _____

4. ask (someone) + explain _____

   _____

5. want (someone) + go _____

   _____

6. remind (someone) + call _____

   _____

Part 5
Contrast: Verb + Gerund or Infinitive

VERB + GERUND OR INFINITIVE

➠ In Parts 3 and 4, you learned that certain verbs must be followed by gerunds and certain verbs must be followed by infinitives. In the exercises that follow, you will have to choose the correct form, gerund or infinitive. Use the reference lists on pages 368-370 if you need help.

➠ **Exercise 1** Choose a gerund or an infinitive to complete each sentence below.

1. We finished _____studying_____ the chapter on modals two weeks ago.

   a. to study   **b.** studying

2. Our teacher always offers _____ students after class when they have a problem.

   a. to help   **b.** helping

3. When I was sick, I couldn't go to class, so my friend volunteered _____ me the class notes and homework assignments.

   a. to bring   **b.** bringing

4. The students appreciate _____ homework on the weekend.

   a. not to get   **b.** not getting

5. Where were you yesterday? You promised _____ me in the library, but you didn't show up.

   a. to meet   **b.** meeting

6. I'd like to stay home tonight, but I have to go _____ for my mother's birthday present.

   a. to shop   **b.** shopping

7. My daughter sometimes pretends _____ sick when she wants to stay home from school.

   a. to be   **b.** being

8. My parents encouraged me _____ a savings account, and now I have $500 in the bank.

   a. to open   **b.** opening

9. I dislike _____ on the weekend because the stores are too crowded.

   a. to shop   **b.** shopping

10. I don't mind _____ my sister's children because they are very well-behaved.

   a. to babysit   **b.** babysitting

VERB + GERUND OR INFINITIVE

➡ **Exercise 2** Choose a gerund or an infinitive to complete each sentence below. When you are finished, compare your answers in a small group or with a partner.

The Great Outdoors

I

My family and I enjoy **(1. pack)** ___*packing*___ the car and **(2. head)** ___*heading*___ for the mountains every summer. Last year we went **(3. camp)** _____ at Sequoia National Park in California. We were planning **(4. stay)** _____ at the Sequoia Lodge, but my children begged us **(5. go)** _____ camping instead. They wanted **(6. sleep)** _____ in tents and **(7. cook *)** _____ all our meals over a campfire. When we got to the park, the park rangers greeted us and directed us to the campgrounds. They advised us **(8. not / leave)** _____ food out on the picnic tables because the food might attract the grizzly bears in the area. The bears seem **(9. be)** _____ friendly, but they can be very dangerous to campers.

II

Every morning our family enjoyed **(10. plan)** _____the day's activities. One morning my husband suggested **(11. hike)** _____to a beautiful lake about three miles away. By the time we got to the lake, we were hot and sweaty, so we decided to go **(12. swim)** _____. We enjoyed **(13. swim)** _____ in the cool, clear mountain lake until we got hungry. Around noon we got out of the water and hiked back to the picnic area for lunch. To our surprise, two big, brown grizzly bears were sitting at our picnic table. They were just finishing our lunch of fried chicken and potato salad. We decided **(14. not / join)** _____ them, and we silently and very carefully made our way back down the mountain to our campground.

III

That night our family spent the evening close to the campfire at our campground. We enjoyed **(15. sing)** _____ songs, **(16. roast)** _____ marshmallows, and **(17. tell)** _____ the other campers about our adventure with the bears that afternoon. This year we are considering **(18. go)** _____ to either Yellowstone National Park or Yosemite National Park. Of course, wherever we go, we'll remember **(19. not / leave)** _____ our food out for the bears!

Note: When two or more infinitives are connected by <u>and</u>, it is not necessary to repeat <u>to</u>.
    <u>Example:</u> They wanted to sleep in tents and ✗ cook all our meals over a campfire.

VERB + GERUND OR INFINITIVE

➡ Some people enjoy giving parties. Other people dread giving parties and entertain as seldom as possible. Good organization is the key to a successful party. If you don't like to entertain, try some of the tips below. Then you, too, can relax and enjoy your own parties.

➡ **Exercise 3** Choose either a gerund or an infinitive to complete each sentence below. Then compare your answers with a partner. Do your answers agree?

How to Entertain Successfully

theme: *subject, one major idea*

¹A successful party requires **(be)** __being__ organized. ²First, before you do anything else, you need **(have)** _____ a theme* . ³For example, if you decide to give a farewell party for a neighbor who is moving to Mexico, the party should have a Mexican theme. ⁴Next, after you find your party theme, you need **(decide)** _____ if you want to have a formal party or an informal party. ⁵For instance, in the summertime, you might want **(have)** _____ an informal barbecue* outdoors on the patio*, especially for large groups. ⁶However, whether it is indoors or outdoors, formal or informal, you have **(make)** _____ a list of what you need for the party. ⁷You might have **(borrow)** _____ extra chairs, tables, dishes, and so on. ⁸Next, you have **(decide)** _____ on your invitations and decorations. ⁹You can easily purchase these items* at a stationery store, or you might enjoy **(make)** _____ your own invitations and decorations. ¹⁰Finally, you need **(plan)** _____ the menu. ¹¹What kind of food will you serve? ¹² How much time will you need **(prepare)** _____ the food? ¹³How much can you prepare in advance? ¹⁴In short, good organization is the key to a successful party. ¹⁵The host* who enjoys **(give)** _____ parties plans well in advance. A harried* host is never a successful host!

barbecue: *outdoor meal where food is cooked on a grill*

patio: *a cement area in the backyard outside the house*

items: *things, objects*

host: *a person who invites guests to a dinner, a party, or some other social occasion*

harried: *worried, harassed, not calm*

SPECIAL POINT – VERBS FOLLOWED BY EITHER A GERUND OR AN INFINITIVE

➠ On the preceding pages, you learned that some verbs must be followed by gerunds, and some verbs must be followed by infinitives. However, there are a few verbs that can be followed by either a gerund or an infinitive with **no change in meaning.**

Example: 1. It began <u>raining</u>. = It began <u>to rain</u>.
            ↑   ↑
        gerund   **infinitive**

2. I like <u>walking</u> in the rain. = I like <u>to walk</u> in the rain.
          ↑   ↑
      gerund   **infinitive**

VERBS FOLLOWED BY EITHER A GERUND OR AN INFINITIVE			
begin	like	prefer	(can't) stand
hate	love	start	

➠ **Exercise 4** The verbs in the sentences below can be followed by either a gerund or an infinitive with no change in meaning. Complete each sentence in two ways.

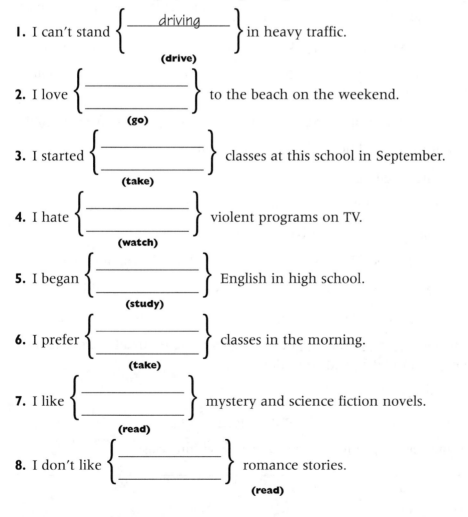

1. I can't stand { _____driving_____ } in heavy traffic.
                        (drive)

2. I love { _____ } to the beach on the weekend.
                 (go)

3. I started { _____ } classes at this school in September.
                   (take)

4. I hate { _____ } violent programs on TV.
                (watch)

5. I began { _____ } English in high school.
                 (study)

6. I prefer { _____ } classes in the morning.
                  (take)

7. I like { _____ } mystery and science fiction novels.
                (read)

8. I don't like { _____ } romance stories.
                      (read)

REFERENCE LIST: VERBS FOLLOWED BY GERUNDS

List 1: The verbs in the list below are followed by gerunds. Do not use infinitives after these verbs.

VERBS FOLLOWED BY GERUNDS

1.	admit	The student <u>admitted</u> <u>cheating</u> on the test and apologized to the teacher.
2.	appreciate	I <u>appreciated</u> <u>receiving</u> your get-well card.
3.	avoid	I always <u>avoid</u> <u>driving</u> in rush-hour traffic if possible.
4.	complete	We finally <u>completed</u> <u>painting</u> the house last weekend.
5.	consider	I <u>considered</u> <u>not returning</u> to school last semester because it's hard to work full-time and study at night.
6.	deny	The shoplifter <u>denied</u> <u>taking</u> the jewelry, but the security guard found it in her purse.
7.	discuss	My friend and I <u>discussed</u> <u>taking</u> a trip to Europe in the spring.
8.	dislike	I <u>dislike</u> <u>getting</u> phone calls from telephone solicitors, especially during dinner.
9.	dread	I <u>dreaded</u> <u>going</u> to the dentist when I was a child.
10.	enjoy	We <u>enjoyed</u> <u>looking</u> at the pictures and souvenirs from our trip to Alaska.
11.	finish	The mechanic didn't <u>finish</u> <u>fixing</u> the brakes until 5:00, so I picked up my car on the way home from work.
12.	keep	My father will probably <u>keep</u> <u>working</u> until he's eighty. He loves his job!
13.	mention	My aunt <u>mentioned</u> <u>not feeling</u> well last night.
14.	mind	I don't <u>mind</u> <u>waiting</u> for you after class.
15.	miss	My friend <u>misses</u> <u>not seeing</u> his family. They still live in Vietnam.
16.	postpone	She <u>postponed</u> <u>taking</u> the driving test until next week.
17.	practice	If you <u>practice</u> <u>speaking</u> outside of class, your English will improve.
18.	quit	Karen <u>quit</u> <u>buying</u> lottery tickets because she never won anything.
19.	recommend	The doctor <u>recommended</u> <u>cutting</u> down on salt and getting more exercise.
20.	regret	My nephew <u>regrets</u> <u>dropping</u> out of high school. He finally understands the importance of a good education.
21.	resist	Little children often <u>resist</u> <u>going</u> to bed.
22.	stop	The children can't go outside until it <u>stops</u> <u>raining</u>.
23.	suggest	The counselor <u>suggested</u> <u>taking</u> a business writing class.

REFERENCE LIST: VERBS FOLLOWED BY INFINITIVES

List 2: The verbs in the list below are followed by infinitives. Do not use gerunds after these verbs.

	VERBS FOLLOWED BY INFINITIVES
1. afford to	We can't <u>afford</u> <u>to buy</u> a new sofa until we save another $200.00.
2. agree to	The bank finally <u>agreed</u> <u>to approve</u> the loan on our house.
3. decide to	I <u>decided</u> <u>not to move</u> out of my apartment. I'm not happy with the location, but the rent is reasonable.
4. deserve to	Nancy <u>deserves</u> <u>to get</u> a good raise. She is an excellent worker.
5. expect to	My aunt <u>expects</u> <u>to get</u> out of the hospital in a day or two. She is feeling much better.
6. forget to	Don't <u>forget</u> <u>to lock</u> the door when you leave.
7. hope to	Jeff <u>hopes</u> <u>to get</u> a scholarship from the University of California.
8. learn to	Children must <u>learn</u> <u>not to speak</u> to strangers.
9. mean to	I'm sorry. I didn't <u>mean</u> <u>to offend</u> you.
10. need to	I <u>need</u> <u>to stop</u> at the grocery store on my way home from work.
11. offer to	Our neighbors <u>offered</u> <u>to pick</u> up our mail while we were on vacation.
12. plan to	I <u>plan</u> <u>to visit</u> the Smithsonian Institution on my trip to Washington, D. C.
13. pretend to	My sister sometimes <u>pretends</u> <u>to be</u> sick on Monday morning.
14. promise to	We <u>promised</u> <u>to take</u> the children to Disneyland this summer.
15. refuse to	I <u>refused</u> <u>to lend</u> my cousin any more money. He already owes me $500.00.
16. remember to	He never <u>remembers</u> <u>to turn</u> off the TV when he leaves the room.
17. seem to	Tom <u>seems</u> <u>to be</u> worried about something. I hope that everything is alright.
18. try to	I'll <u>try</u> <u>to leave</u> work early on Friday.
19. volunteer to	My friend <u>volunteered</u> <u>to drive</u> me to work when my car was in the shop.
20. wait to	I can't <u>wait</u> <u>to leave</u> on my trip to Europe. Our tour goes to London, Paris, and Rome!
21. want to	Do you <u>want</u> <u>to go</u> to the movies tonight?

REFERENCE LISTS OF GERUNDS AND INFINITIVES

List 3: The verbs in the list below follow the pattern *verb + someone + infinitive.*

<table>
<tr><td colspan="2" align="center">**VERB + (SOMEONE) + INFINITIVE**</td></tr>
<tr><td>1. advise (someone) to</td><td>The doctor advised me to get more exercise.</td></tr>
<tr><td>2. allow (someone) to</td><td>Mr. and Mrs. Lee do not allow their children to watch TV before dinner.</td></tr>
<tr><td>3. ask (someone) to</td><td>I asked my neighbor to take in my mail while I was on vacation.</td></tr>
<tr><td>4. encourage (someone) to</td><td>The teacher always encourages us to practice English outside of class.</td></tr>
<tr><td>5. expect (someone) to</td><td>Our boss expects everyone to be at work on time.</td></tr>
<tr><td>6. forbid (someone) to</td><td>The law forbids people to smoke in most public places.</td></tr>
<tr><td>7. help (someone) to</td><td>My cousin helped me to find an apartment when I moved here from Reno.</td></tr>
<tr><td>8. instruct (someone) to</td><td>My piano teacher instructed me to practice at least one hour a day.</td></tr>
<tr><td>9. permit (someone) to</td><td>Most movie theaters do not permit people to bring their own food.</td></tr>
<tr><td>10. remind (someone) to</td><td>The teacher reminded us to turn in our compositions at the end of class.</td></tr>
<tr><td>11. require (someone) to</td><td>The clerk required the young man to show his ID before he could buy beer</td></tr>
<tr><td>12. tell (someone) to</td><td>Parents always tell their children to be careful when they cross the street.</td></tr>
<tr><td>13. trust (someone) to</td><td>I don't trust him to give me the right directions. I'd better check the map.</td></tr>
<tr><td>14. want (someone) to</td><td>Someday I want to travel to Australia and New Zealand.</td></tr>
<tr><td>15. warn (someone) to</td><td>My supervisor warned me not to be late for work again.</td></tr>
</table>

List 4: The verbs in the list below can be followed by either a gerund or an infinitive without a change in meaning.

<table>
<tr><td colspan="2" align="center">**VERBS FOLLOWED BY EITHER A GERUND OR AN INFINITIVE**</td></tr>
<tr><td>1. begin</td><td>We began {studying / to study} gerunds and infinitives two weeks ago.</td></tr>
<tr><td>2. hate</td><td>I hate {waiting / to wait} in line at the supermarket.</td></tr>
<tr><td>3. like</td><td>Mrs. Stanton likes {making / to make} clothes for her granddaughter.</td></tr>
<tr><td>4. love</td><td>The children love {going / to go} to the beach.</td></tr>
<tr><td>5. prefer</td><td>I prefer {buying / to buy} my fresh fruit and vegetables at the fruit stand near my house.</td></tr>
<tr><td>6. (can't) stand</td><td>I can't stand {driving / to drive} in heavy traffic.</td></tr>
<tr><td>7. start</td><td>I just started {doing / to do} my homework. It will probably take me two hours to finish.</td></tr>
</table>

✔ CHECK YOUR UNDERSTANDING

▸ Use the pairs of verbs below to write sentences with gerunds or infinitives. Remember that some of the verbs must be followed by a gerund, and some of the verbs must be followed by an infinitive. A few verbs can be followed by either a gerund or an infinitive. Use any verb tense (present, past, or future). Refer to the lists on pages 368 - 370 if necessary.

1. promise + go   *I promised to go to the movies with a friend on Friday night.*

2. finish + write

3. invite (someone) + go

4. go + shop

5. like + play

6. decide + not/move

7. enjoy + see

8. remind (someone) + call

9. begin + study

10. hope + visit

11. need + do

12. ask (someone) + help

Part 6
Using Gerunds after Prepositions

VERB + PREPOSITION + GERUND

> ▶ **Learning Point**
>
> A preposition is often followed by a gerund. We <u>cannot</u> use an infinitive after a preposition.

Example: 1. correct: The student apologized for <u>leaving</u> class early.
                                     ↑   ↑
                                prep gerund

            not correct: The student apologized for ~~to leave~~ class early.
                                     ↑   ↑
                                 prep infinitive

2. correct: The class complained about <u>having</u> too much homework.
                                ↑   ↑
                              prep gerund

            not correct: The class complained about ~~to have~~ too much homework.
                                ↑   ↑
                              prep infinitive

➡ Before you go on to the gerund exercises that follow, it is important to remember that we use certain prepositions with certain verbs. Take a few minutes to study the verb + preposition combinations in the box below. You will use these combinations in the exercises on pages 373 - 374.

VERB + PREPOSITION COMBINATIONS

<u>verb + prep</u>	<u>verb + prep</u>	<u>verb + prep</u>
argue about	concentrate on	accuse (someone) of
complain about	congratulate (someone) on	apologize (to someone) for
dream about/of	insist on	blame (someone) for
forget about	feel like	excuse (someone) for
talk (to someone) about	believe in	forgive (someone) for
think about	succeed in	thank (someone) for
warn (someone) about		prevent (someone) from
worry about		

VERB + PREPOSITION + GERUND

▶ **Exercise I** Complete the sentences below with a preposition and gerund. If you need help with the prepositions, refer to the list on page 372.

At School

1. The teacher always insists ___on___ ___starting___ class on time.
   <small>prep</small>   <small>(start)</small>

2. The teacher excused the students _____ _____ class last week.
   <small>prep</small>   <small>(miss)</small>

3. Students often worry _____ _____ bad grades.
   <small>prep</small>   <small>(get)</small>

4. Students should concentrate _____ _____ their grades.
   <small>prep</small>   <small>(improve)</small>

5. The teacher accused three students _____ _____ on the last test.
   <small>prep</small>   <small>(cheat)</small>

6. I don't believe _____ _____ more than 12 or 15 units a semester.
   <small>prep</small>   <small>(take)</small>

7. I'm worried about Angela. She is talking _____ _____ out of school.
   <small>prep</small>   <small>(drop)</small>

8. Some of my friends are thinking _____ _____ to a four-year college.
   <small>prep</small>   <small>(transfer)</small>

9. Martin's work schedule prevented him _____ _____ school full time.
   <small>prep</small>   <small>(attend)</small>

10. I'm planning _____ _____ for a job as a computer programmer after I graduate.
    <small>prep</small>   <small>(apply)</small>

▶ **Exercise 2** Follow the same directions as in Exercise 1.

At Work

1. The employees complained _____ _____ too much overtime.
   <small>prep</small>   <small>(work)</small>

2. The supervisor warned Henry _____ _____ too many coffee breaks.
   <small>prep</small>   <small>(take)</small>

3. The director thanked everyone _____ _____ the job on schedule.
   <small>prep</small>   <small>(complete)</small>

4. Carla apologized to the group _____ _____ the last meeting.
   <small>prep</small>   <small>(miss)</small>

5. Everyone congratulated Dave _____ _____ a promotion.
   <small>prep</small>   <small>(get)</small>

6. One of my friends at work is dreaming _____ _____ in a few months.
   <small>prep</small>   <small>(retire)</small>

7. The members of the union argued _____ _____ the new contract.
   <small>prep</small>   <small>(accept)</small>

8. My boss blamed me _____ _____ the copy machine, but it wasn't my fault.
   <small>prep</small>   <small>(break)</small>

9. Kim doesn't like her job. She's talking _____ _____ to another department.
   <small>prep</small>   <small>(transfer)</small>

10. I never feel _____ _____ to work on Monday morning.
    <small>prep</small>   <small>(go)</small>

VERB + PREPOSITION + GERUND

➡ **Exercise 3** Complete the sentences below with the correct preposition and a gerund. If you need help, refer to the list on page 372.

Paragraph 1   **The Importance of School Counselors**

Many schools with budget problems think **(1)** <u>about</u> <u>eliminating</u> counselors, but I don't
                                                    prep   (eliminate)

agree. For example, when my son was a junior in high school, he hated his classes and almost

dropped out of school. He complained **(2)** _____ _____ too much
                                              prep   (have)

homework. He never concentrated **(3)** _____ _____ his assignments in
                                            prep   (get)

on time, and he often felt **(4)** _____ _____ class. Then his
                                     prep   (cut)

counselor warned him **(5)** _____ _____ out of school. He also talked
                                prep   flunk)

(6) _____ _____ the future without an education. Fortunately, the
          prep   (face)

counselor succeeded **(7)** _____ _____ my son's attitude. By the end of
                               prep   (change)

the school year, my son brought up his grades and passed all of his classes. Clearly, one way or

another, schools must manage not to sacrifice our children's counselors.

Paragraph 2   **A Dream**

A friend of mine always talks **(1)** _____ _____ it rich in the lottery.
                                          prep   (strike)

She dreams **(2)** _____ _____ at least $5 million. In fact, to make this a
                      prep   (win)

reality, she plans to buy 100 tickets for next week's drawing. If she wins, she'll never have to

worry **(3)** _____ _____ her bills. She can forget **(4)** _____
                 prep   (pay)   prep

_____ to work ever again. Instead, she and her husband will travel around
     (go)

the United States in a brand new RV motor home. Of course, she doesn't know that her chances

are about one in a billion. I doubt that I'll ever have the chance to congratulate her

(5) _____ _____. However, the world would be a dreary place if we
          prep   (win)

couldn't dream!

✔ CHECK YOUR UNDERSTANDING

A. Choose the correct preposition from the box for each verb below. A preposition can be used more than one time. If you need help, refer to the list on page 372.

about	for	from	in	like	of	on

verb	preposition	verb	preposition
1. believe	_____in_____	11. argue	_____
2. blame (someone)	_____	12. dream	_____
3. talk (to someone)	_____	13. succeed	_____
4. concentrate	_____	14. accuse (someone)	_____
5. complain	_____	15. think	_____
6. excuse (someone)	_____	16. thank (someone)	_____
7. forgive (someone)	_____	17. feel	_____
8. forget	_____	18. warn (someone)	_____
9. apologize (to someone)	_____	19. worry	_____
10. congratulate (someone)	_____	20. insist	_____

B. Write your own sentences with the words below. Use the correct preposition with each verb. Use a gerund after the preposition. Use any tense.

1. argue + prep _We argued about spending too much money on entertainment._

_____

2. feel + prep _____

_____

3. thank (someone) + prep _____

_____

4. think + prep _____

_____

5. congratulate (someone) + prep _____

_____

6. worry + prep _____

_____

ADJECTIVE + PREPOSITION + GERUND

> ▶ **Learning Point**
>
> It is common to use certain prepositions with certain <u>adjectives</u> such as **angry about**, **worried about**, **afraid of**. We use a gerund after the preposition.

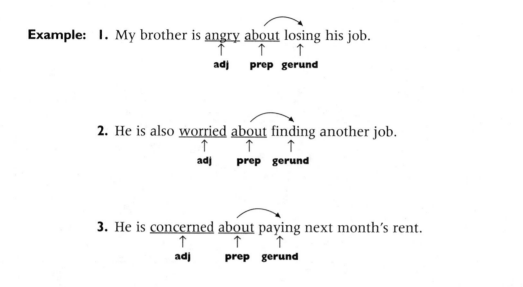

Example: **1.** My brother is <u>angry</u> <u>about</u> losing his job.
                                  ↑   ↑   ↑
                                adj   **prep** **gerund**

2. He is also <u>worried</u> <u>about</u> finding another job.
                     ↑   ↑   ↑
                   adj   **prep** **gerund**

3. He is <u>concerned</u> <u>about</u> paying next month's rent.
                  ↑   ↑   ↑
                adj   **prep** **gerund**

⇒ We usually use an adjective + preposition combination after the verb <u>Be</u> (am, is, are, was, were). Study the adjective + preposition combinations in the box below. You will use these combinations in the gerund exercises on page 377.

ADJECTIVE + PREPOSITION COMBINATIONS

<u>adjective + prep</u>	<u>adjective + prep</u>	<u>adjective + prep</u>
active in	* concerned about	afraid of
* interested in	conscientious about	guilty of
* involved in	* excited about	proud of
* arrested for	sorry about	* scared of
grateful (to someone) for	* worried about	* tired of
responsible for		good at

The words with an asterisk (*) are past participles of verbs used as adjectives.

ADJECTIVE + PREPOSITION + GERUND

➠ **Exercise 4** Complete the sentences below with the correct preposition and a gerund.

1. I'm not interested __in__ __looking__ for another job.
   prep **(apply)**

2. I am excited _____ _____ a big promotion.
   prep **(get)**

3. I'm sorry _____ _____ the meeting early. I had a doctor's appointment.
   prep **(leave)**

4. Someone is guilty _____ _____ paper and other office supplies.
   prep **(steal)**

5. I'm not very good _____ _____ in front of a group of people.
   prep **(speak)**

6. I'm afraid _____ _____ my car pool. I can't stay any longer.
   prep **(miss)**

➠ **Exercise 5** Complete the dialogs below with the correct adjective + preposition + gerund.

1. **A:** What a great party! Who was __responsible for making__ the arrangements?
   (responsible / make)

   B: Ted was _____ the restaurant and _____
   (responsible / find) **(make)**

   the reservations. Marnie was _____ the band.
   (responsible / hire)

   A: Well, they both should be _____ such a good job!
   (proud / do)

2. **A:** Our planet is in trouble. Everyone should be _____
   (concerned / protect)

   the environment.

   B: Yes, I agree with you. My family is always _____ water and
   (conscientious / save)

   _____ disposable items.
   (recycle)

   A: Would you be _____ our group? We are _____ to
   (interested / join) **(active / help)**

   educate the public about environmental issues.

3. **A:** Did you hear about our neighbor's son? He was _____ drugs.
   (arrested / sell)

   B: Yes, Mrs. Henderson told me. She said that he was _____
   (involved / break)

   into several houses in the neighborhood too. I feel sorry for his family.

✔ CHECK YOUR UNDERSTANDING

A. Choose the correct preposition from the box for each adjective below. A preposition can be used more than one time. If you need help, refer to the list on page 376.

about	at	for	in	of

adjective	**preposition**	**adjective**	**preposition**
1. be interested	in	10. be worried	_____
2. be arrested	_____	11. be active	_____
3. be responsible	_____	12. be proud	_____
4. be excited	_____	13. be concerned	_____
5. be afraid	_____	14. be guilty	_____
6. be tired	_____	15. be involved	_____
7. be good	_____	16. be conscientious	_____
8. be scared	_____	17. be grateful (to someone)	_____
9. be sorry	_____		

B. Complete the sentences below. Use a gerund after the adjective + preposition combination in each sentence.

1. Parents are responsible for _____ _teaching their children to be good citizens._ _____

2. I am sorry about _____

3. Many students are interested in _____

4. Last week I was very worried about _____

5. Children are always excited about _____

6. Some people are afraid of _____

7. The students in my class were tired of _____

8. I am concerned about _____

9. I am grateful to my parents for _____

10. I am good at _____

Part 7
Gerunds and Infinitives Used as Subjects of Verbs

GERUNDS USED AS SUBJECTS OF VERBS

Learning Point

1. We can use gerunds as subjects of verbs.

   Example: Running (s, gerund) is (v) good exercise.

2. Gerund subjects are always singular, so the verb must also be singular to agree with the subject.

Exercise 1 Complete the sentences below with a gerund subject. Use the verbs in the box. Use each verb only once.

smoke	eat	walk	listen	learn
✔ write	ski	speak	speed	camp

1. __Writing__ improves with practice. Students should write as often as possible.
2. __________ in front of an audience makes me nervous.
3. __________ a foreign language is difficult.
4. __________ is a popular winter sport in most countries of the world.
5. __________ is my favorite hobby, so we take several trips to the mountains every summer.
6. __________ to music is my favorite pastime.
7. __________ can cause lung cancer, emphysema, and heart disease.
8. __________ is dangerous and irresponsible. Careless drivers can kill people.
9. __________ a lot of fast food is not good for you.
10. __________ a mile a day is a good form of exercise.

GERUNDS USED AS SUBJECTS OF VERBS

➠ There are many different ways to enjoy a vacation. Some people like to rent a house at the beach and just relax for a week or two. Other people like to take trips in recreational vehicles (RVs) and explore and sightsee at their convenience. In the paragraph below, Linda Martin, an instructor at a local community college, is describing her favorite way to travel.

My Favorite Way to Travel

Taking a tour is my favorite way to travel. For one thing, you can explore more places in a short time. Last summer, for example, my husband and I took a seven-day tour to the British Isles, and we traveled all over England, Scotland, Wales, and Northern Ireland. Second, sightseeing is easy with a good tour director. Our tour director was always well-informed and showed us two or three important places a day. For example, on our first day, we visited Stonehenge and the beautiful city of Bath in England, and we never felt rushed. Third, a tour helps you to meet people from all over the world. We met people from British Colombia, New Zealand, Australia, South Africa, and the United States. We also met a very interesting Chinese family from Hong Kong. Finally, a tour is a good way to learn about a country's customs and culture. For example, driving on the opposite side of the road in England was difficult for us at first. Paying for our purchases with pounds and shillings* was also a challenge.* Carrying raincoats and umbrellas everywhere was important because of the frequent showers in the British Isles. To conclude, a tour is a good way to learn about a country for the first time.

➠ **Exercise 3** Five of the sentences in the paragraph above have gerund subjects. Write the five sentences on the lines below. Circle the gerund subject and mark the verb.

                 ᵛ
1. (Taking) a tour is my favorite way to travel. _____

_____

2. _____

_____

3. _____

_____

4. _____

_____

5. _____

_____

Vocabulary Notes   ***pounds and shillings:*** *money used in England*
                                       challenge: *something that is difficult to do*

INFINITIVES USED AS SUBJECTS OF VERBS

> ► **Learning Point**
>
> Just as we can use a gerund as the subject of a verb, we can also use an infinitive as the subject of a verb.

    s   **v**
<u>Traveling</u> by train is fun and educational. **(gerund used as subject of verb)**

    s   **v**
<u>To travel</u> by train is fun and educational. **(infinitive used as subject of verb)**

➠ Although it is possible to use an infinitive as the subject of a verb, it is not common. It is more common to use <u>it</u> as the subject. We use the pattern **it + infinitive**.

<u>To travel</u> by train is fun and educational. **(not common)**
  infinitive

It is fun and educational <u>to travel</u> by train. **(more common)**
                   infinitive

➠ **Exercise 4** Change the gerund subjects in the sentences below to the pattern **it + infinitive**. Work with a partner.

Leisure Time Activities

1. Touring Hoover Dam in Nevada is an interesting experience.

   It is an interesting experience to tour Hoover Dam in Nevada.

2. Camping at Yosemite National Park is fun for the whole family.

_____

3. Fishing for trout in a clear mountain stream is restful.

_____

4. Joining a health club to improve your health is a good idea.

_____

5. Reading a good book in your free time is a pleasure.

_____

6. Water skiing on one of California's beautiful lakes is enjoyable.

_____

Writing Assignment

➠ Your writing assignment in this chapter is to write a paragraph about one of the topics below.

▶ What to do ◀

1. Choose <u>one</u> of the topic sentences to write about.

_____ **Topic 1:** _____ is my favorite hobby.
        (gardening, reading, coin collecting, etc.)

Everyone has a favorite activity to do in his or her leisure time. What is your favorite hobby? Why do you like it? What makes it enjoyable for you?

_____ **Topic 2:** _____ is difficult.
        (learning a foreign language, learning to play golf, learning to drive, etc.)

Some things take a lot of time and effort to learn to do well. What is one thing that you think is especially difficult to learn? What makes it difficult?

_____ **Topic 3:** _____ has many advantages.
        (living with your parents, living with a roommate, living alone, etc.)

How do you prefer to live? What are the advantages of living with parents or living with a roommate? What are the advantages of living alone?

2. Write the first draft and the final draft of your paragraph on separate sheets of paper.

3. Follow the writing steps below.

STEP 1   Before you begin to write, take a few minutes to think about your topic. Then make a *list* of your ideas.

STEP 2   Choose three ideas from your list, and write a *first draft (practice paragraph)*.

STEP 3   *Revise* and *edit* your practice paragraph.

STEP 4   Write your *final draft (final paragraph)*.

Chapter 15
Present Perfect Tense and Present Perfect Progressive Tense

To the Student:

In previous chapters, you learned that English verbs have five forms:

1	2	3	4	5
ROOT FORM (SIMPLE FORM)	**-S FORM**	**PAST FORM**	**PRESENT PARTICIPLE (ing)**	**PAST PARTICIPLE**
talk	talks	talked	talking	talked
eat	eats	ate	eating	eaten

You will begin this chapter by reviewing the fifth form of the verb, the past participle.

Part I
Forming the Present Perfect Tense

THE PAST PARTICIPLES OF REGULAR AND IRREGULAR VERBS

➠ You have learned that regular verbs end in -ed in the past form and past participle (wait -waited -waited). Irregular verbs do not end in -ed in the past form and past participle. Irregular verbs usually change spelling (eat - ate - eaten). Refer to the chart below.

	ROOT FORM (SIMPLE FORM)	PAST FORM	PAST PARTICIPLE
regular verbs	wait	waited	waited
	attend	attended	attended
	study	studied	studied
	live	lived	lived
irregular verbs	eat	ate	eaten
	go	went	gone
	write	wrote	written
	know	knew	known

➠ **Exercise I** Write the past participle of the verbs in the chart below. If you need help with the past participles of the irregular verbs, refer to the verb list on the next page.

root form	past form	past participle		root form	past form	past participle
I. learn	learned	_____		II. do	did	_____
2. come	came	_____		12. drink	drank	_____
3. decide	decided	_____		13. get	got	_____
4. stop	stopped	_____		14. practice	practiced	_____
5. think	thought	_____		15. leave	left	_____
6. make	made	_____		16. speak	spoke	_____
7. wash	washed	_____		17. try	tried	_____
8. give	gave	_____		18. apply	applied	_____
9. copy	copied	_____		19. read	read	_____
10. finish	finished	_____		20. have	had	_____

REFERENCE CHART – THE PAST PARTICIPLES OF IRREGULAR VERBS

➡ Study the list of irregular verbs below. You must memorize the past participles of irregular verbs. *Note:* There is also a verb list on page 410 in the Appendix.

root form	past form	past participle	root form	past form	past participle
1. be	was, were	**been**	44. lend	lent	**lent**
2. become	became	**become**	45. let	let	**let**
3. begin	began	**begun**	46. lie	lay	**lain**
4. bite	bit	**bitten**	47. lose	lost	**lost**
5. blow	blew	**blown**	48. make	made	**made**
6. break	broke	**broken**	49. mean	meant	**meant**
7. bring	brought	**brought**	50. meet	met	**met**
8. build	built	**built**	51. pay	paid	**paid**
9. buy	bought	**bought**	52. put	put	**put**
10. catch	caught	**caught**	53. quit	quit	**quit**
11. choose	chose	**chosen**	54. read	read	**read**
12. come	came	**come**	55. ride	rode	**ridden**
13. cost	cost	**cost**	56. ring	rang	**rung**
14. cut	cut	**cut**	57. rise	rose	**risen**
15. do	did	**done**	58. run	ran	**run**
16. draw	drew	**drawn**	59. say	said	**said**
17. drink	drank	**drunk**	60. see	saw	**seen**
18. drive	drove	**driven**	61. sell	sold	**sold**
19. eat	ate	**eaten**	62. send	sent	**sent**
20. fall	fell	**fallen**	63. set	set	**set**
21. feed	fed	**fed**	64. shake	shook	**shaken**
22. feel	felt	**felt**	65. shoot	shot	**shot**
23. fight	fought	**fought**	66. shut	shut	**shut**
24. find	found	**found**	67. sing	sang	**sung**
25. fly	flew	**flown**	68. sit	sat	**sat**
26. forget	forgot	**forgotten**	69. sleep	slept	**slept**
27. forgive	forgave	**forgiven**	70. speak	spoke	**spoken**
28. freeze	froze	**frozen**	71. spend	spent	**spent**
29. get	got	**gotten**	72. stand	stood	**stood**
30. give	gave	**given**	73. steal	stole	**stolen**
31. go	went	**gone**	74. sweep	swept	**swept**
32. grow	grew	**grown**	75. swim	swam	**swum**
33. hang	hung	**hung**	76. take	took	**taken**
34. have	had	**had**	77. teach	taught	**taught**
35. hear	heard	**heard**	78. tear	tore	**torn**
36. hide	hid	**hidden**	79. tell	told	**told**
37. hit	hit	**hit**	80. think	thought	**thought**
38. hold	held	**held**	81. throw	threw	**thrown**
39. hurt	hurt	**hurt**	82. understand	understood	**understood**
40. keep	kept	**kept**	83. wake	woke	**woken**
41. know	knew	**known**	84. wear	wore	**worn**
42. lay	laid	**laid**	85. win	won	**won**
43. leave	left	**left**	86. write	wrote	**written**

FORMING THE PRESENT PERFECT TENSE

> ### ▶ Learning Point
>
> **1.** We form the Present Perfect Tense with the helping (auxiliary) verb **have** and the **past participle** of the main verb.
>
> **2.** The helping verb <u>have</u> changes to <u>has</u> when the subject is *he, she,* or *it.*
>
> <u>Example:</u> I have walked ⟶ he / she / it has walked

⇒ Forms of the Present Perfect Tense

AFFIRMATIVE

		helping verb	past participle				helping verb	past participle	
1.	I	have	eaten	(I've eaten)	**1.**	we	have	eaten	(we've eaten)
2.	you	have	eaten	(you've eaten)	**2.**	you	have	eaten	(you've eaten)
3.	he she it	has	eaten	(he's eaten) (she's eaten) (it's eaten)	**3.**	they	have	eaten	(they've eaten)

NEGATIVE

		helping verb	past participle			helping verb	past participle
1.	I	have not (haven't)	eaten	**1.**	we	have not (haven't)	eaten
2.	you	have not (haven't)	eaten	**2.**	you	have not (haven't)	eaten
3.	he she it	has not (hasn't)	eaten	**3.**	they	have not (haven't)	eaten

YES-NO QUESTIONS and SHORT ANSWERS

	helping verb		past participle			helping verb		past participle	
1.	Have	I	eaten?	Yes, you have. No, you haven't.	**1.**	Have	we	eaten?	Yes, you have. No, you haven't.
2.	Have	you	eaten?	Yes, I have. No, I haven't.	**2.**	Have	you	eaten?	Yes, we have. No, we haven't.
3.	Has	he she it	eaten?	Yes, he she it has.	**3.**	Have	they	eaten?	Yes, they have. No, they haven't.
				No, he she it hasn't.					

EXAMPLES OF PRESENT PERFECT TENSE SENTENCES

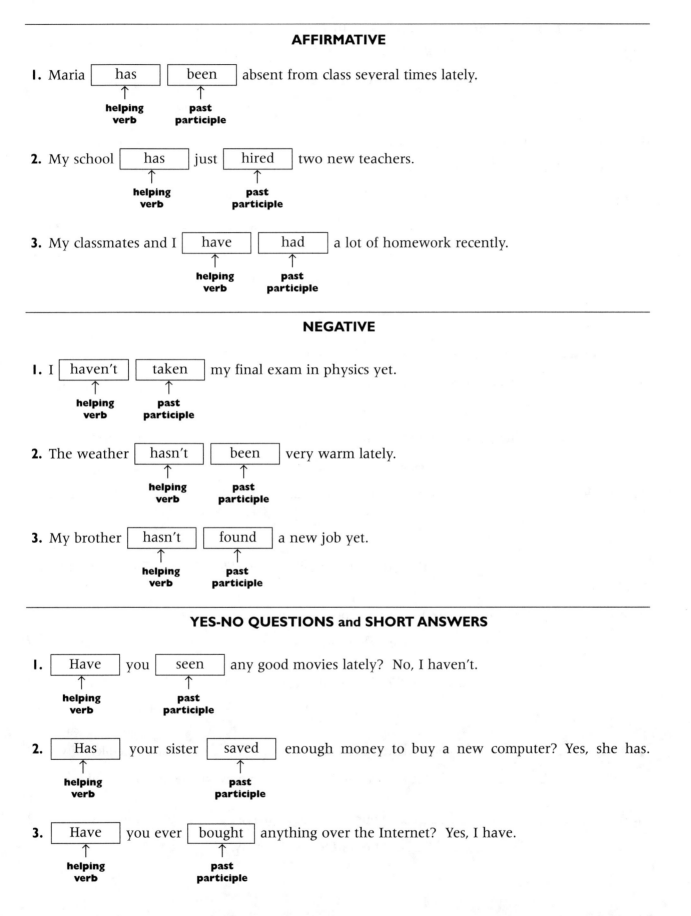

AFFIRMATIVE

1. Maria ⎡has⎤ ⎡been⎤ absent from class several times lately.
         helping   past
         verb   participle

2. My school ⎡has⎤ just ⎡hired⎤ two new teachers.
         helping   past
         verb   participle

3. My classmates and I ⎡have⎤ ⎡had⎤ a lot of homework recently.
         helping   past
         verb   participle

NEGATIVE

1. I ⎡haven't⎤ ⎡taken⎤ my final exam in physics yet.
         helping   past
         verb   participle

2. The weather ⎡hasn't⎤ ⎡been⎤ very warm lately.
         helping   past
         verb   participle

3. My brother ⎡hasn't⎤ ⎡found⎤ a new job yet.
         helping   past
         verb   participle

YES-NO QUESTIONS and SHORT ANSWERS

1. ⎡Have⎤ you ⎡seen⎤ any good movies lately? No, I haven't.
    helping   past
    verb   participle

2. ⎡Has⎤ your sister ⎡saved⎤ enough money to buy a new computer? Yes, she has.
    helping   past
    verb   participle

3. ⎡Have⎤ you ever ⎡bought⎤ anything over the Internet? Yes, I have.
    helping   past
    verb   participle

FORMING THE PRESENT PERFECT TENSE

➡ **Exercise 2** Use the Present Perfect Tense to complete the AFFIRMATIVE sentences in the paragraph. Use the helping verb <u>have</u>, <u>has</u> and the past participle of the verb in parentheses.

A World Traveler

My next-door-neighbor loves to travel, and he **(1. travel)** <u>has traveled</u> all over the world. He particularly enjoys traveling in Asia. He **(2. be)** _____ to Japan, China, Singapore, and India. He **(3. see)** _____ many of the wonders of the world such as Mt. Fuji, the Taj Mahal, and the Great Wall of China. He **(4. take)** _____ part in many of the cultural events and festivities of these countries. He **(5. meet)** _____ many interesting people over the years, and he **(6. make)** _____ many good friends. Someday, I hope to be able to travel, too!

➡ **Exercise 3**   Use the NEGATIVE form of the Present Perfect Tense to complete the sentences below.

1. I've been to Europe, but I **(be)** _____<u>haven't been</u>_____to Australia.

2. My family and I have met Mr. Lane, but we **(meet)** _____ his wife.

3. Martha has paid the phone bill, but she **(pay)** _____ the electricity bill.

4. I've finished Exercise 2, but I **(finish)** _____ Exercise 3.

5. Ed has taken several math classes, but he **(take)** _____ calculus.

➡ **Exercise 4** Use the Present Perfect Tense to complete the YES-NO QUESTIONS and SHORT ANSWERS below.

1. **A:** _____<u>Have</u>_____ you **(eat)** _____<u>eaten</u>_____ at any good restaurants lately?

   B: Yes, _____<u>I have</u>_____. The White Dove Cafe is especially good.

2. **A:** _____ your sister and brother-in-law **(get)** _____ back from their trip?

   B: No,_____. They should be back in a couple of days.

3. **A:** _____ you and your classmates **(review)** _____ the past participles of verbs?

   B: Yes, _____. In fact, we had a quiz, and everyone did very well.

4. **A:** _____ your friend Jan **(start)** _____ her new job yet?

   B: Yes, _____. She started last Monday.

Part 2
The Meaning of the Present Perfect Tense

UNSPECIFIED TIME IN THE PAST

> ### ▶ Learning Point 1
>
> We use the Present Perfect Tense to talk about an action that happened at an unspecified time in the past. <u>Unspecified</u> means that the exact time of the action is not given.
>
> <u>Example:</u> Tom has already finished his homework.
> **(The exact time is not given. We do not know exactly when Tom finished his homework.)**

> ### ▶ Learning Point 2
>
> We also use the Present Perfect Tense to talk about actions that were repeated many times in the past. We do not know when the actions happened because the exact times are not given.
>
> <u>Example:</u> Rosa has seen the movie, *Titanic*, several times.
> **(The exact times of the actions are not given. We do not know exactly when Rosa saw the movie, *Titanic*.)**

▪▪▶ We use the Present Perfect Tense when we do not give the exact time of the action. We use the Simple Past Tense when we give the exact time of the action. Study the examples below.

1. Present Perfect Tense:
(exact time is not given)
Ruth <u>has</u> already <u>started</u> her new job at E-Com Systems.

Simple Past Tense:
(exact time is given)
She <u>started</u> there last Monday.

2. Present Perfect Tense
(exact time is not given)
The weather <u>has been</u> very warm lately.

Simple Past Tense:
(exact time is given)
It <u>was</u> 98° yesterday.

3. Present Perfect Tense:
(exact time is not given)
I'<u>ve spoken</u> with the counselor about my schedule three times.

Simple Past Tense:
(exact time is given)
In fact, I <u>spoke</u> with him yesterday afternoon.

4. Present Perfect Tense:
(exact time is not given)
My brother <u>has gotten</u> several speeding tickets recently.

Simple Past Tense:
(exact time is given)
He got another ticket last Friday night.

USING THE PRESENT PERFECT TENSE AND THE SIMPLE PAST TENSE

▶ **Exercise I** Choose the Present Perfect Tense or the Simple Past Tense to complete the dialogs below. Remember to use the Present Perfect Tense when the exact time of the action is not given. Use the Simple Past Tense when you know the exact time of the action.

Note: We often use the time words **recently, lately,** and **yet** with the Present Perfect Tense because these words do not show exact time.

I. **A:** ___Have___ you **(see)** ___seen___ any good movies lately?

   B: Yes, I _have_. My sister and I (see) _saw_ the new movie with Tom Hanks last weekend. It was great!

2. **A:** _____ your son **(find)** _____ a new job yet?

   B: No, he_____. He **(have)** _____ an interview last week, but he **(not / get)** _____ he job.

3. **A:** _____ Kathy and Tony **(save)**_____ enough money to buy a house?

   B: No, they_____ . They still need several thousand dollars to make the down payment. Tony **(start)** _____ a second job two weeks ago to make extra money.

4. **A:** _____ you **(buy)** _____ your new computer yet?

   B: Yes, I _____. I **(buy)** _____ it at Fry's Electronics last Friday night and **(set)** _____ everything up on Saturday. I really like it. It's much faster than my old one.

5. **A:** _____ you **(have)** _____ a physical exam recently?

   B: No, I _____. I have an appointment next Thursday. I'm a little worried about my blood pressure. It **(be)** _____ 145 / 90 when I **(take)** _____ it at the pharmacy yesterday. That's pretty high.

6. **A:** _____ your sister **(have)** _____ her baby yet?

   B: Yes, she _____. She **(have)** _____ a baby girl last Saturday night.

7. **A:** _____ you **(eat)** _____ in the new cafeteria yet?

   B: Yes, I _____. I **(meet)** _____ some friends there for lunch yesterday. The food was excellent.

USING THE PRESENT PERFECT TENSE AND THE SIMPLE PAST TENSE

➡ **Exercise 2** Complete the dialogs below with the Present Perfect Tense and Simple Past Tense. Use the time word **already** with the Present Perfect Tense. **Already** does not show exact time.

1. A: It's almost April 15. Are you going to work on your income tax return tomorrow?

   B: Oh, __I've already finished__ it. I __finished__ it last Sunday. I'm getting $500.00 back.*
         (already, finish)   **(finish)**

2. A: Are you and your family going to take a vacation this year?

   B: We _____ our vacation. We _____ it in February.
             (already, take)   **(take)**

   We went skiing in Canada.

3. A: Are you going to buy a lottery ticket for the Big Spin next Saturday? The jackpot is $3 million!

   B: I _____ a ticket. In fact, I _____ several tickets
            (already, buy)   **(buy)**

   yesterday at a little grocery store near my house. It's supposed to be a lucky place to buy tickets.

4. A: Are you ready for your husband's surprise party on Saturday? Do you need any tables or

   chairs?

   B: No, thanks. I _____ them. I _____ them from Abbey Rents yesterday.
           (already, rent)   **(rent)**

5. A: When are you going to have your English exam?

   B: We _____ it. We _____ it last
            (already, have)   **(have)**

   Tuesday night. I hope I passed. I'll find out tomorrow night.

6. A: You have a lot of responsibility in your new job. You should ask your boss for a raise.

   B: I _____ to him about it. I _____
            (already, speak)   **(speak)**

   to him after last Friday's meeting. He said that he would think about it.

7. A: Don't forget to call the eye doctor and make an appointment for your yearly eye exam.

   B: I _____ him. I _____ yesterday
            (already, call)   **(call)**

   afternoon.   I have an appointment at 4:30 next Thursday.

Vocabulary Note * **_I'm getting $500 back.:_** _I'm getting a $500 refund._

PRESENT PERFECT AND SIMPLE PAST

Exercise 3 Rewrite the paragraph below. Use the Present Perfect Tense or the Simple Past Tense of each verb in parentheses.

TO DO
✔ pack boxes
✔ clean oven and refrigerator
✔ wash windows
✔ clean rugs
✔ clean tile and shower in the bathroom
clean out garage

Moving Day

Mike and Ana **(1. be)** very busy lately. They **(2. just, buy)*** a new house, and they are getting ready to move. They **(3. already, pack)** all their dishes, books, clothes, and other personal belongings, but they still have to finish cleaning the apartment. They must leave the apartment in perfect condition if they want to get their cleaning deposit back. They **(4. already, wash)** all the windows and **(5. shampoo)** the rugs. Last night, they **(6. work)** until after midnight. Ana **(7. clean)** the oven and **(8. defrost)** the refrigerator, and Mike **(9. scrub)** the shower and all the tile. As soon as they clean out the garage, they will be ready for the landlord's inspection.

_____

_____

_____

_____

_____

_____

_____

_____

_____

_____

_____

_____

_____

_____

Note: The time word **just** can be used in the Present Perfect Tense or the Simple Past Tense without a change in meaning. _Example:_ They have **just** eaten = They **just** ate.

ANSWERING QUESTIONS WITH <u>EVER</u>

▶ **Learning Point**

It is very common to use the time word <u>**ever**</u> with the Present Perfect Tense to ask about a person's experiences. The time word <u>ever</u> means <u>at any time in your life</u>.

➤ Study the examples below.

        1. Have you <u>ever</u> had to attend traffic school?

<u>affirmative:</u>   Yes, I have. I've had to attend traffic school twice.

<u>negative:</u>   No, I haven't. I've never had to attend traffic school.

        2. Have you <u>ever</u> run out of gas on the highway?

<u>affirmative:</u>   Yes, I have. I've run out of gas a few times.

<u>negative:</u>   No, I haven't. I've never run out of gas on the highway.

        3. Have you and your family <u>ever</u> been to New York?

<u>affirmative:</u>   Yes, we have. We've been there many times.

<u>negative:</u>   No, we haven't. We've never been to New York.

        4. Have you <u>ever</u> taken a cruise?

<u>affirmative:</u>   Yes, I have. I've taken several cruises.

<u>negative:</u>   No, I haven't. I've never taken a cruise.

        5. Have you <u>ever</u> had an operation?

<u>affirmative:</u>   Yes, I have. I've had three operations.

<u>negative:</u>   No, I haven't. I've never had an operation.

        6. Have you <u>ever</u> read a novel in English?

<u>affirmative:</u>   Yes, I have. I've read two or three novels in English.

<u>negative:</u>   No, I haven't. I've never read a novel in English.

<u>*Note:*</u> once = one time, twice = two times

ANSWERING QUESTIONS WITH <u>EVER</u>

▶ **Exercise 4**   Write <u>true</u> answers to the questions below. Give a short answer and a long answer.

Example: Have you ever gone skiing?

    Yes, I have. I've gone skiing many times (once, twice, several times, etc.).

or

    No, I haven't. I've never gone skiing.

1. Have you ever visited Washington, D.C.?

_____

2. Have you ever taken a data processing class?

_____

3. Have you ever eaten sushi?

_____

4. Have you ever gotten a ticket for speeding?

_____

5. Have you ever been in an automobile accident?

_____

6. Have you ever had a garage sale?

_____

7. Have you ever told a lie?

_____

8. Have you ever lost your wallet?

_____

9. Have you ever locked your keys in the car?

_____

10 Have you ever bounced a check* ?

_____

11. Have you ever borrowed money from a friend?

_____

12. Have you ever been in love?

_____

Vocabulary Note   * <u>bounce a check</u>: *write a check without sufficient money in your checking account*

✓ CHECK YOUR UNDERSTANDING

A. Answer the questions below.

1. How do we form the Present Perfect Tense?

_____

2. When do we use the Present Perfect Tense?

    a. _____

    _____

    b. _____

    _____

3. What is the difference between the Present Perfect Tense and the Simple Past Tense?

_____

_____

    a. Write a sentence in the Present Perfect Tense. Use a time word in your sentence.

    _____

    b. Write a sentence in the Simple Past Tense. Use a time word in your sentence.

    _____

B. *EDITING* - The sentences below have verb errors. Rewrite each sentence correctly. <u>Note</u>: In some of the sentences, there is more than one way to correct the error.

1. I have bought my books for the new semester yesterday.

_____

2. Have you saw the new movie at the Century Theater yet?

_____

3. I haven't felt very well last night.

_____

4. He just written a letter to his cousin.

_____

5. Have you ever ate raw fish?

_____

✓ CHECK YOUR UNDERSTANDING

C. Complete the paragraphs below with the correct form of the verbs in parentheses. Use the Present Perfect Tense or the Simple Past Tense.

Paragraph 1   **A Great Film**

I enjoy foreign films very much, and I **(1. see)** _____ several excellent films lately. In fact, I **(2. see)** _____ two very good Spanish films last month. My favorite of the two films **(3. be)** _____ La Cantante. This film **(4. win)** _____ many important awards recently. In fact, it **(5. win)** _____ the Academy Award for Best Foreign Film a few days ago.

Paragraph 2   **Work Hard, Get Rich!**

My brother is a very successful real estate agent. It is only July, and he **(1. already, sell)** _____ twelve properties. In fact, in the spring he **(2. sell)** _____ several houses in a new development near the ocean and three condominiums in the city. In addition, he **(3. just, buy)** _____ four "fixer-uppers". He plans to paint and wallpaper, repair the plumbing, landscape the yards, and sell the houses for a good profit. My brother hopes to retire before he is forty!

Paragraph 3   **A Famous Classmate**

In October, I am going to attend my twentieth high school reunion. I hope that one of my old classmates, Tom Adams, will be there. Tom **(1. become)** _____ a very famous author over the years. He **(2. write)** _____ articles for many well-known newspapers and magazines. In addition, he **(3. write)** _____ three very successful novels. One of his novels **(4. be)** _____ on the best-seller list for sixteen weeks last year. A few months ago, *Time* magazine **(5. publish)** _____ an interview with him, and he **(6. appear)** _____ on several TV talk shows last month. I wonder if Tom will remember me. I am the classmate who used to help him with his homework!

Part 3
Another Meaning of the Present Perfect Tense

USING <u>FOR</u> AND <u>SINCE</u>

> ▶ **Learning Point 1**
>
> We often use the words <u>for</u> and <u>since</u> with the Present Perfect Tense to talk about actions that began in the past and continue to the present time.

1. Peter <u>has lived</u> in San Jose for ten years.
(Peter moved to San Jose ten years ago, and he still lives in San Jose at the present time.)

2. Mr. and Mrs. Lopez <u>have studied</u> English for six months.
(They began to study English six months ago, and they still study English at the present time.)

3. Mr. Olson <u>has taught</u> at this school since February.
(Mr. Olson began to teach at this school in February, and he still teaches here at the present time.)

4. My uncle <u>has owned</u> his Ford Mustang since 1967.
(My uncle bought his Mustang in 1967, and he still has it at the present time.)

> ▶ **Learning Point 2**
>
> <u>For</u> tells how long an action has been in progress.
>
> <u>Since</u> tells when an action began in the past.

FOR→ how long	**SINCE**→ when the action began
for six months	since 1988
for a long time	since last week
for about five years	since last month
for three days	since 10:00
1. I have worked at Cisco <u>for</u> six months.	**1.** I have known Mr. Lee <u>since</u> 1988.
2. Mary has needed a new car <u>for</u> a long time.	**2.** My neighbor has been sick <u>since</u> last week.
3. I have worn glasses <u>for</u> about five years.	**3.** I haven't heard from Kim <u>since</u> last month.
4. Tom hasn't been in class <u>for</u> three days.	**4.** The computer has been down <u>since</u> 10:00.

FOR AND SINCE

➡ **Exercise 1** Answer each question below with the Present Perfect Tense. Answer in two ways, using <u>for</u> and <u>since</u>.

Situation 1:   It's 9:30 a.m. Mary got to work at 7:30. How long has Mary been at work?

<u>Mary has been at work</u> ⟨ <u>for two hours.</u>
<u>since 7:30.</u>

Situation 2:   It's Tuesday. Dang's toothache started on Saturday. How long has he had a toothache?

Situation 3:   It's August. Elaine and Bob bought a new house six months ago. How long have they owned their house?

Situation 4:   It's October. Paula and her husband got married in June. How long have they been married?

Situation 5:   The year is 2002. Dr. Razavi became a doctor in 1997. How long has she been a doctor?

➡ **Exercise 2** Write <u>true</u> sentences about yourself with the Present Perfect Tense. Answer in two ways, using <u>for</u> and <u>since</u>.

1. How long have you lived here?

2. How long have you attended this school?

3. How long have you known your teacher?

FOR AND SINCE

▶ **Exercise 3** Complete the sentences below with the Present Perfect Tense. Use either <u>for</u> or <u>since</u> in each sentence.

1. Mr. and Mrs. Garcia **(own)** <u>have owned</u> a restaurant in downtown San Francisco <u>since</u> 1988, and they've been very successful.

2. We **(want)** _____ to go to Canada _____ several years, but we've never had the time or the money to make the trip.

3. My sister speaks French very well. She **(take)** _____ French lessons _____ about five years.

4. Rakesh **(expect)** _____ a letter from his family in India _____ several days, but he hasn't heard from them. He plans to call them tonight.

5. Shirley's husband **(be)** _____ out of work _____ March 3. They're worried about their house payments.

6. My neighbor had a heart attack, and he **(be)** _____in the hospital _____ last week. He hopes to go home in a few days.

▶ **Exercise 4** Follow the same directions as in Exercise 3.

1. I **(have)** _____ this car _____ over a year, and I've never had a problem with it.

2. Mr. Hall is a very good friend of ours. We **(know)** _____ him _____ about fifteen years.

3. My son **(have)** _____ a bad cold _____ Tuesday, and he's still not feeling very well.

4. Ted graduated from college last June, and he **(work)** _____ for City Bank _____ his graduation. He works in the financial planning department.

5. My parents just celebrated their Silver Wedding Anniversary. They **(be)** _____ married _____ twenty-five years.

6. My sister's little boy is getting big. He **(grow)** _____ two inches _____ his last birthday.

SPECIAL POINT - TIME CLAUSES WITH SINCE

> ### Learning Point
>
> 1. In Present Perfect Tense sentences, we can use <u>since</u> to introduce a time clause to tell when the action began.
>
>   s   v   c
>
>   <u>Example:</u> I've known Frank <u>since I was a child</u>.
>
>   **present perfect**   **time clause**
>
> 2. The verb in the main clause is in the Present Perfect Tense. The verb in the time clause is in the Simple Past Tense.

MAIN CLAUSE **Present Perfect Tense**	**TIME CLAUSE WITH <u>SINCE</u>** **(tells when the action began)** **Simple Past Tense**
	s v c
1. I've known Frank	since I <u>was</u> a child.
2. Tina <u>has worn</u> glasses	since she <u>was</u> twelve years old.
3. Margaret <u>hasn't worked</u>	since she <u>won</u> the lottery.
4. I've had a headache	since I <u>woke</u> up this morning.

▸ **Exercise 5** Add a time clause with <u>since</u> to complete each Present Perfect sentence below. Be sure to use the Simple Past Tense in the time clause.

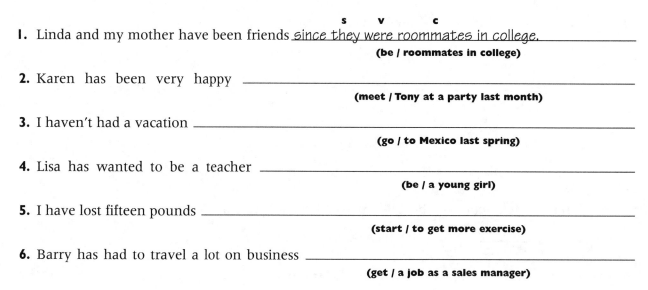

                                                    s   v   c

1. Linda and my mother have been friends <u>*since they were roommates in college.*</u>
                                                  (be / roommates in college)

2. Karen has been very happy _____
                                       (meet / Tony at a party last month)

3. I haven't had a vacation _____
                                  (go / to Mexico last spring)

4. Lisa has wanted to be a teacher _____
                                  (be / a young girl)

5. I have lost fifteen pounds _____
                                (start / to get more exercise)

6. Barry has had to travel a lot on business _____
                                  (get / a job as a sales manager)

✓ CHECK YOUR UNDERSTANDING

➡ Think carefully about the meaning of the sentences below. Then write **true, false,** or **I don't know** on the line after each sentence.

1. Peter has studied Russian for three years.

    a. Peter still studies Russian.   **a.** _____true_____

    b. Peter has been to Russia.   **b.** _____I don't know._____

    c. Peter doesn't study Russian any more.   **c.** _____false_____

2. The children haven't eaten lunch yet.

    a. The children are going to eat lunch in a few minutes.   **a.** _____

    b. The children had a big lunch today.   **b.** _____

    c. The children are hungry.   **c.** _____

3. Susan worked for Intel from 1999 to 2001.

    a. Susan still works for Intel.   **a.** _____

    b. Susan went to work for another company in 2001.   **b.** _____

    c. Susan was working for Intel in 2000.   **c.** _____

4. Mr. and Mrs. Taylor's son just started his first year at college.

    a. Mr. and Mrs. Taylor's son is in college now.   **a.** _____

    b. Mr. and Mrs. Taylor's son graduated from high school a few months ago.   **b.** _____

    c. Mr. and Mrs. Taylor's son started college about two years ago.   **c.** _____

5. Lan has forgotten to bring her dictionary to class several times.

    a. Lan forgot her dictionary yesterday.   **a.** _____

    b. Lan doesn't like to use a dictionary.   **b.** _____

    c. Lan has forgotten her dictionary more than once.   **c.** _____

6. Paul has lived in Los Angeles since last March.

    a. Paul moved to Los Angeles in March.   **a.** _____

    b. Paul lives in Los Angeles now.   **b.** _____

    c. Paul plans to move to San Diego soon.   **c.** _____

7. Marta has been on a diet for five weeks.

    a. Marta wants to lose weight.   **a.** _____

    b. Marta has already lost several pounds.   **b.** _____

    c. Marta's doctor told her to lose weight.   **c.** _____

Part 4
The Present Perfect Progressive Tense

THE MEANING OF THE PRESENT PERFECT PROGRESSIVE TENSE

➠ In previous parts of this chapter, you studied the Present Perfect Tense. In Part 4, you will study the Present Perfect <u>Progressive</u> Tense.

> ▶ **Learning Point**
>
> We use the Present Perfect Progressive Tense to tell how long an action has been in progress. We often use the words <u>for</u> and <u>since</u> with the Present Perfect Progressive Tense.

➠ Study the examples below.

1. Rita is talking on the phone now.

   She <u>has been talking</u> on the phone for over an hour.
   (Present Perfect Progressive Tense tells how long the action has been in progress.)

2. Paul is waiting for the bus right now.

   He <u>has been waiting</u> for the bus for twenty minutes.
   (Present Perfect Progressive Tense tells how long the action has been in progress.)

3. I'm studying for a big math test right now.

   I<u>'ve been studying</u> for my math test since 9:00 this morning.
   (Present Perfect Progressive Tense tells how long the action has been in progress.)

4. My brother is watching TV in the family room right now.

   He<u>'s been watching</u> TV since the baseball game began an hour ago.
   (Present Perfect Progressive Tense tells how long the action has been in progress.)

5. It's raining outside now.

   It<u>'s been raining</u> since early this morning.
   (Present Perfect Progressive Tense tells how long the action has been in progress.)

FORMING THE PRESENT PERFECT PROGRESSIVE TENSE

▶ **Learning Point**

To form the Present Perfect Progressive Tense, we use:

have, has	+	been	+	-ing form
↑		↑		↑
helping verb		**past participle of <u>Be</u>**	**present participle of the main verb**	

◉▶ **Forms of the Present Perfect Progressive Tense**

AFFIRMATIVE

		helping verb	past participle	main verb -ing form				helping verb	past participle	main verb -ing form
1.	I	have	been	working		**1.**	we	have	been	working
2.	you	have	been	working		**2.**	you	have	been	working
3.	he she it	has	been	working		**3.**	they			

NEGATIVE

		helping verb	past participle	main verb -ing form				helping verb	past participle	main verb -ing form
1.	I	have not	been	working		**1.**	we	have not	been	working
2.	you	have not	been	working		**2.**	you	have not	been	working
3.	he she it	has not	been	working		**3.**	they			

YES-NO QUESTIONS

	helping verb		past participle	main verb -ing form			helping verb		past participle	main verb -ing form
1.	Have	I	been	working?		**1.**		we	been	working?
2.	Have	you	been	working?		**2.**	Have	you	been	working?
3.	Has	he she it	been	working?		**3.**		they		

<u>Note:</u>   We do not use the Present Perfect Progressive Tense with non-action (non-progressive) verbs such as <u>like</u>, <u>know</u>, <u>understand</u>, <u>own</u>. If you need to review non-progressive verbs, refer to Chapter 5, page 125.

THE PRESENT PERFECT PROGRESSIVE TENSE

▶ **Exercise 1** Complete the sentences below with the Present Perfect Progressive Tense to show <u>how long</u> the actions have been in progress.

1. I'm looking for my car keys. I <u>'ve been looking</u> for them **for over an hour.** I can't find them anywhere.

2. Joe is working at IBM now. He _____ there **since last March.** He likes his job a lot and gets along well with his manager and co-workers.

3. My friend Helga is dating Ron Davis. She _____ Ron **for nearly a year.** They plan to get married in September.

4. I'm waiting for my sister. I _____ for her **since 5:00.** She's never on time.

5. We're studying the Present Perfect Progressive Tense. We _____ the Present Perfect Progressive Tense **for about twenty minutes.**

6. My neighbor's son is practicing the drums. He _____ the drums **since 8:00 this morning.** He's a drummer in a rock band. I wish that he would move!

▶ **Exercise 2** Use the Present Perfect Progressive Tense to answer the questions below. Give <u>true</u> answers. Use <u>for</u> or <u>since</u> in each answer.

1. How long have you been studying at this school?

_____

2. How long has your teacher been teaching at this school?

_____

3. How long have you been trying to learn English?

_____

4. How long have you been living in this city?

_____

5. How long have you been living at your present address?

_____

PRESENT PROGRESSIVE VS. PRESENT PERFECT PROGRESSIVE

▶ **Exercise 3** Everybody loves a garage sale! People always hope to find a bargain, a valuable antique, or some hidden treasure among the articles for sale. Even if they don't find a bargain, it's always fun to browse through other people's "junk". Choose the Present Progressive Tense or the Present Perfect Progressive Tense to complete the sentences below.

A Successful Garage Sale

1. Bob and Sandy _____are having_____ a garage sale today.

   a. are having   **b.** have been having

2. People _____ since 9:00 this morning.

   a. are coming and going   **b.** have been coming and going

3. Right now several people _____ at Bob's old stamp collection.

   a. are looking   **b.** have been looking

4. Bob _____ stamps for many years, and he has decided to sell some of his duplicate stamps and albums.

   a. is collecting   **b.** has been collecting

5. On the other side of the yard, Sandy _____ to a man about her exercise bike now. The bike is several years old, but it's still in good condition.

   a. is talking   **b.** has been talking

6. The man _____ to bargain with Sandy for several minutes. He wants her to lower the price of the bike to $35.00, but Sandy wants $50.00.

   a. is trying   **b.** has been trying

7. Bob and Sandy's son Bradley _____ price tags on several of his old trucks, cars, games, and other toys right now.

   a. is putting   **b.** has been putting

8. Their daughter Jenny is in charge of the cash box. At the moment, she _____ the money. She is happy because the cash box is filling up!

   a. is counting   **b.** has been counting

☑ CHECK YOUR UNDERSTANDING

A. Answer the questions below.

  1. How do we form the Present Perfect Progressive Tense?

       _____

  2. When do we use the Present Perfect Progressive Tense?

       _____

  3. What words do we often use with the Present Perfect Progressive Tense to show how long an action has been in progress?

       _____

  4. Do we use non-action (non-progressive) verbs such as <u>like</u>, <u>know</u>, <u>understand</u>, <u>own</u> in the Present Perfect Progressive Tense?

       yes _____   no _____

B. *EDITING* - The postcard below has 5 errors in the use of the Present Perfect Progressive Tense. Find and correct the errors. The first one is done for you.

Hi, Lorraine!

    Here we are on our way to Acapulco. A cruise is definitely the best way to travel. We ~~has~~ *have* been sailing for three days, and we've been have a wonderful time on the ship. There are activities all day long. We've been swimming, sunbathing, watch movies, and gambling in the casino. In the evenings, we've been attended the stage shows and dancing in the grand ballroom. Of course, we've been eaten! Every day, we have three delicious meals and a wonderful midnight buffet!

                     See you soon!

                     Joe and Pat

Ms. Lorraine Baxter
1234 Willow Street
San Jose, CA 95125

VERB REVIEW

My brother and sister-in-law love the ocean and have always wanted to live in Hawaii. At the end of last year, they had the opportunity to buy a small resort on the island of Maui. The resort opened a few months ago and has been full almost every night. My brother and sister-in-law are finding it difficult to keep up with the comings and goings of their guests. Running a resort in Hawaii is not a vacation. It's hard work!

▶ Look at the guest register below. Then work with a partner to answer the questions on the next page.

Sunday, May 24

Guests	Check-In	Check-Out
Ms. Judith Marks and daughter	5/20	
Mr. and Mrs. Bob Hale	5/17	5/23
Mr. Jonathan Peterson	5/12	
Mr. and Mrs. Andres Garcia	5/15	5/20
Ms. Wendy Thorpe	5/23	
Ms. Mei Chen	5/23	
Mr. and Mrs. Tom Finnegan	5/22	
Dr. Peter Sung	5/23	
Mr. and Mrs. Howard Watanabe	5/18	
Ms. Kathy Schumer	5/19	5/22

ALOHA RESORT

VERB REVIEW

➤ Use the information from the guest register on page 407 to answer the questions below. Use complete sentences in your answers. Be careful with the verb tenses. Work with a partner.

1. How long have Judith Marks and her daughter been at the resort?

   They have been at the resort since May 20.

2. Who has been at the resort the longest?

   _____

3. Is Wendy Thorpe still a guest at the resort?

   _____

4. How many guests have checked out?

   _____

5. Which guest stayed at the resort the shortest time?

   _____

6. How long did Mr. and Mrs. Hale stay at the resort?

   _____

7. Are Bob Hale and his wife still guests at the resort?

   _____

8. When did Mr. and Mrs. Garcia leave the resort?

   _____

9. How long have Mr. and Mrs. Watanabe been guests at the resort?

   _____

10. How long was Kathy Schumer a guest at the resort?

    _____

11. How many guests are staying at the resort now (on May 24)?

    _____

12. How many people were staying at the resort on May 21?

    _____

✎ Writing Assignment

▸ Your writing assignment in this chapter is to write a paragraph about one of the topics below.

▶ What to do ◀

1. Choose **one** of the topic sentences below to write about.

_____ **Topic 1:** My life has changed in several ways since I came to the United States.

Living in a foreign country requires a person to make adjustments in many areas of his/her life: language, customs, climate, etc. What are the biggest changes that have occurred in your life since you came to the United States?

_____ **Topic 2:** There have been many changes in the world since my parents were young.

Change has become more and more rapid, and the world has changed in many ways over the last decades. What are some of the major changes that have occurred since your parents were young?

2. Write the first draft and the final draft of your paragraph on separate sheets of paper.

3. Follow the writing steps below.

STEP 1	Before you begin to write, take a few minutes to think about your topic. Then make a *list* of your ideas.
STEP 2	Choose two or three ideas from your list, and write a *first draft (practice paragraph)*.
STEP 3	*Revise and edit* your practice paragraph.
STEP 4	Write your *final draft (final paragraph)*.

THE FIVE FORMS OF ENGLISH VERBS

1 ROOT FORM (SIMPLE FORM)	2 -S FORM	3 PAST FORM	4 PRESENT PARTICIPLE (ing)	5 PAST PARTICIPLE
argue	argues	argued	arguing	argued
arrive	arrives	arrived	arriving	arrived
bake	bakes	baked	baking	baked
become	becomes	became	becoming	become
begin	begins	began	beginning	begun
bite	bites	bit	biting	bitten
blow	blows	blew	blowing	blown
borrow	borrows	borrowed	borrowing	borrowed
break	breaks	broke	breaking	broken
bring	brings	brought	bringing	brought
build	builds	built	building	built
burn	burns	burned	burning	burned
buy	buys	bought	buying	bought
call	calls	called	calling	called
catch	catches	caught	catching	caught
change	changes	changed	changing	changed
choose	chooses	chose	choosing	chose
come	comes	came	coming	come
cost	costs	cost	costing	cost
cut	cuts	cut	cutting	cut
dig	digs	dug	digging	dug
do	does	did	doing	done
draw	draws	drew	drawing	drawn
drink	drinks	drank	drinking	drunk
drive	drives	drove	driving	driven
eat	eats	ate	eating	eaten
erase	erases	erased	erasing	erased
expect	expects	expected	expecting	expected
explain	explains	explained	explaining	explained
fall	falls	fell	falling	fallen
feed	feeds	fed	feeding	fed
feel	feels	felt	feeling	felt
fight	fights	fought	fighting	fought
find	finds	found	finding	found
finish	finishes	finished	finishing	finished
fix	fixes	fixed	fixing	fixed
fly	flies	flew	flying	flown
forget	forgets	forgot	forgetting	forgotten
forgive	forgives	forgave	forgiving	forgiven
freeze	freezes	froze	freezing	frozen
get	gets	got	getting	gotten
give	gives	gave	giving	given
go	goes	went	going	gone
grow	grows	growing	grew	grown
hang	hangs	hung	hanging	hung

THE FIVE FORMS OF ENGLISH VERBS

1 ROOT FORM (SIMPLE FORM)	2 -S FORM	3 PAST FORM	4 PRESENT PARTICIPLE (ing)	5 PAST PARTICIPLE
have	has	had	having	had
hear	hears	heard	hearing	heard
help	helps	helped	helping	helped
hide	hides	hid	hiding	hid
hit	hits	hit	hitting	hit
hold	holds	held	holding	held
hope	hopes	hoped	hoping	hoped
hurt	hurts	hurt	hurting	hurt
invent	invents	invented	inventing	invented
keep	keeps	kept	keeping	kept
know	knows	knew	knowing	known
laugh	laughs	laughed	laughing	laughed
lay	lays	laid	laying	laid
learn	learns	learned	learning	learned
leave	leaves	left	leaving	left
lend	lends	lent	lending	lent
let	lets	let	letting	let
lie (recline)	lies	lay	lying	lain
lie (tell a lie)	lies	lied	lying	lied
like	likes	liked	liking	liked
listen	listens	listened	listening	listened
live	lives	lived	living	lived
look	looks	looked	looking	looked
lose	loses	lost	losing	lost
love	loves	loved	loving	loved
make	makes	made	making	made
mean	means	meant	meaning	meant
meet	meets	met	meeting	met
memorize	memorizes	memorized	memorizing	memorized
need	needs	needed	needing	needed
open	opens	opened	opening	opened
order	orders	ordered	ordering	ordered
own	owns	owned	owning	owned
pay	pays	paid	paying	paid
plan	plans	planned	planning	planned
play	plays	played	playing	played
practice	practices	practiced	practicing	practiced
put	puts	put	putting	put
quit	quits	quit	quitting	quit
read	reads	read	reading	read
realize	realizes	realized	realizing	realized
recite	recites	recited	reciting	recited
remember	remembers	remembered	remembering	remembered
rent	rents	rented	renting	rented
return	returns	returned	returning	returned

THE FIVE FORMS OF ENGLISH VERBS

1 ROOT FORM (SIMPLE FORM)	2 -S FORM	3 PAST FORM	4 PRESENT PARTICIPLE (ing)	5 PAST PARTICIPLE
ride	rides	rode	riding	ridden
ring	rings	rang	ringing	rung
rise	rises	rose	rising	risen
run	runs	ran	running	run
say	says	said	saying	said
see	sees	saw	seeing	seen
sell	sells	sold	selling	sold
send	sends	sent	sending	sent
set	sets	set	setting	set
shake	shakes	shook	shaking	shaken
shoot	shoots	shot	shooting	shot
shut	shuts	shut	shutting	shut
sing	sings	sang	singing	sung
sink	sinks	sank	sinking	sunk
sit	sits	sat	sitting	sat
sleep	sleeps	slept	sleeping	slept
smoke	smokes	smoked	smoking	smoked
speak	speaks	spoke	speaking	spoken
spend	spends	spent	spending	spent
stand	stands	stood	standing	stood
steal	steals	stole	stealing	stolen
study	studies	studied	studying	studied
sweep	sweeps	swept	sweeping	swept
swim	swims	swam	swimming	swum
take	takes	took	taking	taken
talk	talks	talked	talking	talked
teach	teaches	taught	teaching	taught
tear	tears	tore	tearing	torn
tell	tells	told	telling	told
think	thinks	thought	thinking	thought
throw	throws	threw	throwing	thrown
try	tries	tried	trying	tried
turn	turns	turned	turning	turned
understand	understands	understood	understanding	understood
use	uses	used	using	used
visit	visits	visited	visiting	visited
wait	waits	waited	waiting	waited
wake	wakes	woke	waking	woken
walk	walks	walked	walking	walked
want	wants	wanted	wanting	wanted
wash	washes	washed	washing	washed
watch	watches	watched	watching	watched
wear	wears	wore	wearing	worn
win	wins	won	winning	won
work	works	worked	working	worked
write	writes	wrote	writing	written
yell	yells	yelled	yelling	yelled

INDEX